I0818506

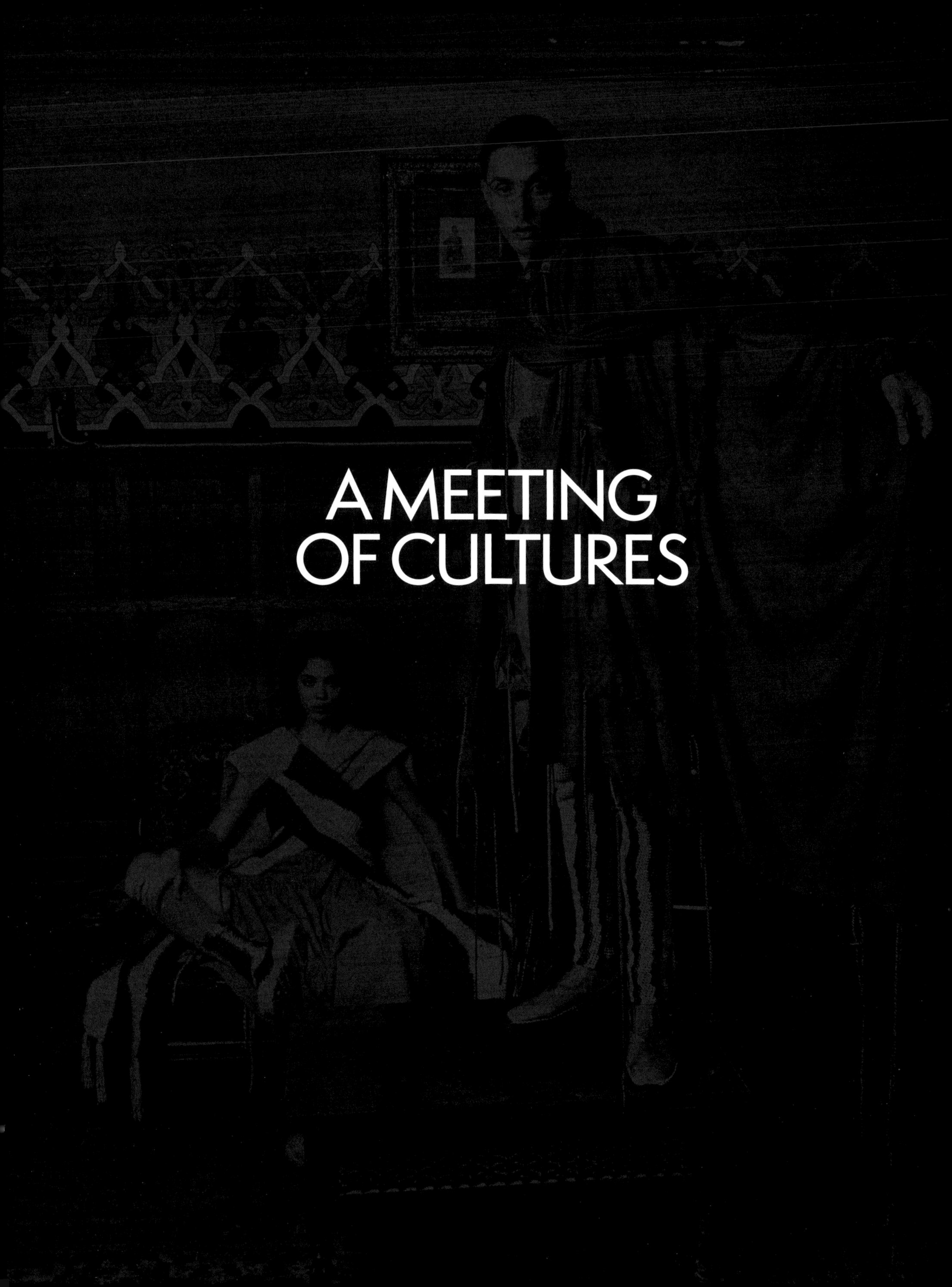

A MEETING OF CULTURES

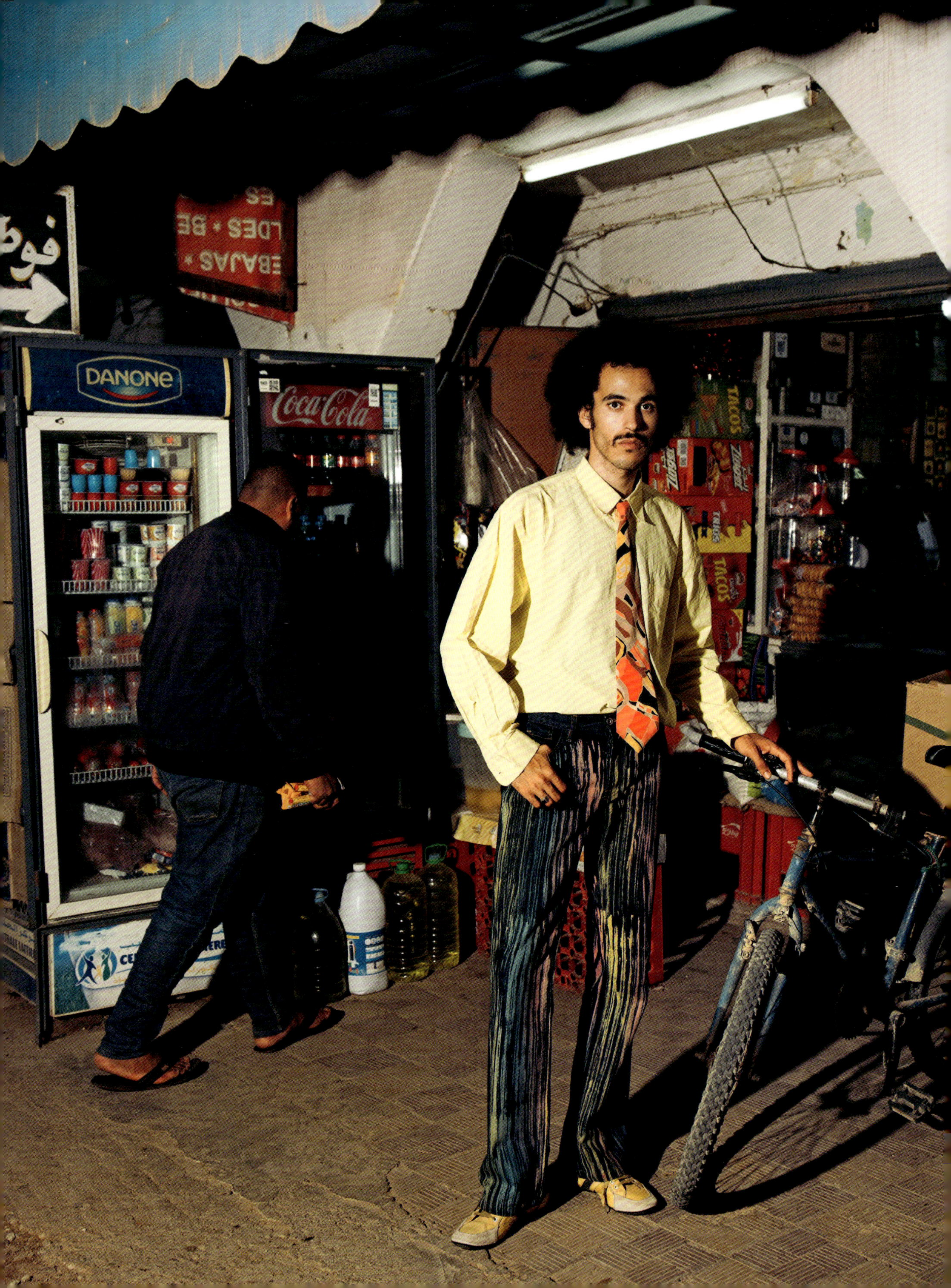
DANONE
Coca-Cola
TACOS
TACOS

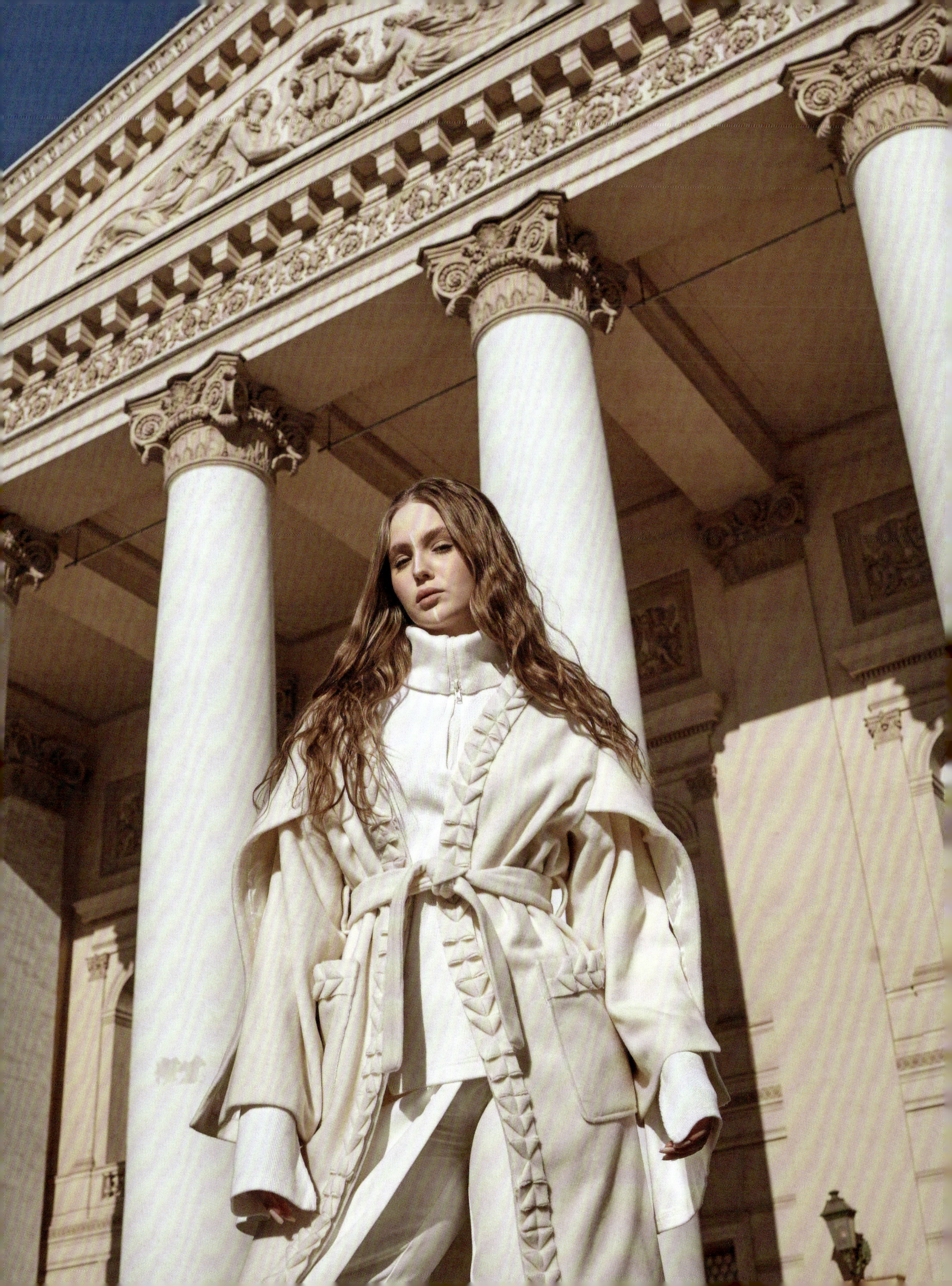

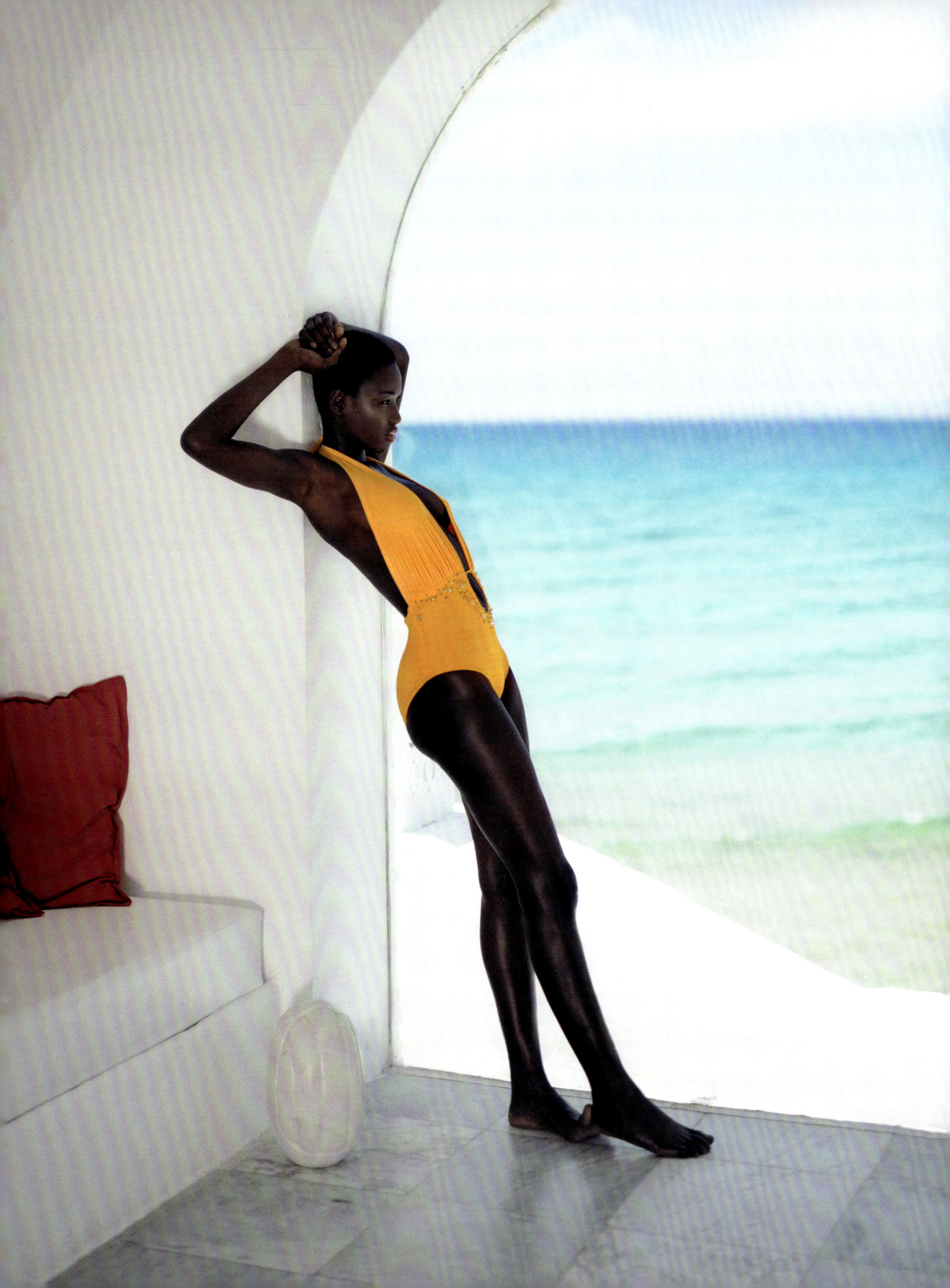

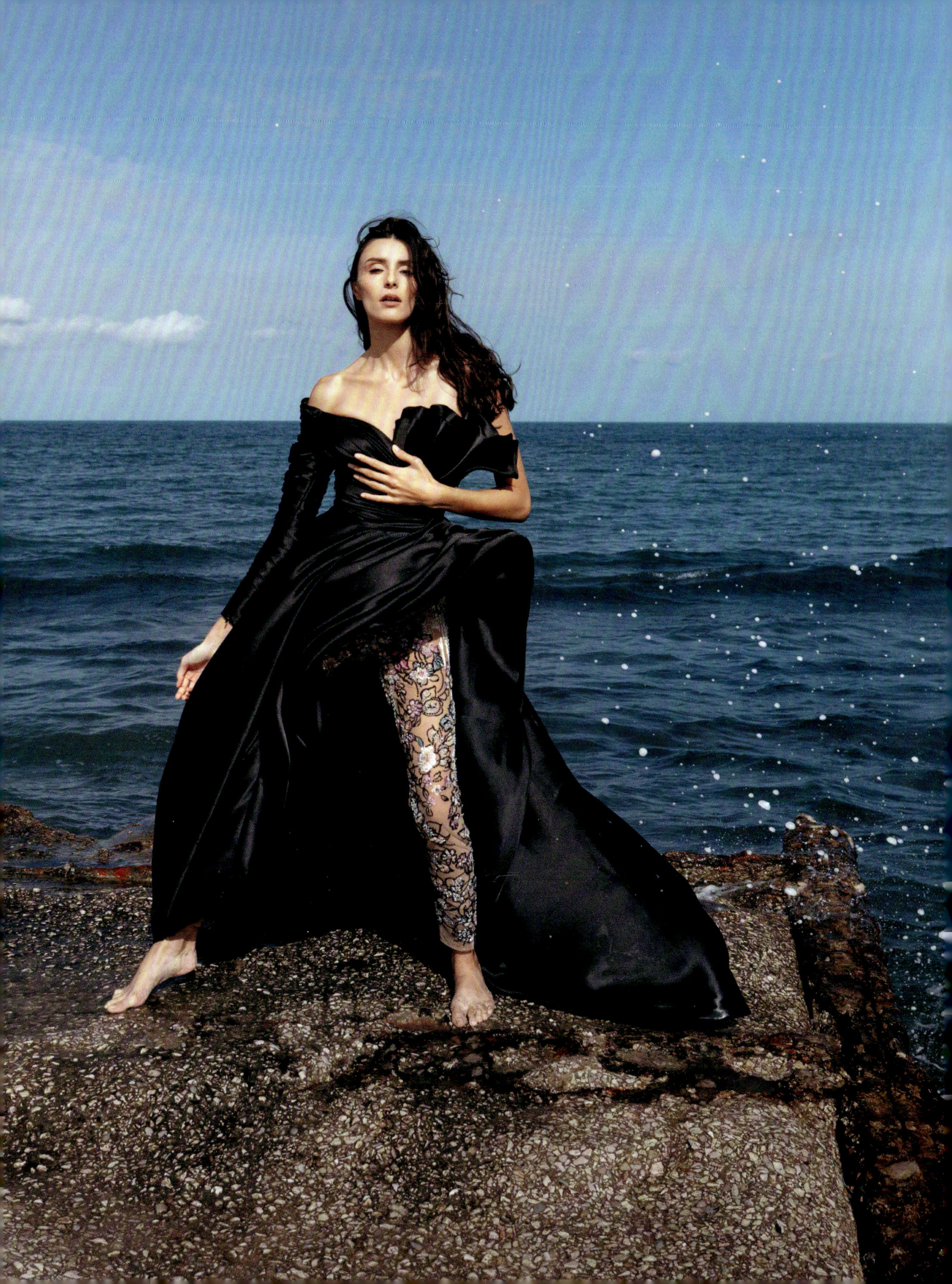

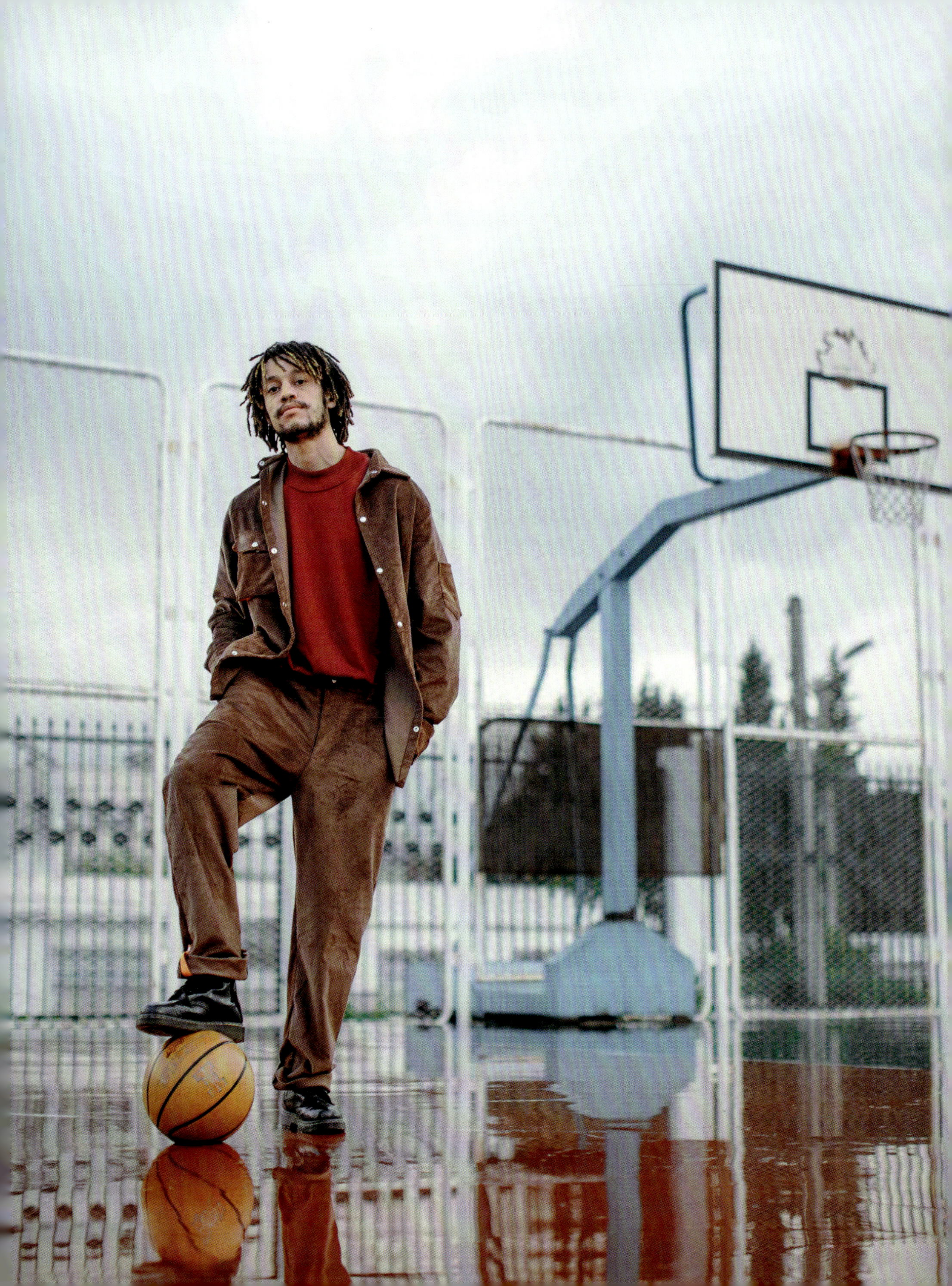

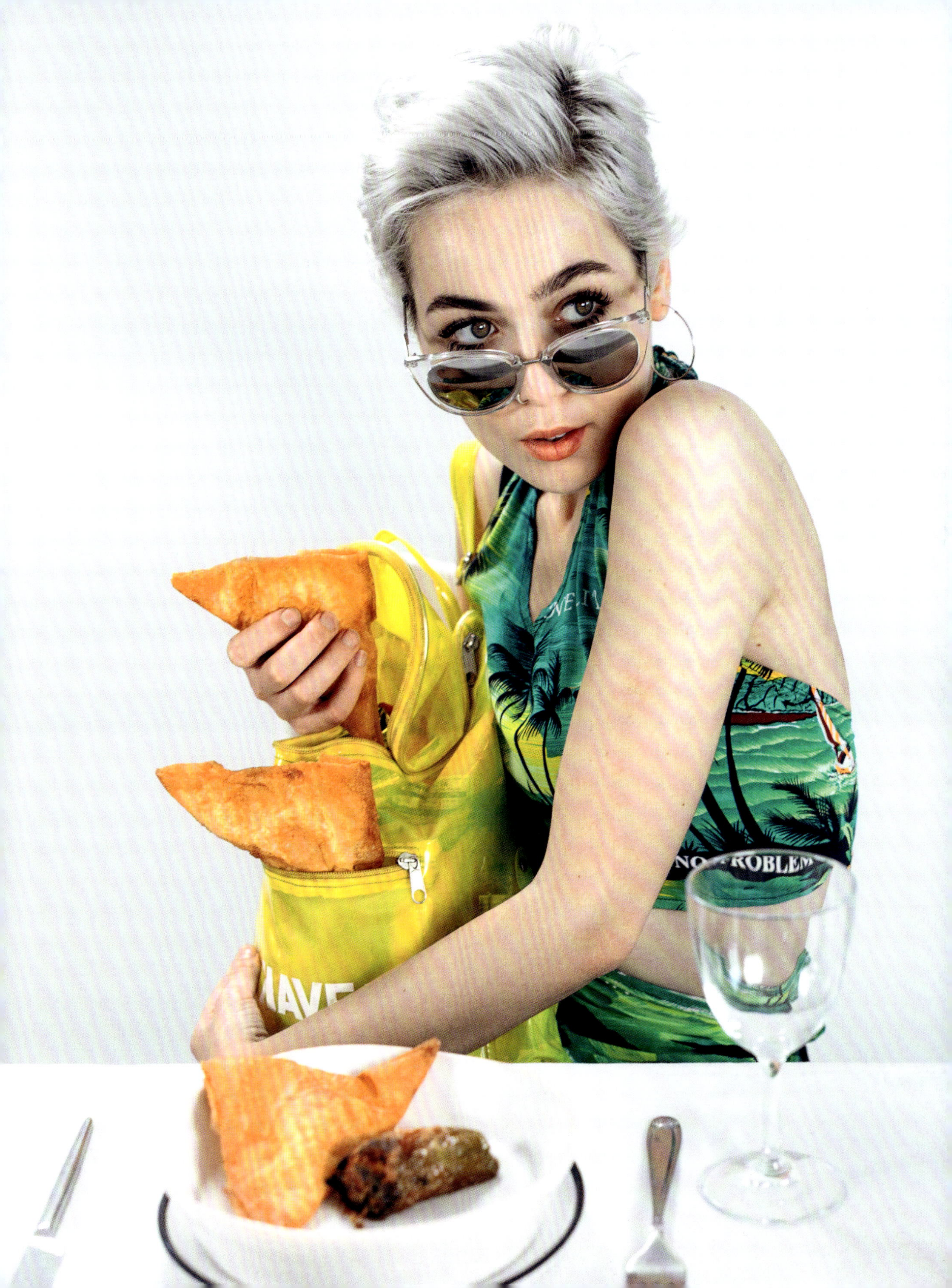

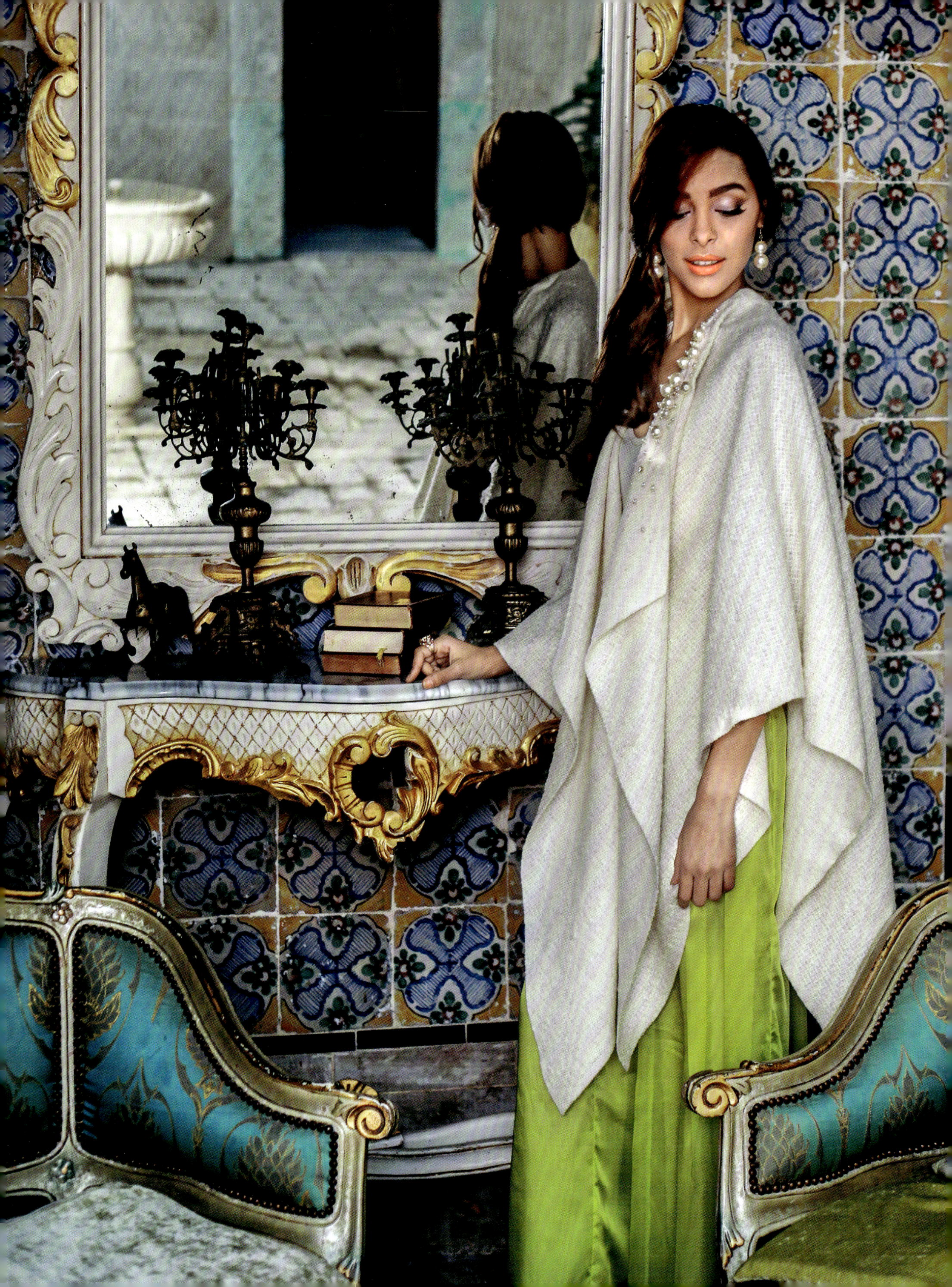

A MEETING OF CULTURES

FASHIONING NORTH AFRICA

ملتقى الثقافات: أزياء شمال أفريقيا

HIRMER

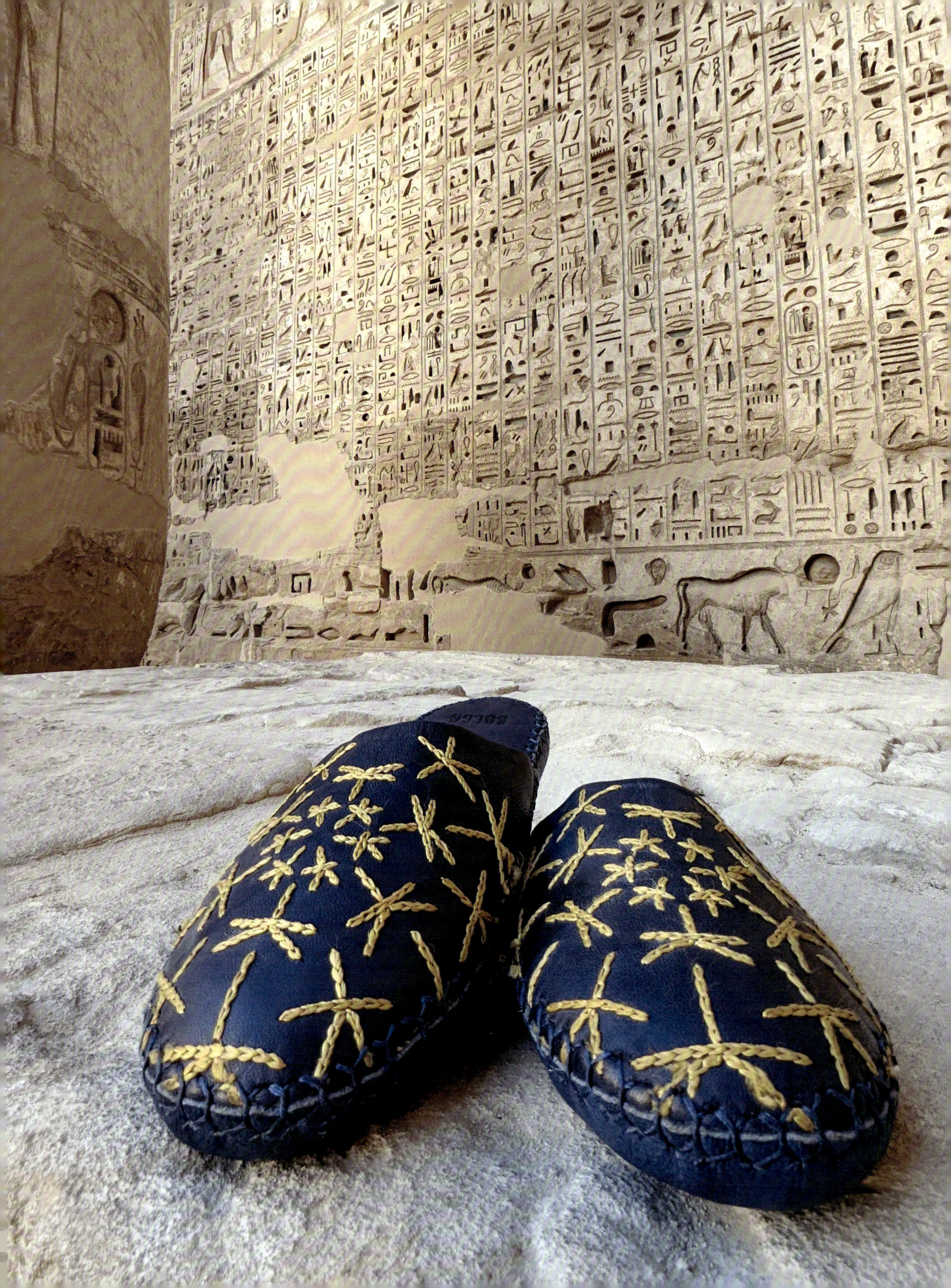

TABLE OF CONTENTS

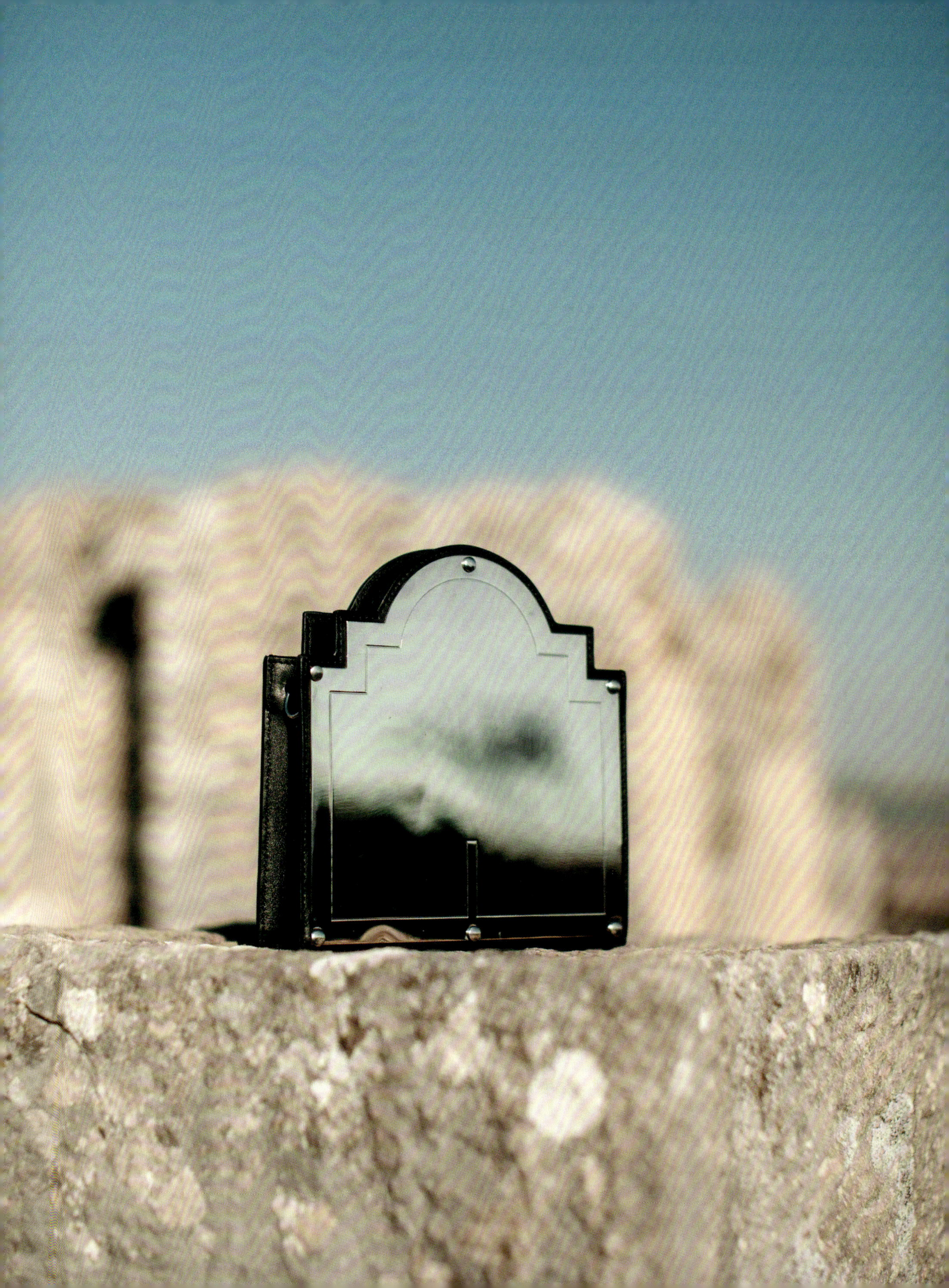

FOREWORD

A *Meeting of Cultures: Fashioning North Africa* is not only the title of this beautiful and thought-provoking exhibition, but it also describes a core purpose of museums: a place where cultures can meet, be examined, discussed, and understood from new perspectives. Because of the way collections in Eurocentric museums were historically gathered, there are inherent biases and limited perspectives that often ignore the voice of the original culture and its people. It is not sufficient to be aware of these dilemmas. Museums must take actions through their collecting policies and exhibition programs to counter historic biases and allow new voices to tell *their* stories.

A Meeting of Cultures continues the KSU Museum's commitment to changing perspectives and inspiring conversations that encourage non-Western voices to be seen and heard. In 2016, KSU Museum curator Dr. Sara Hume presented *Fashions of Southern Africa* that showcased distinctive contemporary designers and perspectives from this region of Africa to counter the binary clichés of Western versus African dress. In 2021, the KSU Museum organized its most ambitious exhibition to date, *TEXTURES: the history and art of Black hair*, synthesizing research in history, fashion, art, and visual culture to assess the "hair story" of peoples of African descent. This was followed by a 2023 traveling photography exhibition, *Posing Beauty in African American Culture.* To ensure a deep and authentic perspective of the contemporary designers currently working in Algeria, Egypt, Morocco, and Tunisia, Dr. Hume engaged Nada Koreish as co-curator. Ms. Koreish is founder of the Fashion Liberation Collective, an organization supporting North African fashion, as well as a fashion designer and lecturer with a deep network and profound insights into North Africa's fashion and design community.

The KSU Museum's commitment to the project includes purchasing garments from several of the exhibition's designers for the permanent collection and the publication of a catalogue in partnership with Hirmer Verlag, who will produce and distribute the volume internationally.

Changes often come slowly to institutions, but with the commitment and vision of individuals like Dr. Hume, Ms. Koreish, and the exhibited designers who generously participated in the project, the KSU Museum continues to take steps to change perspectives and understandings of what a global society looks like.

Sarah J. Rogers,
former Director of the KSU Museum

ACKNOWLEDGEMENTS

Every museum exhibition is the result of incredible teamwork, and that is especially true of this exhibition, which depended on coordination across oceans, across continents. The project even spanned the tenure of two directors at the Kent State University Museum, Sarah J. Rogers and Dr. Sarah Spinner Liska. Both leaders were strong champions of this ambitious project and each in her way ensured its success from vision to realization.

I am deeply indebted to my co-curator, Nada Koreish, who contributed boundless energy and a deep knowledge of the subject. I also enjoyed the assistance of three tremendous students, Curatorial Intern Kathryn Anderson, KSU Museum Fellow Sophie Bessell, and Curatorial Assistant Sefra Protch. Joanne Fenn, KSU Museum Collections Manager, Registrar, and Professor, managed to coordinate loans and shipping from dozens of lenders with the support of student collections assistants Sabrina Adjiri, Olivia Carpenter and Likitha Kalla. James Williams, KSU Museum Senior Exhibition Designer, worked closely with the curators to create a stunning installation design that supports their vision. He also benefited from the efforts of student assistants Babz Glines, Art Mooneyham, and Vic Williams. Exceptional recognition is due to the hard work of Special Assistant Bianka Hausknecht, who negotiated the challenges of layers of bureaucracy. This publication is the KSU Museum's second partnership with Hirmer Verlag and we are grateful to Elisabeth Rochau-Shalem, Rainer Arnold, and designer Sophie Friederich for their care in translating the curatorial vision into this publication.

As always, Diane Petrella, Dean of KSU's College of the Arts, was an early and enthusiastic supporter of the project, as were Mourad Krifa, Director of the Shannon Rodgers and Jerry Silverman School of Fashion Design and Merchandising, and Ikram Toumi, Associate Professor in the School of Communication Studies.

Such ambitious projects depend on the great generosity of many donors and sponsors, including the lead sponsor of the exhibition, Linda Harper, and the on-going support of the Ohio Arts Council.

I want to thank the talented writers who made such insightful contributions to this volume. Thank you Kazna Askar, Norhan El Sakkout, and Kenza Vandeput-Taleb. To all the artists and lenders, who have graciously agreed to part with their objects for the duration of the exhibition, we are most grateful. You have each shared your time, your insights, your pride in your culture, and I hope that the profiles we have included here in these pages attest to our appreciation.

Finally we are grateful for the support of those who have made this exhibition and publication possible. They include Lead Sponsor Linda Harper, the Ohio Arts Council, and the Louise H. and David S. Ingalls Foundation.

Dr. Sara Hume, Curator/Professor

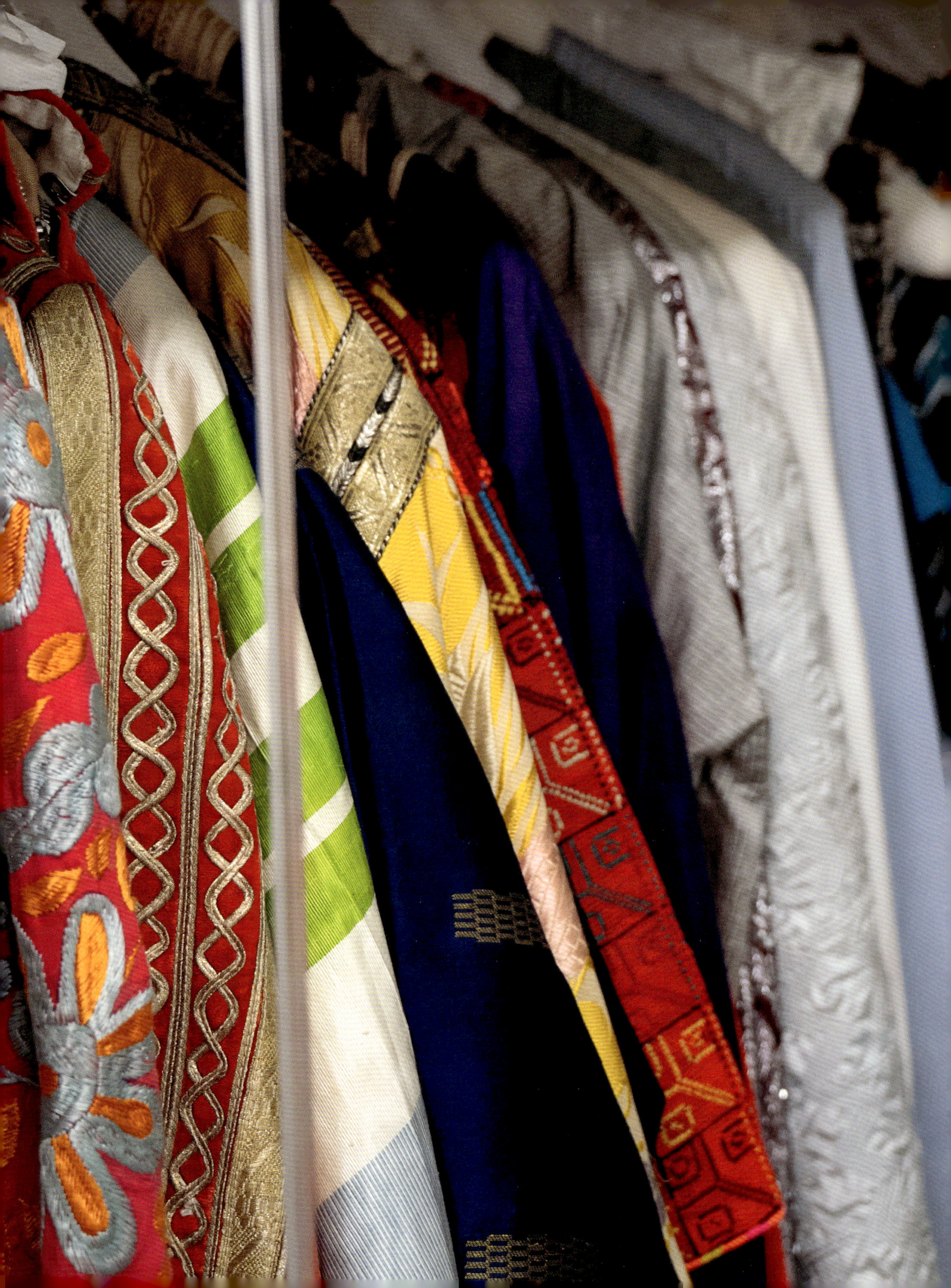

RETHINKING COLLECTING PRACTICES

Dr. Sara Hume

As the curator of *A Meeting of Cultures*, it seems that the task I have set for myself is to define what North African fashion means. But that is a project too complex, too fraught to be taken on by anyone let alone a person whose education has been in the field of European history and whose experience in museums has focused largely on collections of Western dress. To overcome the limitations of my own perspective, I have joined forces with Nada Koreish, who has dedicated her career to supporting North African designers and broadening the focus of fashion studies to create space for underrepresented voices. It has been important for me not to allow the specificity of my own educational background to circumscribe the range of exhibitions and scholarship that is produced at the Kent State University Museum. For too long the field of fashion history has focused largely on the dress practices in Europe and the United States—more specifically on the wealthy elite of urban centers.

This exhibition represents the second in a series I have organized on fashion on the African continent. Rather than pack the tremendous diversity of African fashion into a single exhibition, we have developed exhibitions looking at smaller regions. In this way we counter the mistaken notion that Africa is a single monolith. Instead, the continent is vast in its expanse and varied in its cultural production. In 2016 we began the series with *Fashions of Southern Africa,* which featured looks from South Africa and Namibia (fig. 1). These exhibitions aim to correct the misconception that the increasing globalization of the fashion industry will ultimately lead to growing homogenization by showcasing how place plays an important role shaping the work of African designers active today.

Drawing together all of the pieces in the exhibition is the idea of North Africa as a place where diverse cultures meet. The Mediterranean connects the five countries of North Africa with

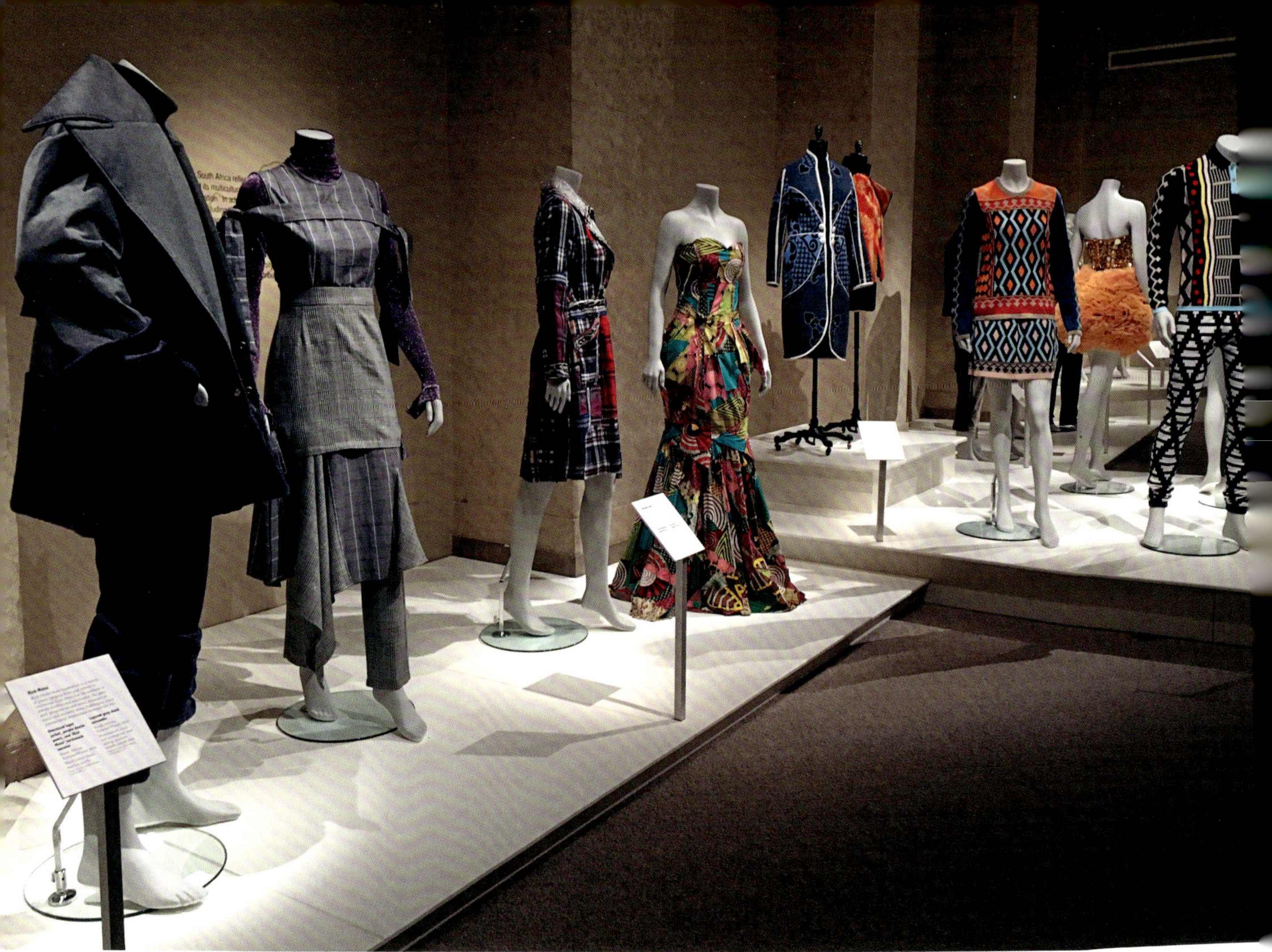

each other but also to Europe and the Middle East. Since ancient times, people and goods have traveled across the Mediterranean, creating a space of exchange. In celebrating this potential for creativity and openness we must not ignore the dark side of these cultural contacts. The Roman invasion and conquest of Carthage, in present-day Tunisia, is evidence of a succession of violent impositions of foreign domination and control. While now we think of North Africa as being part of the Arab world, Muslim control of the area starting in the seventh century occurred at the expense of earlier regimes and cultures. In its turn the Ottoman empire established control over the coastal area of most of North Africa. Through the nineteenth century European powers sought to control North Africa along with sub-Saharan Africa and the Middle East. France became a dominant player in the Maghreb, consolidating colonial power over Algeria, while exercising de facto control over Morocco and Tunisia. Similarly the British ruled over Egypt as a protected state.[1]

Fig. 1: Gallery view of *Fashions of Southern Africa* on view at the Kent State University Museum August 2026–July 2027. Photograph by Sara Hume

As a result of the political and economic domination, the relationship between Europe and North Africa has been asymmetrical. Seeking to maximize their educational and economic opportunities, people from North Africa have immigrated in significant numbers to Europe. However, the displacement is not always permanent—rather there is a dynamic movement of people back and forth between Europe and North Africa. Many of the designers included in this exhibition have spent part of their life in Europe and have clientele on both sides of the Mediterranean. Similarly, the Middle East has been an important market for North African designers. Recognizing the continual flow of goods and the movement of the population, this exhibition includes designers and artists who identify as North African but are part of the broader diaspora, as well as those who have a permanent home in the region.

The asymmetry in the historic relationship between Europe and North Africa has also resulted in the perception of European culture as being modern, dynamic, and advancing, while North African culture is seen as traditional, static, and backward. While the word "traditional" is not necessarily pejorative, its juxtaposition against the idea of progress and modernity situates it as inferior. The aim of *A Meeting of Cultures* is to counter this prevailing dichotomy. Fashion and design in North Africa is dynamic and progressive not despite but because of a rich legacy of expert craftsmanship and cultural heritage. To explore this dynamism, the exhibition is organized around three themes: Disruptors, Threads, and Our Land. These themes each bring together the work of designers from different countries and draw out the diverse approaches to retaining cultural distinctiveness, while adapting to contemporary concerns ranging from sustainability to gender identity. The first theme, "Disruptors," looks at how designers present streetwear styles that call into question conventional rules such as the distinctions between menswear and women's wear. The second theme, "Threads," concentrates on how designers are committed to couture techniques, locally sourced materials, and sustainability. "Our Land" honors designers who take inspiration from familiar elements of the region's rich dress heritage and built environment and interpret them in modern designs.

Collecting Challenges

In addition to reshaping the view of fashion presented to the public, this series of exhibitions of African fashion has broadened the way the KSU Museum collects the dress of non-Western cultures. In fact, it has led to a rethinking of the distinctions drawn between "Western" and "non-Western" dress. The very terminology is problematic, first because much of North Africa is actually west of Europe—Marrakesh lies further west than London! But the greater concern is the construction of this opposition itself, which "is tightly interwoven with a colonial-racist worldview."[2] Despite the imprecision of the words, I will continue with these designations because they articulate a distinction which underpins the collection. The KSU Museum is typical of museums in the United States and Europe which collect costumes and textiles. Historically, examples of dress from the Arab world, like those from elsewhere in Africa, South America, and Asia have been segregated within the museum from fashions of Europe and the United States. While the storage of the latter is organized by time period and designer, the non-Western fashions are grouped geographically and often lack documentation indicating when and by whom the pieces were made. The collecting and storage practices reflect a belief that non-Western fashion is timeless and unchanging, based on traditions and long-standing customs rather than individual creativity.

The founders and early staff of the KSU Museum drew a distinction between Western and non-Western fashion not simply through the organization of the collection but in the very mission statement of the institution. Written in 1986, just a year after the Museum opened its doors to the public, the mission statement asserted:

> The Kent State University Museum maintains collections of selected examples of costume, design, interior furnishings and art that reflect the development of fashion and style in society from the late-17th century through the present. These collections emphasize
> i) material from Western urban cultures.
> ii) material from urban cultures of other parts of the world.
> iii) non-urban material as it relates to, or is reflective of, the development of fashion and style in urban cultural contexts.

The early mission had a clear emphasis on urban culture which it linked to fashion and style. While the three bulleted points are not explicitly ranked in order of priority, there is an implied hierarchy centering the West and radiating out from there with other material of interest "as it relates to" fashion and style. For what other reason would there even be a need to differentiate Western cultures from those of "other parts of the world"? Why not simply combine such materials as being from urban cultures?

In contrast, the current mission statement on our website reads:

> The Kent State University Museum advances the understanding of world cultures through collecting, preserving, interpreting and exhibiting fashion, textiles, and related arts to students, scholars, and the general public.

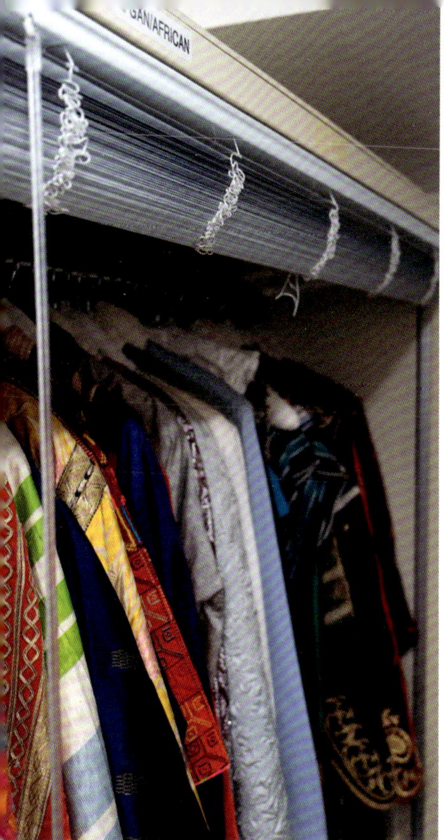

Fig. 2: Kent State University Museum storage of African and Middle Eastern collection. Photograph by Sara Hume

While the initial mission emphasized fashion and style for its own sake, the new mission articulates the value of fashion and textiles in that they provide knowledge of world cultures. There is no hierarchy of culture which distinguishes Western and non-Western, urban and rural. However, in order to live up to the ambitious claims of the current mission, careful attention must be paid to the collecting policies going forward.

The current storage system remains a legacy of the distinctions the KSU Museum has drawn between Western and non-Western fashion. The former collection is currently stored according to two systems of organization. The historic dress—from the eighteenth century through the 1930s—is arranged chronologically. For pieces which date from the 1940s to the present, there are two different storage locations. The storage space located on the first floor of Rockwell Hall is organized alphabetically by designer. Obviously this location is reserved for pieces with known designers. The storage which is located off-site is organized chronologically. Within the chronological organization the pieces are divided by function: suits and separates, cocktail and evening, wedding, menswear, children's wear, knitwear, etc. These two overarching systems of organization reflect the predominant understanding of Western fashion: it changes in meaningful ways over time and is the product of creative genius.

By contrast, the clothing from non-Western cultures as well as European regional dress is stored on the third floor of Rockwell Hall following a different logic. The pieces stored in these cabinets and drawers are arranged geographically. For instance, there are currently two cabinets of hanging storage dedicated to dress from Africa and the Middle East (fig. 2). These two cabinets bring together caftans and burnooses that are attributed to North Africa alongside Liberian and Nigerian pieces, as well as a Bedouin dress and robes that purportedly came from the royal family of King Saud of Saudi Arabia. The pieces are organized geographically without regard for their chronology or maker. While this organization implies an understanding of non-Western clothing as being traditional in the sense of not changing over time, it is also a reflection of a lack of information regarding the date or maker of the pieces.

In many ways museums function through the categorization of the objects in their possession. The process of categorizing and labeling objects reflects the values underlying the institutions. Many scholars have linked the operations of museums and archives as a mechanism for the dominant culture to exercise power over marginalized groups. Rodney G. S. Carter has framed the power dynamic through the idea of silences in the archives: "the powerful can introduce silences into the archives by denying marginal groups their voice and the opportunity to participate in the archives."[3] The silence in many cases comes not from excluding representation of objects from cultures, but in the failure to accompany the objects with their stories and adequate documentation.

While some pieces come with detailed provenance, the majority come with minimal information. For example, the red velvet caftan which bears the accession number 1983.001.0964 is described in the cataloguing information as "African, North African" (fig. 3). The date is alternately recorded as 1950-75 and "late 19th to early 20th century." This particular garment formed part of the original collection of the KSU Museum's founders Shannon Rodgers and Jerry Silverman. They acquired pieces from all over the world both from their travels as well as from dealers in the United States and Europe. Unfortunately, they did not keep scrupulous documentation of their acquisitions and many of their non-Western pieces have only the vaguest of identifying information. Their interest in world dress focused largely on aesthetics. The stunning gold embroidery on a rich, red velvet ground appealed to their love of ostentation and fine workmanship. The lack of detailed knowledge on the part of the collectors deprives future users of the collection of valuable information.

Erica de Greef points out the danger of a collection developed through donation in that such a collection "reflects the donors' notion of cultural value, and their perceptions of, and contribution toward, the making of shared public memories."[4] In the case of African objects, many collectors who donated to American museums have historically been engaged in a range of colonial activities, be they military, administrative, or missionary. As the KSU Museum opened in the 1980s, a couple decades after most countries in Africa had gained independence, the collecting reflected the values of the postcolonial period. The legacy of colonialism endured through the consumption of non-Western culture for the pleasure of the tourist. North Africa was admired among Europeans and Americans as picturesque and exotic. Silverman and Rodgers were typical of many of the KSU Museum's donors in that they did not have deep knowledge of any particular region's culture. As the museum founders, the couple's values pervaded much of the museum's early collecting practices. Founded in conjunction with the establishment of the Shannon Rodgers and Jerry Silverman School of Fashion Design and Merchandising, the KSU Museum served as inspiration for fashion design students. The guidelines for acquisition emphasized that items should be of "particular value for contemporary designers," or "represent a wide variety of structural and surface design techniques." The only interest in non-Western culture would be if it served "cross-cultural comparative purposes."[5] The collecting practices prioritized the physical appearance and construction of the object over the story, function, or significance in its original context.

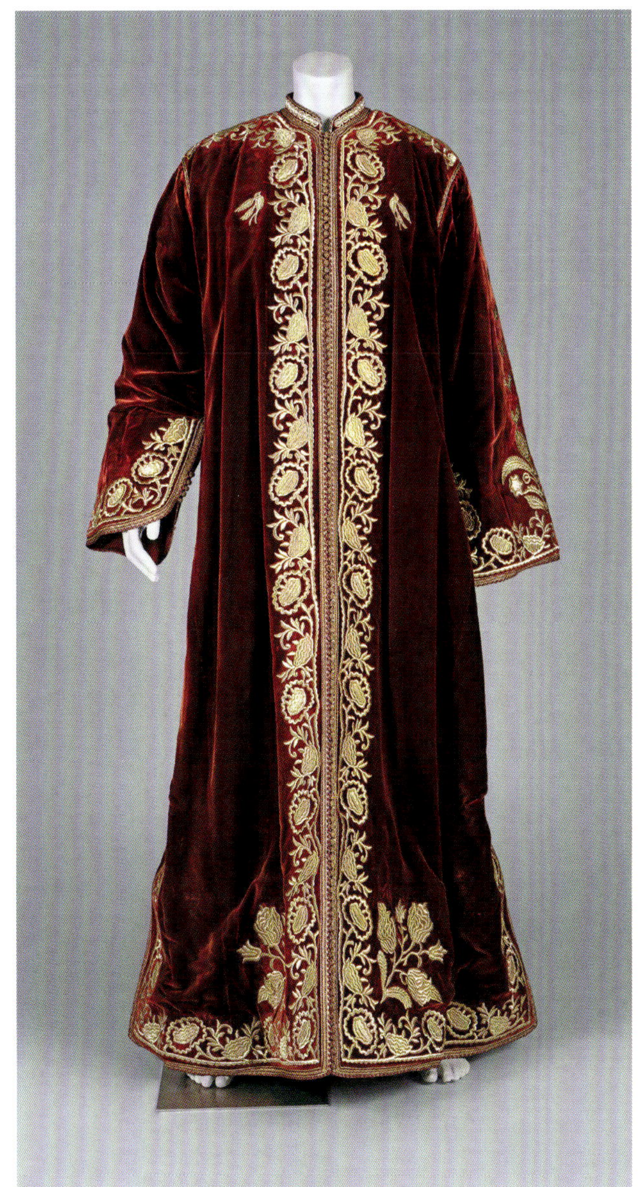

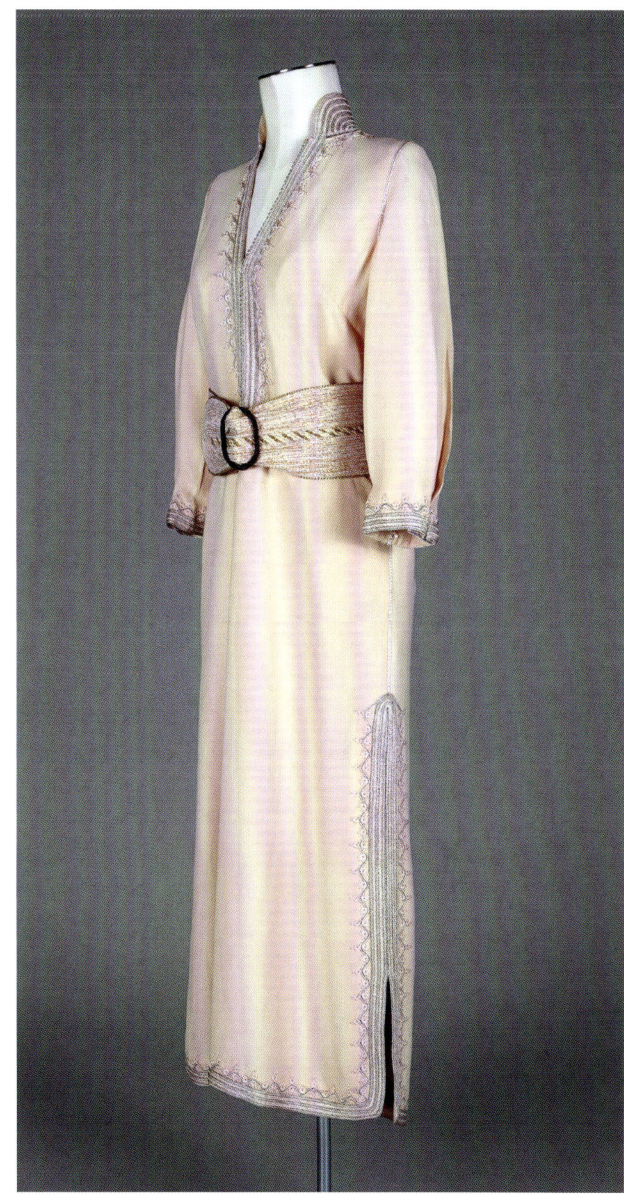

Fig. 3: Red velvet caftan with goldwork embroidery, North African, Silverman/Rodgers Collection, KSUM 1983.001.0964

Fig. 4: Jelabba of peach silk crepe with belt, gift of Salma Gibara (Mrs. Sam Gibara), KSUM 2016.15.2 ab. Photographs by Sara Hume

More recently, many of the collectors traveled to the African continent to engage in scholarship or tourism. While different levels of background knowledge inform the collecting done by scholars as opposed to tourists, there is often still the intervention of an outsider's perspective in the selection of pieces as well as the stories they can tell. In Heather Akou's analysis of collecting practices underlying collections of African fashion and textiles, she contrasts the collection of renowned dress scholar Joanne Eicher, who acquired pieces for her own use, against the wardrobe of a Nigerian woman. As Akou says, the latter collection "not only informs us as collectors and scholars but reflects the cultural values of the Africans who made and/or wore the items of dress."[6]

By and large the collectors who contributed the North African objects to the KSU Museum collection were Americans who acquired pieces on their travels. One notable exception are the ensembles donated in 2016 by Salma Gibara (fig. 4). Mrs. Gibara was born in Cairo to a Lebanese family. She lived along with her husband Sam Gibara in Paris, Casablanca, Brussels, and Toronto as well as Akron, where he worked for Goodyear. The Egyptian pieces she donated are described in the cataloguing as "jelabbas" (*djellabas*) and date to the 1990s. The value of having garments donated by people who are themselves of the culture comes in the known function of the pieces. In contrast, pieces purchased by tourists during their travels often lack detailed information about why and when and by whom they may have been worn—if in fact the pieces were ever worn and not simply made to be sold as souvenirs.

Another example from our collection which highlights some of these challenges is a dress of black cotton with red and blue cross stitch embroidery; it is categorized as "African, North African, Bedouin" and dated between 1875 and 1899 (fig. 5). The description includes the information that it was purchased by the donor Gene LePere in Luxor, Egypt, in 1992, before being donated to the KSU Museum in 1996. Although the piece was purchased in Egypt, it is not clear that that is where the piece was made and worn, in fact, in her correspondence with the museum the donor speculates that it was more likely Yemeni than North African. Bedouins are nomadic peoples who have inhabited the desert regions across North Africa and the Middle East for millennia. The piece may have been worn in Egypt but the knowledge to precisely locate its origin has been lost along the way. On the other hand, perhaps the designation as *Bedouin* is more salient than a classification according to national boundaries that did not exist when it was produced and perhaps were not meaningful to its producers and wearers. The division of North Africa and the Middle East into the countries that we know today was largely imposed by colonial powers rather than reflecting cultural distinctions.

The database in which the KSU Museum stores all of their records has fields for creator, date, and culture. The convention of recording culture as a nationality demonstrates how the institution imposes a prevailing system of values through categorization. As we have seen, the creator field is empty for all of the North African pieces in the collection acquired before this exhibition. The failure of the collectors of the non-Western garments to ascertain the maker indicates that the identity of the artisans who carefully crafted the garments was not

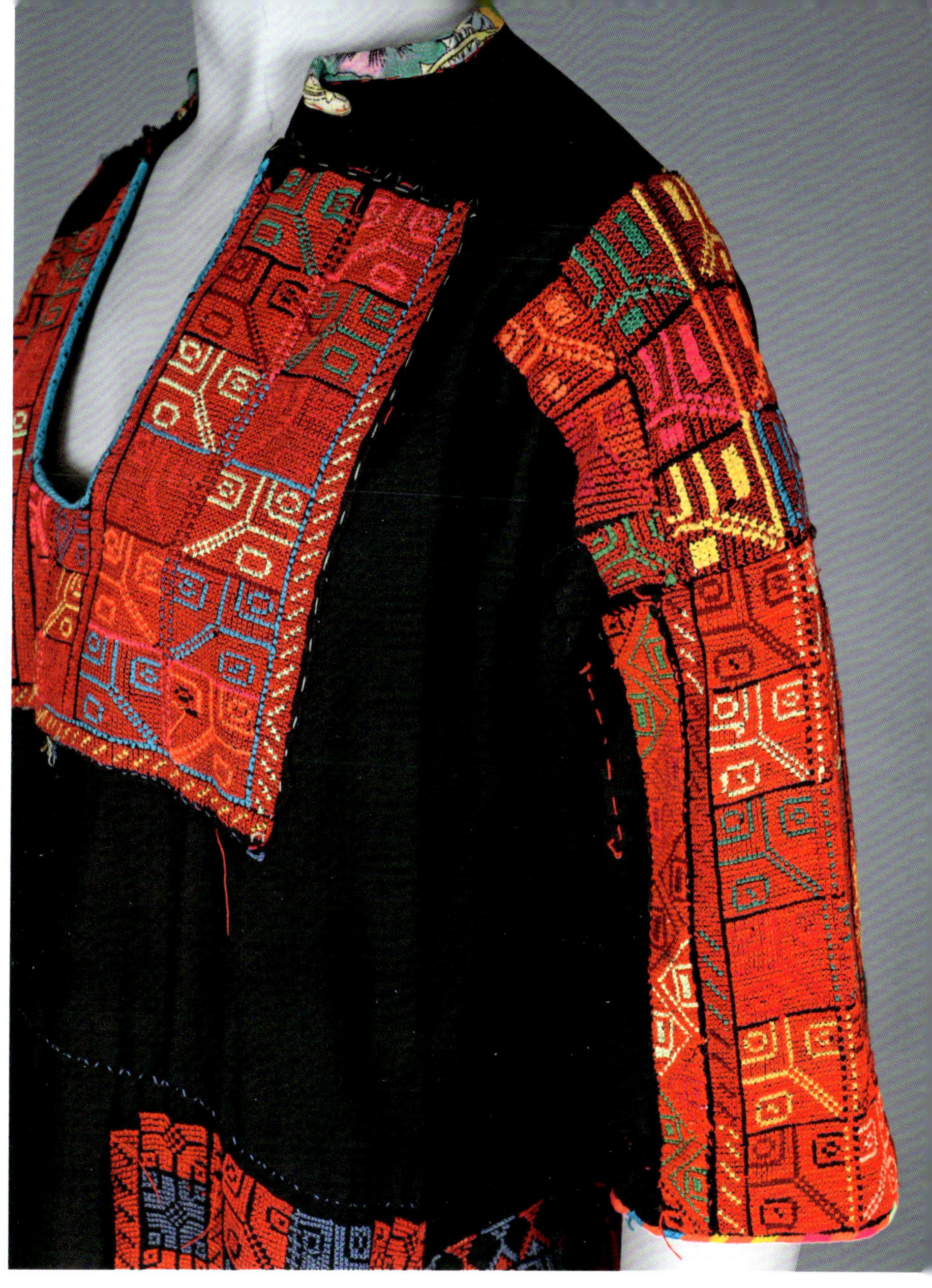

Fig. 5: Sleeve detail of Bedouin robe of black cotton with cross-stitch embroidery, gift of Gene H. LePere, KSUM 1996.026.000. Photograph by Sara Hume

considered noteworthy. This stands in sharp contrast to the collecting practices for Western fashion, where pieces are valued for the designer, the brand, the label. *A Meeting of Cultures* provides an opportunity to change our collecting practices in order to represent and honor the individual creators responsible for North African fashion. Similarly, the date and culture will be known with precision.

The date field is almost always filled but the information is unreliable. For instance, the red velvet caftan from the Silverman/ Rodgers collection has two conflicting dates recorded in different fields. The earlier date may have come when Rodgers purchased the piece from the dealer or at auction. The later date may be based on a comparison between the piece and others with known dates in the collection. The caftan is extremely similar to another piece transferred to the KSU Museum from the Museum at FIT (KSUM 2000.63.3; fig. 6). The date of the piece transferred from FIT is recorded as ca. 1970 and the culture is recorded as Moroccan. However the piece originally belonged to the American fashion designer Adele Simpson, who acquired it to use as design inspiration. The provenance of these two caftans is remarkably similar and while the information from one may be used to enhance knowledge of the other, the underlying loss of context and history cannot be corrected. The preference for these ornate, gold-worked styles among American fashion designers in the 1970s and 80s says as much about American taste as Moroccan design.

Going forward

There are several institutions working on the type of scholarship into the evolution of North African clothing styles that can be both a model and a resource as we collect going forward. The Victoria & Albert Museum in London has been working with Angela Jansen to develop their collection of Moroccan dress. This new collection falls under the purview of the Asian department rather than being part of same department as the rest of contemporary fashion. This distinction parallels the situation of the KSU Museum, where Western and non-Western dress are separated. Furthermore, Jansen laments locating the rich cultural resources in an institution which not only has a long colonial history but also a European location that makes it largely inaccessible for ordinary Moroccans. Despite these drawbacks, the collecting methods entailing detailed information about the makers and original context are exemplary. Most of the pieces from the early postcolonial period are sourced from private collections in Morocco and France. More recent pieces are acquired directly from the designers.[7]

While Jansen's work has been specifically dedicated to Moroccan pieces, the Zay Initiative has collected dress from across the Arab world. Founded by Reem Tariq El Mutwalli, the initiative began with the collection of historic dress from the United Arab Emirates and has expanded to cover North Africa and the Middle East. According to their website, "The Zay Initiative aims to promote an understanding of the evolution of regional culture, building up public awareness and appreciation of this unique heritage, reaching out to like-minded individuals and institutions nationally, regionally, and globally."[8] The collection is accessible not simply through exhibitions and museum loans but more importantly through an

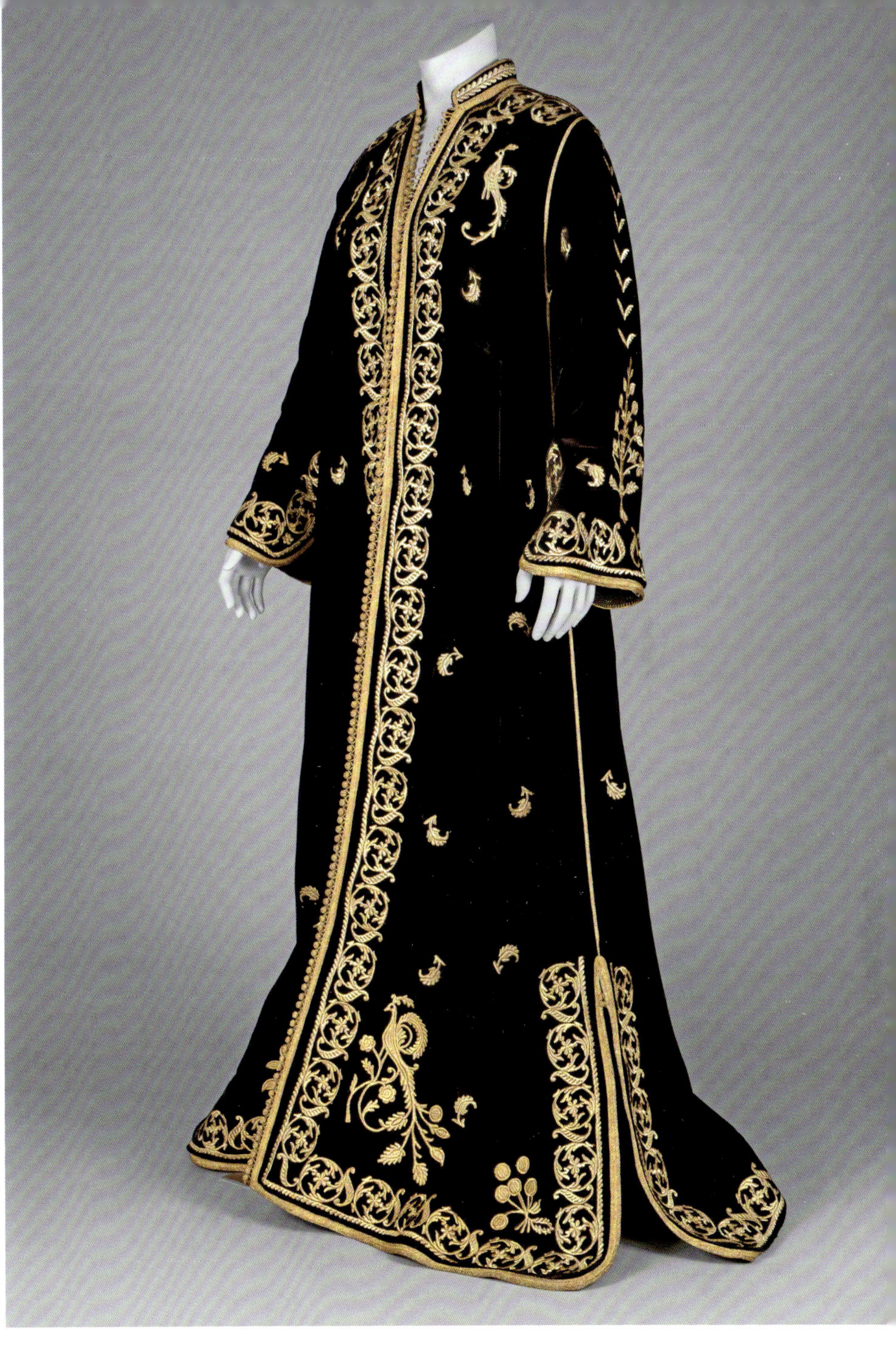

Fig. 6: Black velvet caftan with goldwork embroidery, Moroccan, ca. 1970, from the collection of Adele Simpson, gift of the Museum at FIT, KSUM 2000.063.000. Photograph by Sara Hume

extensive digital archive. The collection of Arab dress can be viewed and searched online with not just images of most pieces but provenance, place of origin, date, a detailed physical description including technique, and a section of further information. The additional information contains important information for the English-speaking reader about vocabulary. For instance, the cataloguing for a Moroccan caftan (ZI2019.500554 MOROCCO) includes the following etymology:

There are multiple names to what is generally called a Moroccan qaftan, such as (mansuriyah), (tahtiyah), (qaftan_khrib), and (qaftan_makhzini). Furthermore, in English the term is often spelt 'caftan' or 'kaftan' changing the [q] from the Arabic letter [qaf] to a hard [c] or [k]. The word qaftan comes from the Persian word khaftan, and entered English by way of Turkish and French.[9]

The Zay Initiative's on-line database makes the private collection of dress into a widely useful source for similar collections worldwide.

The accessibility of the Zay Initiative's collection is both instructive as a means of overcoming the segregation of non-Western dress in the KSU Museum's collection as well as illuminating its challenges. The searchability of an online database allows the user to group the collection according to their own desired terms. While the organization of the collection's physical storage can only sort by one attribute, be it maker, date, or place of origin, the KSU Museum's database on PastPerfect can sort through the records for the entire collection by material, color, technique, or any other desired attribute. The limitation to this system is that the quality of the search results are only as good as the quality of the information entered into the database. We have already seen the limitations of our cataloguing due to a lack of information at the time of acquisition. Additional limitations arise because of imprecision or inconsistency in the lexicon. In the case of the Moroccan garment above the object name could be general, such as dress or robe. Alternately the word *qaftan* could be spelled at least three different ways as described above: with a *q*, *c*, or *k*. This inconsistency comes from the transliteration of a language which does not use the Latin alphabet. That is not to mention the additional options listed by the Zay initiative such as *mansuriyah* or *tahtiyah*. The development of metadata to populate the collections management system is a very complicated process and demands thought and extensive research.

The logistics of integrating another culture's heritage into a museum collection have challenged curatorial and registrarial staffs for the past generation. Beyond the difficulties posed by respecting the languages of diverse cultures, the description of objects can unwittingly express prevailing colonial or racist attitudes. Work is ongoing to develop best practices not simply in collecting and documenting objects but in standardizing vocabulary and lexicon for catalogues. The Philadelphia Museum of Art, for example, has published an "Ethical Cataloguing Statement," in which they "commit to maintaining transparency regarding our policies and procedures. We invite community input and welcome your feedback."[10] As they acknowledge, the efforts to rectify outdated language and best document marginalized cultures is ongoing and feedback from the communities who are represented is essential to ensure improvement.

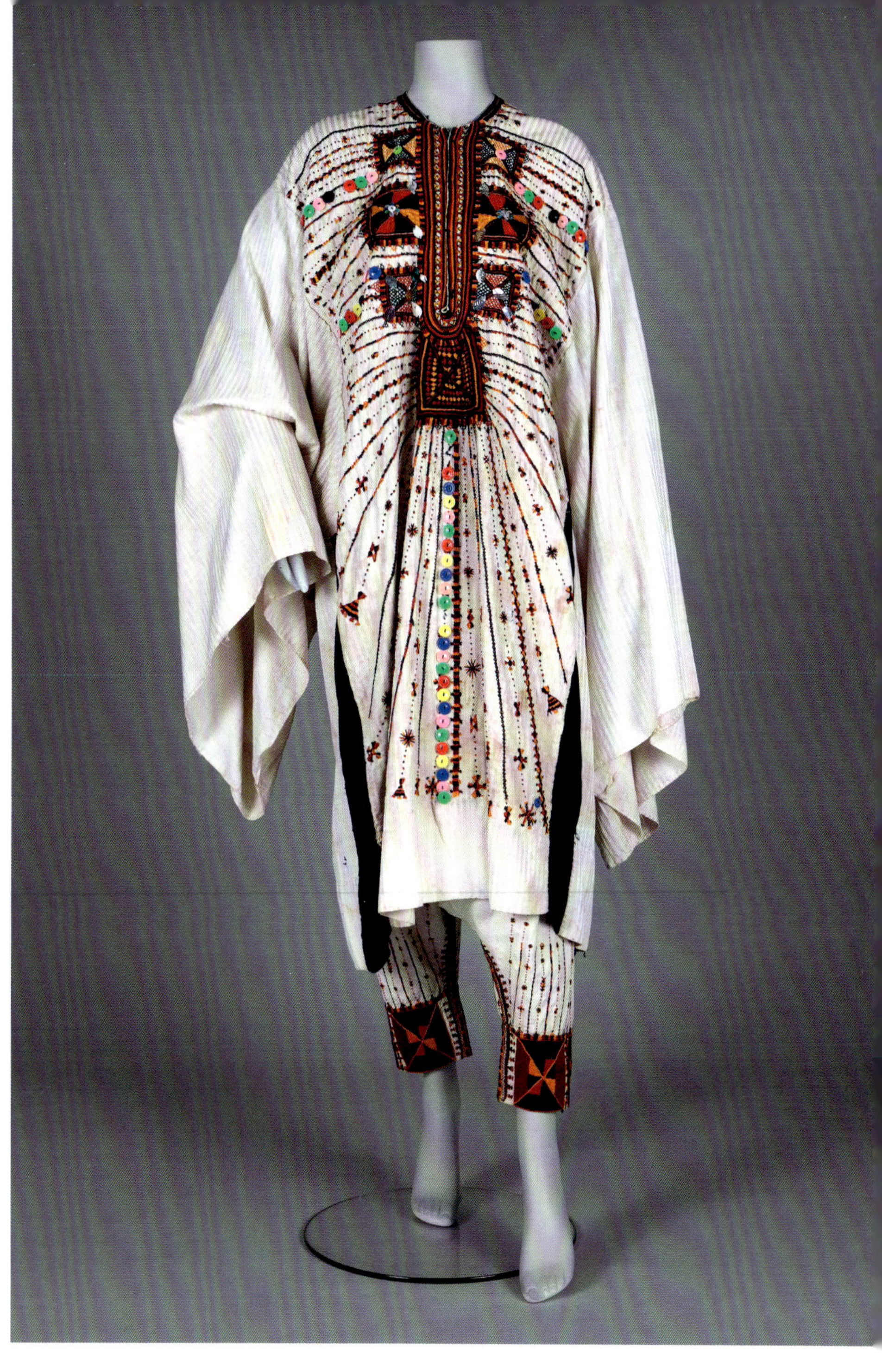

Fig. 7: Bridal tunic and trousers of embroidered white cotton adorned with buttons and sequins, Egyptian, Siwa Oasis, Silverman/Rodgers Collection, KSUM 1983.001.2495 ab. Photograph by Sara Hume

A Meeting of Cultures coincides with the commemoration of the KSU Museum's 40th anniversary. Thus, this is an appropriate opportunity to reflect on our collecting practices and ensure they conform to the principles laid forth in our Mission. In preparation for the exhibition we did a review of the North African pieces in our collection and researched the provenance and sought to determine the dates and cultures of pieces with greater precision than already present in our database. While the amount of information we were able to gain was limited we did have one success story. We discovered a beautiful robe of white cotton adorned with colorful buttons and embroidery accompanied by a matching pair of trousers (fig. 7). Unfortunately the outfit had mistakenly received an accession number which duplicated another piece and we could not locate any records for it. We did know that it was part of the original Silverman/Rodgers collection. Because it had no documentation, we knew nothing about it including where in the world it might have originated. It had been given the same number as a Hausa ensemble from Nigeria and was stored in the African/Middle East cabinet, so we began with the working assumption that it was African. The Museum Fellow, Sally Saindon, researched extensively into the dress of cultures across the African continent in hopes of finding a match. Ultimately, she succeeded in identifying it as a wedding garment of a woman from the Siwa Oasis in Egypt. A very similar example is actually in the collection of the Zay Initiative which includes a detailed description of its cultural context in its database.[11] We were able to give the ensemble a unique accession number (1983.001.2495 ab) and display it in conjunction with our exhibition *As the World Weds: Global Wedding Traditions.* This case demonstrates the value of the dissemination of information on-line relating to North African dress. It also makes evident how pieces in our collection can be more meaningfully displayed to the public if we know their cultural context.

Although we are working hard to compensate for the absence of documentation regarding pieces already in our collection, it remains impractical to reorganize our physical storage of non-Western pieces to integrate them with our Western dress. We cannot retroactively acquire the information about all of the pieces we have already collected. We cannot dispose of the pieces we have which are valuable to us. We cannot undo the different practices and customs of the past. What we can do is change our practices going forward. We can collect important designers from around the world with attention to when the pieces were made as well as where. We recognize through both our words and our actions that the work of designers from around the world are equal in creativity and craftsmanship to the work of a Coco Chanel or an Alexander McQueen. This catalogue as well as the exhibition are testaments to the originality, brilliance, and quality of design coming from North Africa. Our hope is that visitors to the exhibition and readers of the catalogue can appreciate the complicated way that place—in this case North Africa—can inspire and shape the way people dress and make clothes.

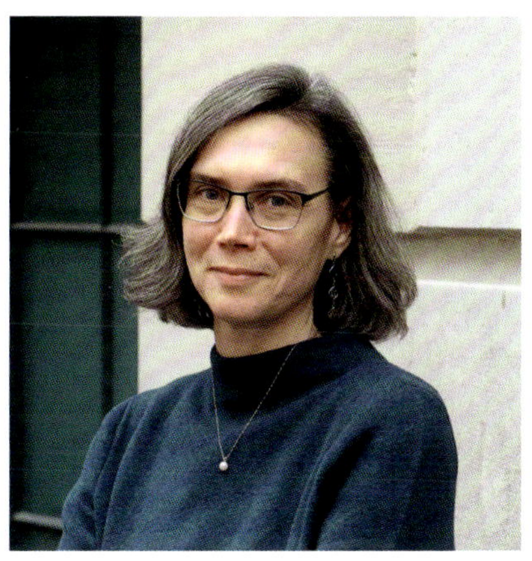

Dr. Sara Hume is Professor and Curator of Kent State University Museum. Her research in the history of dress has focused on the global reach of the fashion industry. She earned her PhD in Modern European History from the University of Chicago, a BA in Art from Yale University and an MA in Museum Studies from the Fashion Institute of Technology. She is the author of *Regional Dress: Between Fashion and Modernity* (Bloomsbury 2022).

1 For modern historical surveys of the countries of North Africa see Susan Gilson Miller, *A History of Modern Morocco* (New York: Cambridge University Press, 2013); Martin Evans and John Phillips, *Algeria: Anger of the Dispossessed* (New Haven: Yale University Press, 2007); Safwan M. Masri and Lisa Anderson, *Tunisia: An Arab Anomaly* (New York: Columbia University Press, 2017); Kenneth J. Perkins, *A History of Modern Tunisia* (Cambridge, UK / New York: Cambridge University Press, 2004); Ronald Bruce St. John, *Libya: From Colony to Revolution* (Oxford: Oneworld Publications, 2012); P. J. Vatikiotis, *The History of Modern Egypt: From Muhammad Ali to Mubarak*, 4th ed. (Baltimore: Johns Hopkins University Press, 1991).

2 Esther Peeren, "Language Cannot Be 'Cleaned Up,'" in *Words Matter: An Unfinished Guide to Word Choices in the Cultural Sector*, Wayne Modest and Robin Lelijveld, eds, (Amsterdam / Berg en Dal/ Leiden/ Rotterdam: Tropenmuseum, Afrika Museum, Museum Volkenkunde, Wereldmuseum, 2018), 45.

3 Rodney G. S. Carter, "Of Things Said and Unsaid: Power, Archival Silences, and Power in Silence," *Archivaria* 61 (Spring 2006): 217.

4 Erica de Greef, "Refashioning Clothing Collections in South African Museums," in *Creating African Fashion Histories: Politics, Museums, and Sartorial Practices*, JoAnn McGregor, Heather Akou, and Nicola Stylianou, eds. (Bloomington: Indiana University Press, 2022), 257.

5 "Kent State University Museum Collections Policies," December 1986, 10.

6 Heather Akou, "Stories behind the Collections and Why They Matter: Examples from Indiana University," in McGregor, *Creating African Fashion Histories*, 247.

7 M. Angela Jansen, "'There Was No Fashion in Morocco Before' (Re)Creating Contemporary Moroccan Fashion History," in McGregor, *Creating African Fashion Histories*, 190–92.

8 "About - The Zay Initiative," accessed June 23, 2024, https://thezay.org/about-zay/.

9 "Qaftan Embroidered with Silk - Morocco," The Zay Initiative, accessed June 23, 2024, https://thezay.org/product/zi2019-500554-moroccocloak-embroidered-with-silk-morocco/.

10 Library Tech Services, "PMA LibGuides: Home: Ethical Cataloging," accessed June 18, 2024, https://philamuseum.libguides.com/home/about-us/ethical-cataloging.

11 "Embroidered Bridal Tunic Dress - Egypt," The Zay Initiative, accessed July 5, 2024, https://thezay.org/product/zi2019-500491-egyptembroidered-bridal-tunic-dress-egypt/.

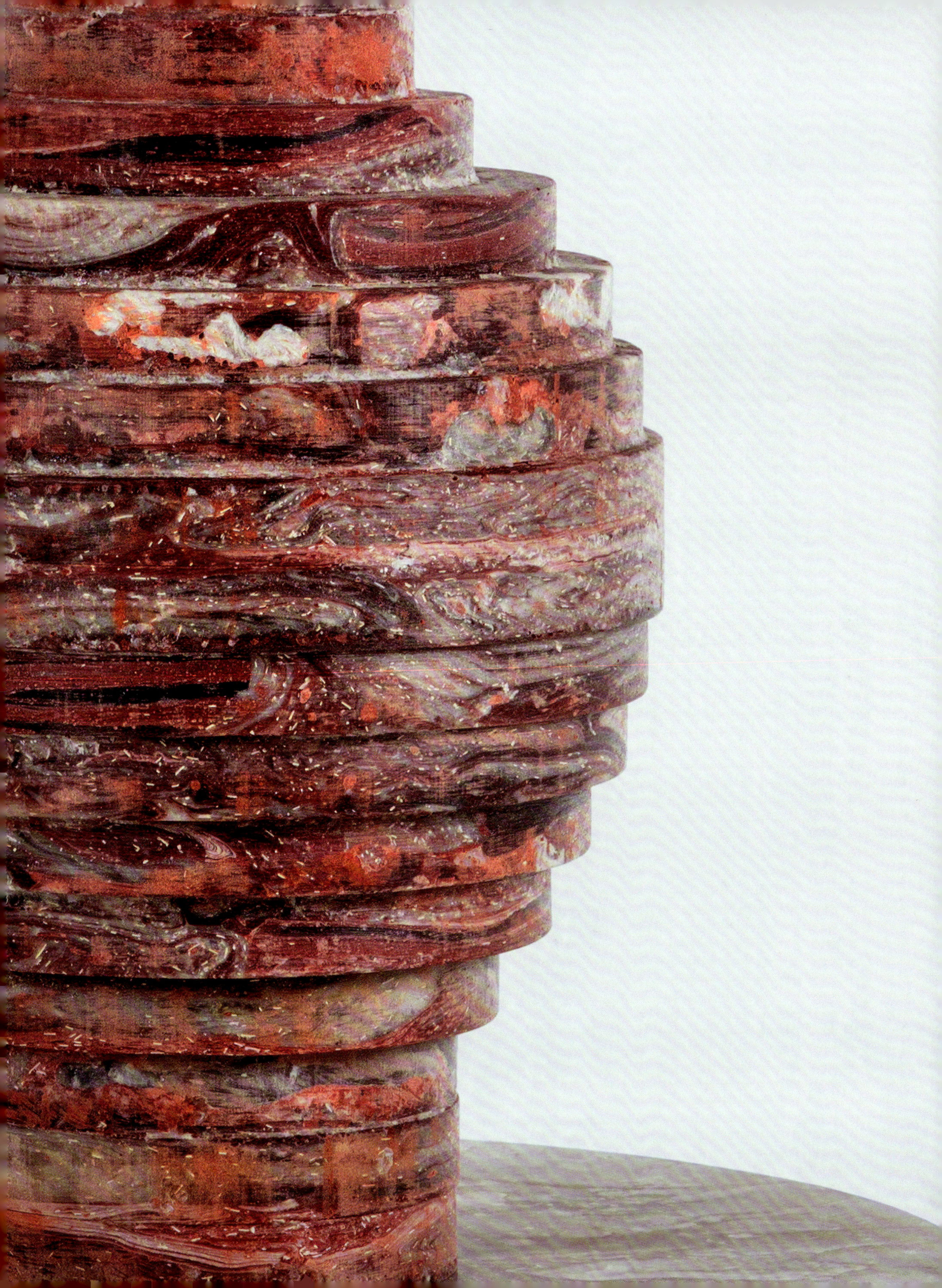

PERCEPTION

Nada Koreish

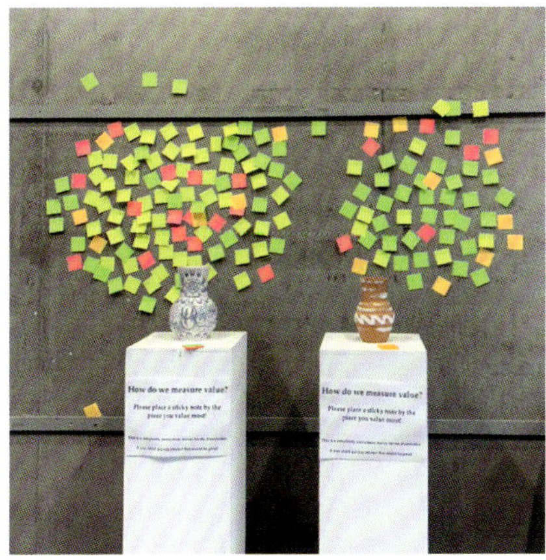

Fig. 1: Testing out ideas of value, by second-year ceramics student Phoebe Grace Wilkes, Cardiff. Image courtesy of Phoebe Grace Wilkes

Perception

A word that, at first glance, seems well, simple. This refers to how we use our senses to take in the world around us. But dive a little deeper, and even within the definition provided by the Oxford Dictionary, it becomes clear that perception is far more complex, more nuanced, more loaded than it first appears. According to the Oxford Languages Dictionary, perception "is the way in which something is regarded, understood, or interpreted—intuitive understanding and insight." The use of terms like "regarded," "understood," and "interpreted" immediately suggests that perception is not just about sensing the world—it is about how we process, filter, and ascribe meaning to what we experience. And in doing so, the concept of perception is thrown into the realm of identity: to what shapes us, to what makes us experience and regard things in particular ways, and to how we assign value to objects, people, and ideas. To nations and cultures. To the OTHER.

Perception

It is more than just a cognitive process. A colonial imperialist conditioning, determining who and what is worthy of recognition, power, and dignity. Used to control the value system. In the opening chapter "On Violence" of Fanon's *Wretched of the Earth,* he unearths the insidious methods of colonialism's conditioning of our self-worth and perception. Fanon argues that the generational power of colonialism is much deeper than territorial: it infects the very spirit of the colonized. To their core, it shapes the way the colonized view and value themselves and the world around them. "It is the colonist who fabricated and continues to fabricate the colonized subject. The colonist derives his validity, i.e., his wealth, from the colonial system."[1] The continuous false narratives and dehumanization leads to the colonized turning their self-perception into a distorted mirror reflecting only inferiority and powerlessness.

Perception

As Casakin and Bernardo explain, identity serves as the foundation for the way individuals perceive, engage with, and appreciate their environment. It facilitates the creation of emotional bonds to places and nurtures a sense of belonging, uniting individuals around shared values and concerns.[2] They (perception, identity, belonging and values) are at their core, linked. Perception, and its effect on identity, dictates how we see

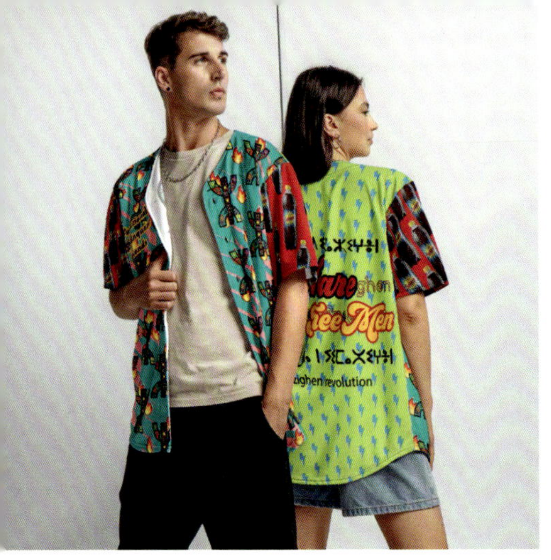

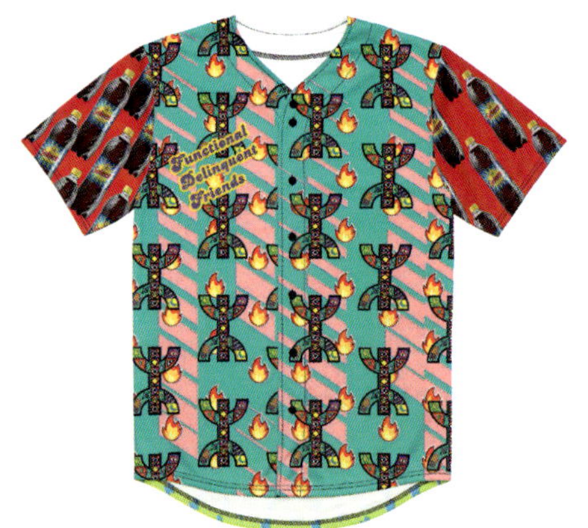

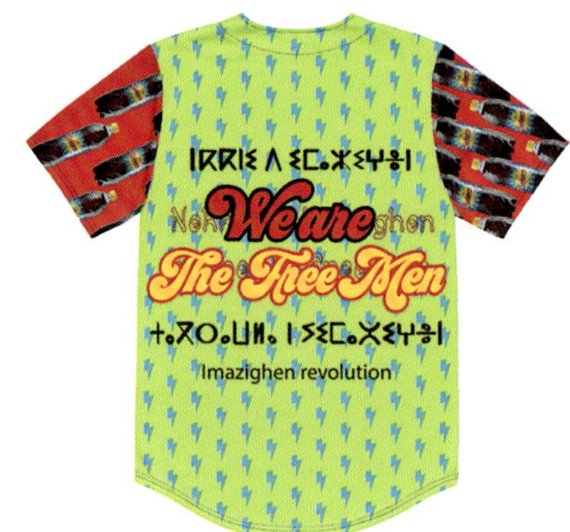

ourselves and how we are seen by others, shaping our sense of worth. And this brings us to the beginning of our exploration, the core of what the FLCNA stands for. This is where our journey into understanding the mind of the "Oriental" begins—a history of how we have been perceived, misrepresented, and how this perception has devalued our heritage, our cultures, and the very way we fashion our bodies.

So, how do we change perception? How do we reclaim our value, both internally and externally? These are the questions we address as we challenge the narratives that have shaped how we see ourselves and how we have been seen by the world. The simple answer would be, as Fanon puts it, "unchanged. Instead, it was the peasants, the 'wretched,' who must find their own human dignity by destroying colonialism, root and branch."[3] Fanon's remedy for this crisis of perception is radical and uncompromising: the process of de-rooting the generational trauma and impact of colonialism, by reclaiming what is ours. By reclaiming the terminology and the way we are spoken of. By rising up against the system that dehumanized them, the colonized affirm their agency, dignity, and humanity.

This "simple" answer leads us back to what FLCNA's purpose is, to reclaim, liberate, and replace the imposed colonial framework with our own sense of value, built on justice, solidarity, and self-recognition. It is a journey of rediscovery, where we not only aim to change our self-worth and value internally but in the rest of the world.

Figs 2–4: All-over print recycled baseball jersey top designed by Nada Koreish for FLCNA, depicting the Yaz, Kabyle writing meaning "we are the free men," to celebrate the liberation of the Algerian people. Images courtesy of Nada Koreish

Perception of "Us" as the "Native"

If you look at the MENA region's image in the West or the West's perception of the 'Orient,' they come hand-in-hand and feed into the self-worth and identity confusion of the region. We cannot discuss the 'Orient" or the "Oriental's journey" without referencing the enlightening work of Edward Said. He defines Orientalismas "a way of coming to terms with the Orient that is based on the Orient's special place in European Western experience. The Orient is not only adjacent to

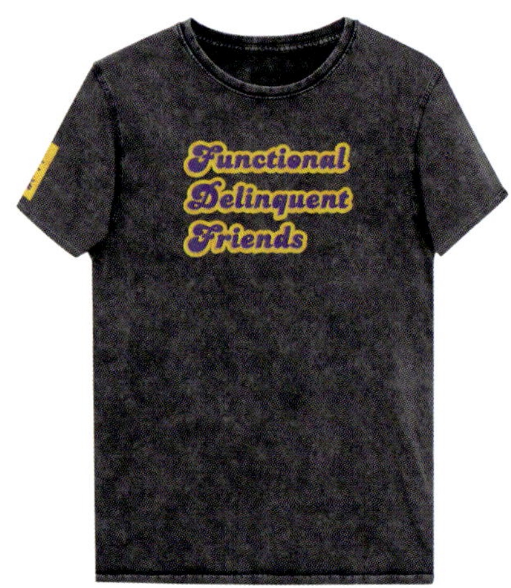

Fig. 5: Unisex denim t-shirt, designed by Nada Koreish for FLCNA, "functional delinquent friends" embroidery signifying the confusion of living in two worlds, with embroidery in Franco-Arab phonetically written as #for life in Arabic letters

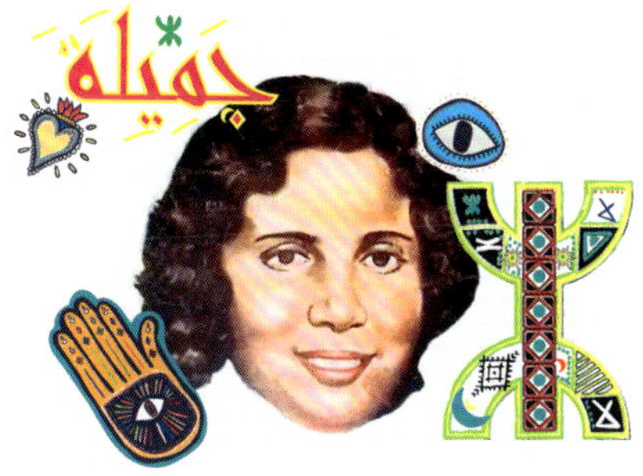

Fig 6: An homage to Algerian heroine and feminist icon Djamila Bouhired, for FLCNA

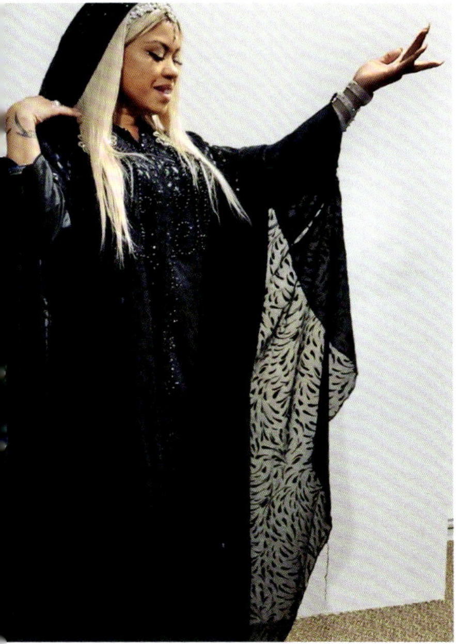

Fig 7: Pandora Gunn, renowned American belly dancer modeling her FLCNA gangsta *abaya*, foiled and beaded chiffon with satin lining, making *abayas* accessible and wearable by all, demystifying the exotic myths and oriental gaze. Image courtesy of Pandora Gunn

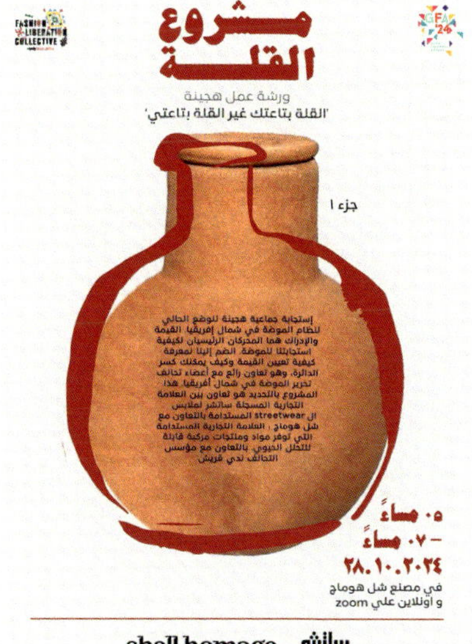

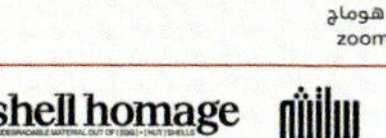

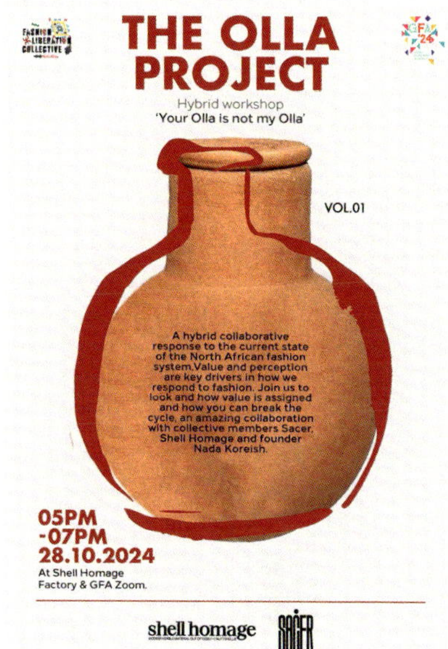

Figs. 8, 9: "Your olla is not my olla." Event flyer designed by the Sacer creative team, for a collaborative event with Shell homage and Sacer. Arabic and English version. This was an intentional play on words. The "olla," a terracotta drinking jug once found in every street of Egypt, is now sold as decorative "folklore art," or regarded as uncivilized. In other parts of North Africa the *olla* is still used daily and adorned. This beautifully made part of our heritage has been discarded, as are items such as the *jalabeya*. Such items, when picked up by an influencer or a celebrity, all of sudden become a trend. People start by superficially reclaiming their heritage, but eventually the process of valuing what is theirs occurs. This was the first of many planned events towards reimagining our native objects

Europe; it is also the place of Europe's greatest and richest and oldest colonies, the source of its civilizations and languages, its cultural contestant, and one of its deepest and most recurring images of the Other. In addition, the Orient has helped to define Europe."[4] Edward Said's definition is unique in that he attributes Europe and Europe's richest cultures to the Orient, he explains this symbiotic (at times parasitic) and strange relationship that the Orient and Europe have, the colonized and colonizer, he also explains simply that Orientalism is the Euro-Western experience, that it is one-sided. Most importantly, it was one of the first places I came across the word and definition of "other." This view of the fictional "Orient" has manifested into a narrative, a reality of a people, stereotyped, labelled, and stripped of their authentic identities and self-worth. Fashion has perpetuated this narrative and nurtured it over centuries. Whether through the fantastical exotification of the other, through the Orientalism movement, or the appropriation of "exotic" textiles and apparel, worn through the colonial era by wealthy Europeans, usually as a form of fetishization. And now down runways and appropriated by celebrities.

Perception will always be the other side of the coin, for value. Value is attributed to oneself, through modes of self-worth, social weight, and taste-making. How we value work, art, or ourselves? As an educator, I constantly tell my students, especially my global majority students, to value themselves. Their perception of the world and how they interact with fashion and other cultural modes are key to the success and added value of any name in fashion. Just look at the rise of streetwear as couture, the influence of Black culture on the ateliers, or YSL—many, many appropriations of North Africa and the rest of the "Orient."

Know your value we shout; yet we, the "wretched of the earth" have forgotten ours.

In the context of fashion, value is everything. In his book *On Decoloniality,* Walter Mignolo discusses how colonialism constructed what we know as the value system today with a focus on aesthetics and culture. It is clear that perception is inherently tied to value. Without a shift in perception, there can be no transformation in value. Value, in this sense, is multifaceted. It can be subjective, cultural, and historical—yet it is very much a colonial construct: value is most definitely a legacy of imperialism.[5]

Ideologies of preordained value emerge as the dominant cultural vector in postcolonial contexts, shaping how we perceive and assign worth. These values, shaped and cemented decades and centuries ago, remain embedded in the world's systems of recognition and worth, dictating what is deemed valuable and what is not. Today, we are paralyzed by our own generational demons, unable to fully unravel these legacies. The confusion surrounding identity—particularly in how we value fashion and taste—stems from these colonial narratives. They have dictated not only global value systems but also ours and the West's individual notions of self-worth, affecting both the colonized and the colonizer.

This peculiar dynamic—a paradoxical coin—remains still: How can we change the world's perception? How can we reimagine our self-worth? How can we dismantle the global value system that continues to weigh on the colonized?

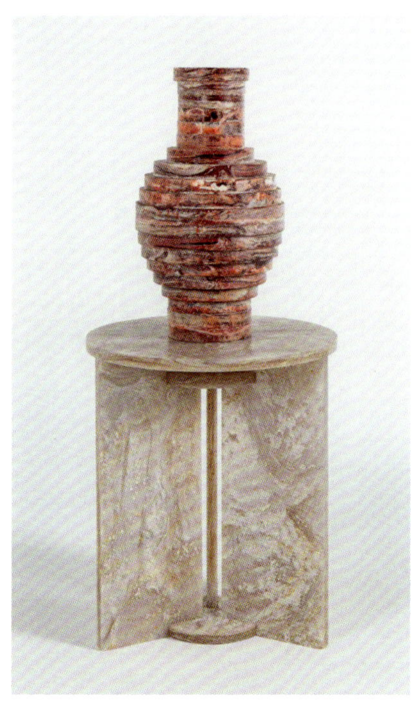

Fig. 10 The *olla* made from Shell Homage patented material, collaboratively designed by FLCNA (Sacer, myself, and Shell Homage founder Rania Elkalla), egg and nut shells patented material, for the Global Fashioning Assembly 2024. Image courtesy SHELL HOMAGE

What Is Our Value? How Are We Perceived?

> Orientalism is not a picture of the East of the Easts. It represents longing, options, and faraway perfection. It is, like Utopia, a picture everywhere and nowhere, save in the imagination. The Orientalist female was a fabrication of the West, attributing Salambō-like license and nudity to figures who escaped Occidental sanction by their placement in an Orientalist world."[6]

The quote above is from the publication accompanying Martin and Koda's Metropolitan Museum exhibition "Orientalism: Visions of the East in Western Dress." We can see how museums have played a role in aesthetics and taste value. Museums were one of the colonial modes of communication, showcasing Orientalist art, stolen artefacts, and other propaganda material to the Western public. This is why we strive to change these ideologies, by using the trusted methods of idea dissemination (such as exhibitions in the West and publications) to rewrite OUR narratives.

This quote highlights the relationship between fashion and Orientalism and how the fashion industry has always used colonialism and Orientalism for its gain. Examples of Orientalism and appropriation in fashion have always been present; this practice is very much alive and has been ever since French and British soldiers set foot on Eastern soil.

Exhibitions such as the aforementioned, although well intended, have always added to the allure of the "Orient." The call of its many mysteries still entices the West. As Said, Codell, Mignolo, Fanon, Gzeky and other scholars of Orientalism explain, "the Orient," a completely fabricated Western construct, inspires and creates an idyllic fantasy where its dwellers are "exotic," superstitious "others." The land is magical, mystical, and deadly. The truth is far, far from this Orientalist view. Codell reiterates Said's concept of "Othering." This is ultimately the longest-lasting effect of Orientalist mindsets. Codell defines the term simply: "'The Orient and the Oriental' became generalized stereotypes that included disparate cultures and ethnicities and crossed boundaries of places, peoples, and cultures. It tended to downplay differences in the interest of creating a homogenous 'Other.'"[7] Codell goes on to reaffirm that nineteenth century art, colonialism, and the birth of Orientalism was visible in anything from literature to stores and consumer goods. There is also a clear link between national and imperial identities. All this is what leads back to the " coin" and the drive to change both sides of it: perception and value.

Which brings us to our final path on our journey, the justification. Why does FLCNA exist and why is there an aching need to decolonize fashion in every crevice, including exhibition spaces?

"OMG! You're so exotic!"

"Oh my god, you're so exotic." A phrase I have heard countless times throughout my life and career—one that has been perceived and internalized differently at various stages. As a young, aspiring fashion designer, it was, for a time, a badge of honor. "Exotic." The word carried an allure, as if being "exotic" made me extraordinary, unique—qualities I believed could propel me to the forefront of the fashion world. It was a label I wore, naively embracing its mystique, unaware of the deeper implications.

Years later, however, the same word began to carry a weightier connotation. The admiration I once felt became intertwined with reductive stereotypes and misguided assumptions. "Do you ride camels?" "Do you live in pyramids?" Questions like these revealed a narrow, often prejudiced lens through which my identity was viewed. Assumptions abounded—that I was "mixed," Black, Hispanic, or the caricature of a "naughty Muslim Arab." The older I became, the more aware I was of how words like "exotic," which I once thought were compliments, were in fact manifestations of unconscious bias, stereotypes, sexism, and even racism.

The image of "exotic" bodies adorned in gold, romanticized within an imagined Oriental wilderness, began to trouble me profoundly. I realized that such portrayals were neither benign nor incidental but rooted in colonial legacies that continue to shape perceptions of non-Western identities. This realization became a turning point. I decided to dedicate my career to challenging and rewriting these narratives, to reclaiming and celebrating our postcolonial identities on our own terms. My work seeks to decolonize perceptions, to foster a deeper understanding of us—our cultures, our histories, and our artistry.

Central to this mission is education. I have committed myself to educating the next generation across the globe about our rich, diverse cultural practices, our ways of knowing, and our creative techniques. I aim to dissect and illuminate the often-blurred lines between cultural appropriation, diffusion, and appreciation, ensuring that our traditions are honored rather than commodified. In doing so, I hope to build bridges of understanding, respect, and equity, reshaping how our identities are perceived, celebrated, and represented in the world.

Today, we strive to dismantle these ideologies by rewriting our narratives through exhibitions and publications. The call to decolonize fashion is urgent and essential—not just for the colonized but also for the global value system. This is why FLCNA exists. We strive to reclaim, educate, exhibit, and transform. FLCNA was founded to create a network of art and design practitioners from the Global South, originally with a focus on the region of North Africa; we have now expanded and will continue to do so.

Can you change perception? We hope we can do this through an exhibition like this. Not only has this exhibition been meticulously curated by me, a North African academic and designer, but it has also used Dr. Sara Hume's wealth of experience of how WE are dealt with in the Western museum system. This includes Dr. Hume's insights on the archiving, display, and labelling of our artefacts in the West. Every

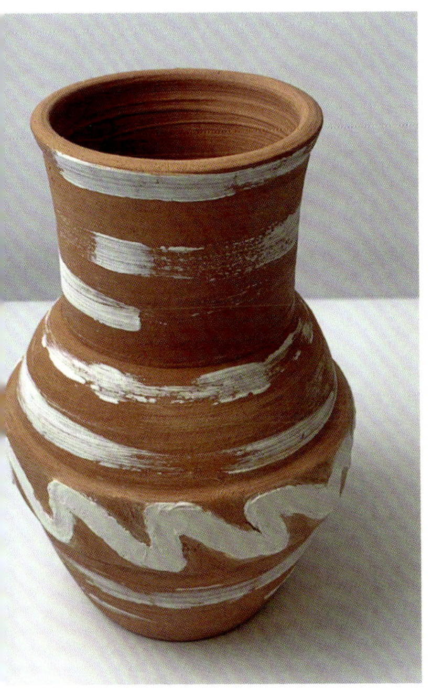
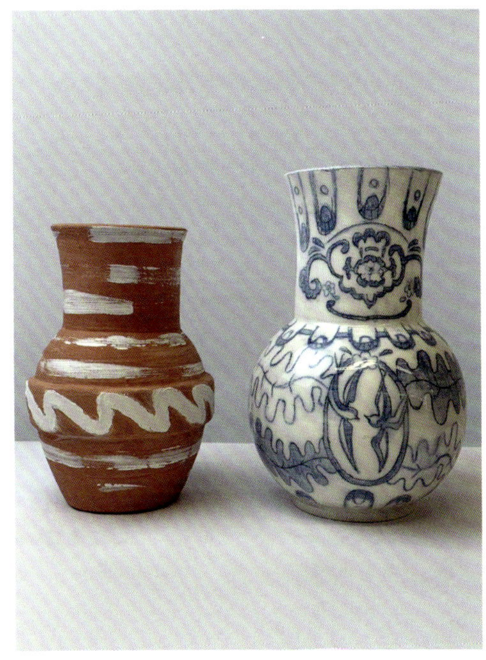
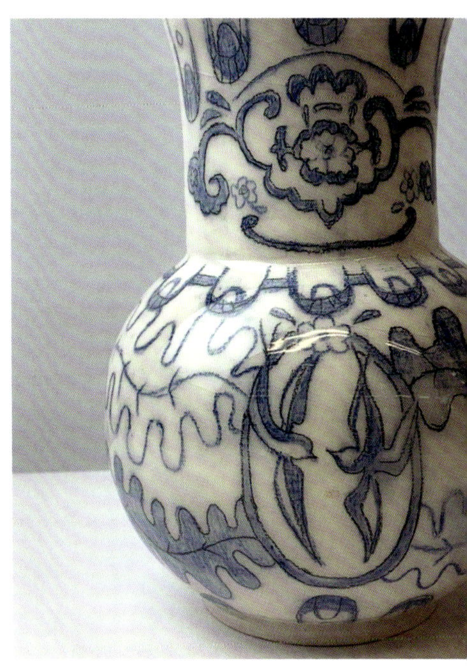

Figs 11, 12, 13: The beautiful inspiring work of my student Phoebe Grace Wilkes, the start of her journey making an authentic Egyptian *olla* from clay. Then making an appropriated glazed and Westernized version. This was then used to test which one people thought would be more valuable. Inspired by my teaching and conversations around our *olla* project. This is what doing decoloniality looks like. Changing perception, the mindsets of the next generation. Phoebe is an extremely talented ceramicist and her treatment of our culture and preserving of it has been beautiful to behold. She truly VALUES the *olla* and the craftmanship necessary to make it. This is how we make change together, changing perception. Continued work of Phoebe Grace Wilkes. Rendered final *olla* and the final glazed Western version with details. Images courtesy of Phoebe Grace Wilkes

aspect of this exhibition has been furthering decoloniality, from my appointment as co-curator to the autonomy given to the exhibitors, the language used to describe the pieces, the labelling of pieces by the designer, and all the details they wish to display alongside it. The exhibitors can display their work in whatever format they choose, and in whatever language, medium, and aesthetic. When embarking on this project, Dr Hume and I decided that to break the colonial legacy of the museum, we must move beyond exhibiting pieces by region. An unknown sea of ambiguity, and, as we have discussed, lack of value. We now have three very relevant sections: Disruptors, Threads, and Our Land. It represents OUR North Africa. The stories and ways of being and fashioning.

Although the above-mentioned Metropolitan Museum exhibition, "Vision of the East in Western Dress" addresses some of the glaring exotification of the "Oriental" and presents the over-the-top stereotypes in clothes, it still is not decolonial. The catalogue and what Martin and Koda writes are decolonial in a sense, but the exhibition itself still featured predominantly well-known designers who fetishized the "East." Such as Yves Saint Laurent, whose dress, clearly inspired by Algeria, was not discussed in much depth. Not even noting that, in fact, the dress was not inspired by Chinese emperors. This is but one example, even the layout of the event was the normal, exhibition standard. Which is again, a Western imposed standard of order and aesthetic deemed worthy of the elite art space. A white space. Our exhibition has allowed designers from all markets, levels, and notoriety to be included. It is breaking the gatekeeping traditions of who is deemed worthy of an exhibition space. In fact, we avoided the customary bigger names purposefully, in order to highlight the work of lesser-known brands, to give them a voice. An example of elevating brands that have achieved a balance between East and West: Sacer is high-end contemporary streetwear, based out of Egypt and now Portugal, selling worldwide. This brand is truly sustainable through and through, as are others in FLCNA and in the exhibition. Tackling topics that are seen as taboo in most of North Africa such as men's mental health, collaborating with the locals from cut off areas of Egypt and causes for awareness. Educating the world on how sustainability can be truly implemented. Sacer is a unique brand that has a vision and voice, which are transported to the West through this exhibition.

Other known brands such as Born in Exile are featured, as well as start-ups such as the Algerian Intique brand. Uniting brands from all the North African countries and giving them this platform with freedom, pure freedom, to showcase however they deem fit has been an act of liberation in itself.

Unlike any other exhibition, the work here is unparalleled, it is a true decolonial reflection of the fashion system in North Africa. This has been a humbling and awakening journey for me as FLCNA's founder, but also for my fellow members who are taking part. We do have a joint project at the exhibition that highlights the sheer variety and depth of this exhibition—from bags to Egyptian Bulga shoes, installations and jewelry. This will be a life-changing experience for us all, and THIS is where our story truly begins in the decolonial plight to reclaim, unlearn, value, and change global perception.

Perception. It will change everything. We will be the change.
We will reclaim our value.

Perception. Has yours changed?

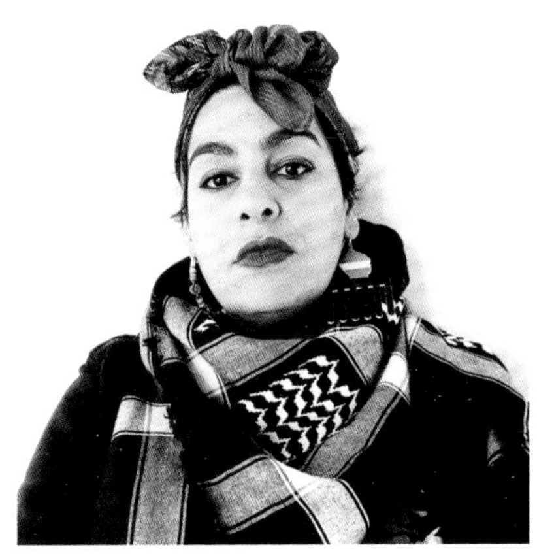

Nada Koreish is a lecturer across multiple disciplines with over fifteen years of experience in the design industry and a doctoral scholar, focusing on decoloniality and fashion in North Africa. She is the founder of the Fashion Liberation Collective North Africa (FLCNA, recently renamed "? Liberation Collective"), a disruptor, and a mother. Always striving to reclaim our history. Our own table. Doing decoloniality through practice, the collective, and in everything she teaches.

1 Frantz Fanon, *The Wretched of the Earth,* trans. Constance Farrington (New York: Grove Press, 1963), 2.
2 Hernan Casakin and Fatima Bernardo, *The Role of Place Identity in the Perception, Understanding, and Design of Built Environments* (Sharjah: Bentham Science Publishers, 2012).
3 Riley Quinn, *An Analysis of Frantz Fanon's The Wretched of the Earth* (London: Routledge, 2017), 15.
4 Edward Said, *Orientalism* (New York: Pantheon Books, 1977), 9.
5 Walter Mignolo and Catherine Walsh, *On Decoloniality: Concepts, Analytics, Praxis* (Durham: Duke University Press, 2018).
6 Richard Martin and Harold Koda, *Orientalism: Visions of the East in Western Dress* (New York: The Metropolitan Museum of Art, 1994), https://www.metmuseum.org/essays/orientalism-visions-of-the-east-in-western-dress (landing page of document).
7 *A Companion to Nineteenth-Century Art.* (United Kingdom: Wiley Online Library, 2018) 121. DOI:10.1002/9781118856321

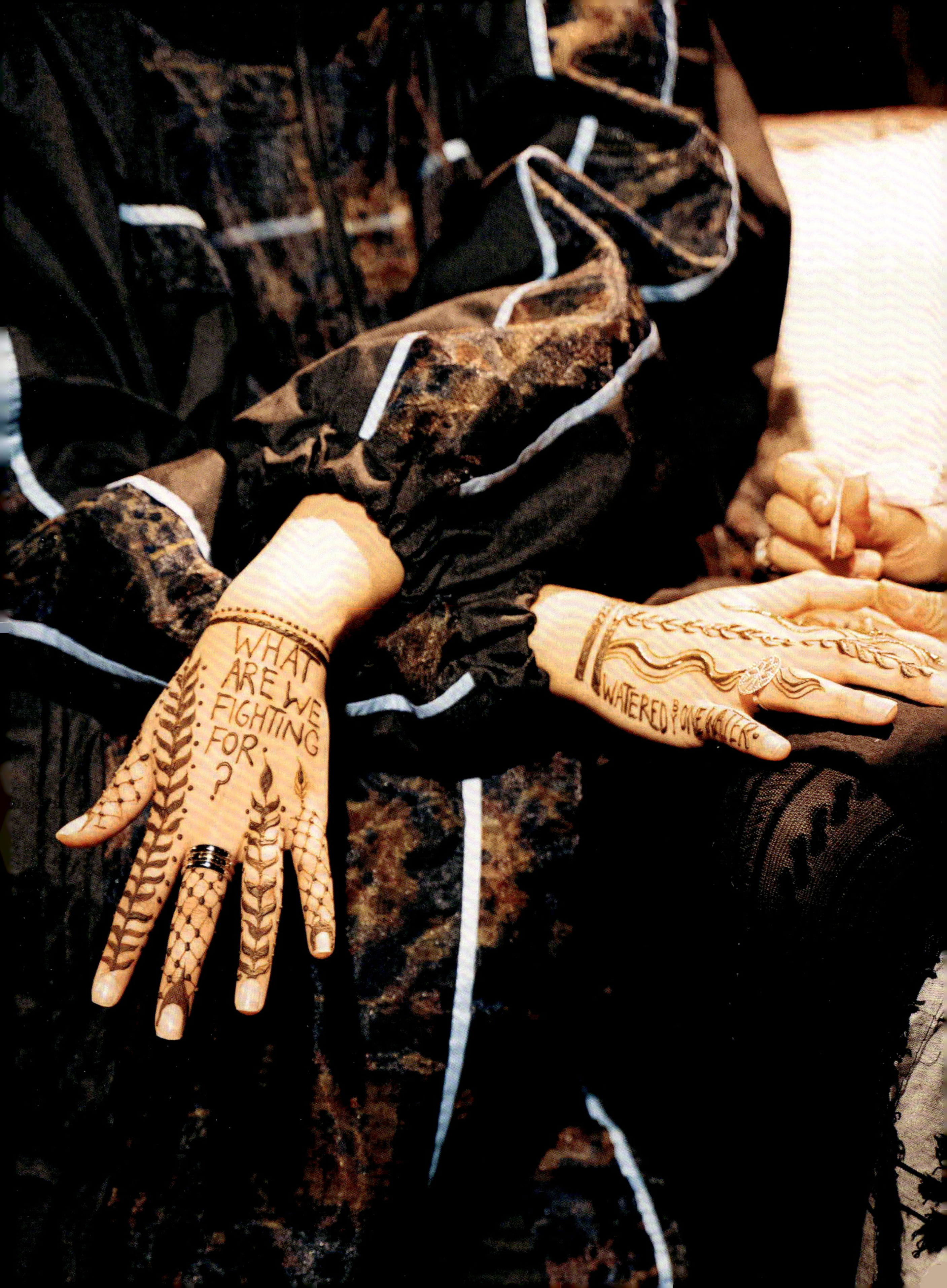
WHAT ARE WE FIGHTING FOR ?
WATERED BY ONE WATER.

HOW DOES FASHION PLAY A ROLE IN CULTURE AND IDENTITY?

Kazna Asker

In contemporary society, the fashion world is often associated with all things luxury, including celebrities and glamour. The industry is widely known as "one of the key value-creating industries for the world economy"[1] and with the rise of social media and accessibility the growing platform has never been in more demand. However, despite the global phenomenon the industry has created in the developed world, the role of fashion goes beyond fleeting trends and metric numbers. Fashion has always been at the forefront of many social and political movements throughout history. It has been a tool to showcase people's "behaviors and manners of doing something"[2] through various styles of clothing and accessories, consequently becoming a vehicle to represent pivotal moments in history. This was most notable in the revolutionary Black Panther's attire of leather, afros, berets, and badges to create a uniform togetherness and through the woven threads of *keffiyeh* scarves to showcase global solidarity with Palestine. Taking this into account, the use of clothing, hair, and behavior has become a form of storytelling for many generations and therefore acts as a voice for cultures and identities in marginalized communities that often go unheard.

Throughout this essay, I will explore how fashion plays a role in culture and identity in communities across the Middle East and North Africa, as well as the diaspora in the UK from my perspective as a British-Yemeni fashion designer. It is important to note that through migration and the knowledge of Islam between the two regions, fashion has been the vehicle to document cultural exchanges throughout history. Using this knowledge, I will then explore my own practice and how my cultural background has used fashion to impact the ideas, customs, and social behavior of a particular people or society generations later.

The Middle East and North Africa

The Middle East and North Africa (MENA) are two distinct regions that share many similarities due to the intersection of history, faith, and culture. While the indigenous people of North Africa are often referred to as the "Amazigh tribes," many historians believe that "some Amazigh tribes have traced their origins to particular Arabized countries such as Yemen and Egypt."[3] Before diving into a more nuanced concept on how fashion reflects these similarities, we must first examine the differentiating tribal identities that have been shaped over centuries and passed down generations.

Tribalism

Tribalism often refers to the social division in a "traditional society consisting of various communities that are linked by social, religious, or blood ties with a common culture."[4] Across the MENA region, each tribe has their own uniform of clothing and accessories that differentiate themselves from each other, showing the clear influence that fashion has on culture and identity. For example, in North Africa, facial tattoos have a historic role in differentiating the Amazigh people from other groups within the region. Similarly, the Yemeni accessory of the *jambiya* has retained strong significance in representing the identity of the Yemeni man. However, the history of Arab nomads travelling across Africa "via trade routes, intellectual debate, and military conquest"[5] resulted in an exchange of shared knowledge, culture, and religion between the regions. This in turn affected "the ideas, customs, and social behavior"[6] within communities, creating a sense of interconnectedness. This is most notable through the use of fashion, since the introduction of Islam across the MENA region has directly influenced both tribal and religious communities' choice of clothing, as many wear traditional clothing, such as head coverings and draped fabrics that modestly cover the body. Therefore, as individuals within these communities choose to follow faith and follow the Islamic dress code, it could be argued that their religious identity has had a direct influence on fashion, consequently creating a wider culture that is relatable to those who practice the faith.

However, some may argue these garments were created for functional purposes within their climate condition. Many tribal communities across the region live in different climates; from deserts to mountains, the varying weather conditions may influence their choice of clothing. This is notable as both MENA regions have adopted light-weight fabric, such as cotton and linen, to create garments that "were simply a very large rectangle of fabric that was folded or draped."[7]

Yet since their establishment, these loose-fitting robes and headscarves are still worn to this day; the culture surrounding these garments has remained strong for centuries and they are now naturally associated with the MENA region. This is clearly shown through the diaspora in Western countries, such as the UK, where these items are worn to remain close to their culture, despite the contrasting climate. Therefore, it could be argued that the role of culture in the MENA region has had centuries worth of history, storytelling, and tribal infrastructure that has directly shaped the way of life and the fashion that currently exists today. In contrast to the Western world of social media, fast fashion, and consumerism, other parts of the world have developed more in faith and sustaining historic craftsmanship, which has built solid foundations rarely infiltrated by outside influences. Consequently, it is difficult to assume that fashion could have the privilege of influencing a culture that is extremely committed to values that go beyond current circumstances. As a result, although fashion once impacted culture and climate, this dynamic has shifted over generations as the diaspora has spread, causing culture to directly influence fashion instead.

My Own Practice

As the daughter of Yemeni immigrants based in the UK, my culture and identity have directly been influenced by both worlds. I was born and raised in Liverpool and then later settled in Sheffield. Growing up in northern England, the influence of sportswear was extremely strong. This approach to fashion influenced me as a designer, since I quickly realized that the Liverpool community's association with football and sports was "driven by the city's need to innovate and stand out from the crowd." This eventually "grew into a lifestyle" and changed "the way football fans dress and behave," proving fashion can directly influence culture and identity.[8] After I moved to Sheffield and grew closer to the Yemeni diaspora, my perspective on the topic broadened when I was exposed to multiculturalism and therefore a wider demographic range of cultures and identities. A particular memory that stimulated my approach to fashion was when I noticed the inter-generational perspectives on fashion within immigrant households. For example, I would see my teenage cousin wearing a Nike tracksuit beside my grandmother in traditional Yemeni clothes.

As a consumer, I used fashion to reflect my culture and the identity of the community I was raised in. However, as a designer, I believe witnessing different approaches to culture and identity inspired my fashion practice. My most recent London Fashion Week (LFW) presentation reflects this, since I was able to create an interactive exhibition exploring the roles of culture and identity in fashion and vice versa.

London Fashion Week Presentation - February 2024

During the February LFW, I created a live presentation called "What are we fighting for?" With everything currently happening in the world, the main goal was to create a space for people to come together to collectively stand for something. The interactive exhibition consisted of a set designed to resemble my grandma's living room; the floor was filled with Persian rugs and models were seated in a Middle Eastern *majlis*, whilst the smell of incense filled the room. The guests were served Yemeni tea and biscuits, and they were able to explore the storyboards of research, read books on the MENA region, interact with the models wearing the collection, get their henna done, and—most importantly—communicate with one another. Although the room resembled the traditions of an Arab household, the music playlist that was heard consisted of UK rap.

The collection itself featured traditional MENA silhouettes to showcase the significance of Islamic modesty. Alongside the traditional woven fabrics and silhouettes, the collection also referenced the sportswear element of technical fabrics inspired by my British northern England upbringing. As shown in the images below, models wore nylon floor-length waterproof coats, inspired by the shapes of the *abaya* and the raincoats of the UK, alongside printed organza featuring the patterns of the traditional fabrics we often see in our households.

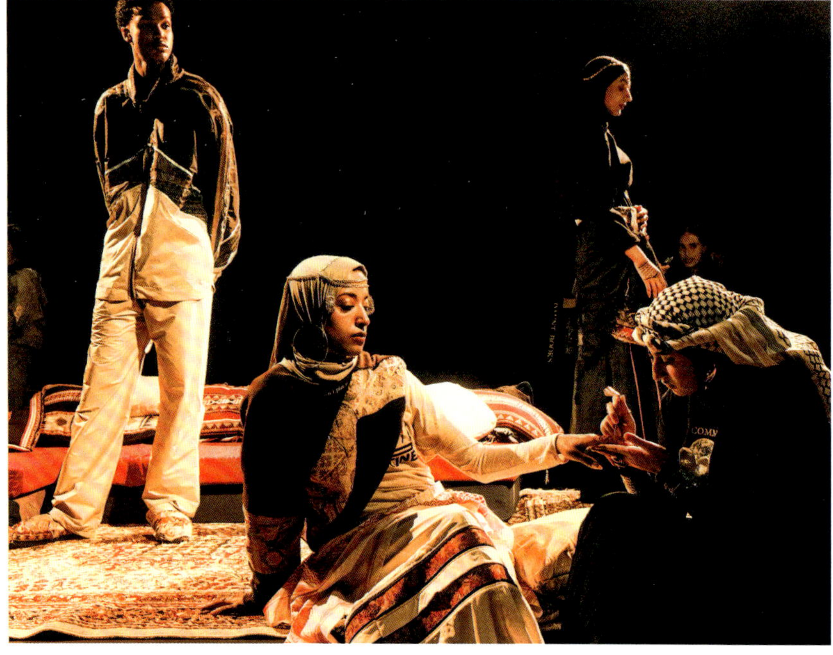

"What are we fighting for?" Kazna Asker London Fashion Week presentation, February 2024. Images courtesy of British Fashion Council

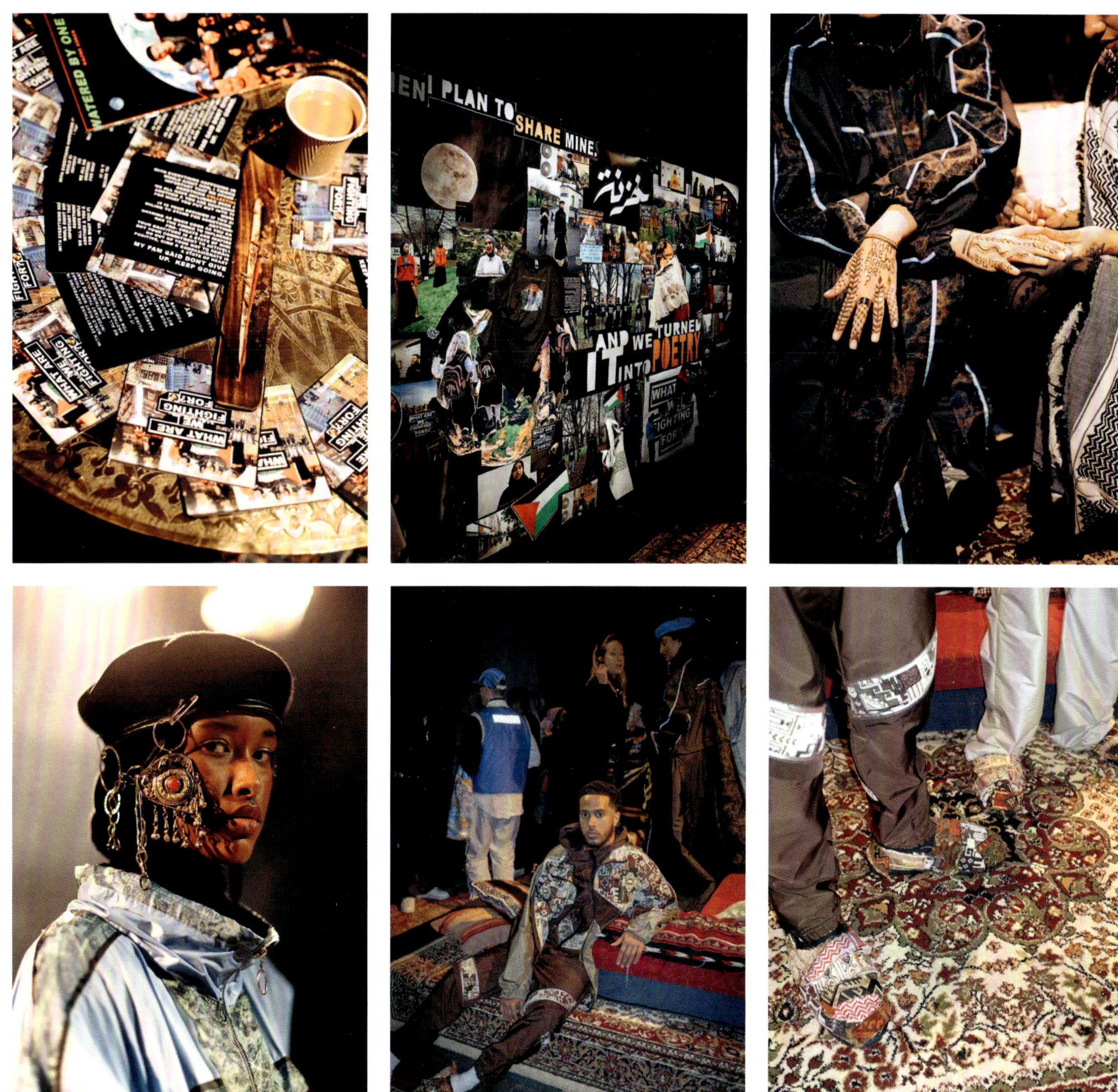

"What are we fighting for?" Kazna Asker London Fashion Week presentation, February 2024. Images courtesy of Sandra Nagel

Overall, the project created a platform that was a true reflection of culture and identity showcasing every part inspired by the "knowledge, beliefs, arts, laws, customs, capabilities, and habits of individuals."[9] From the clothes and diversity of models, to the food and music, to the art, politics, and social movements, every reference in the event was a reflection of my own culture and identity. As a result, fashion played a dominant role in the process of creating.

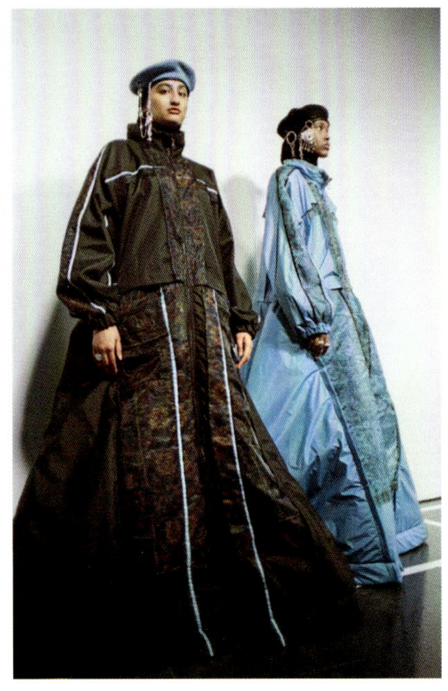

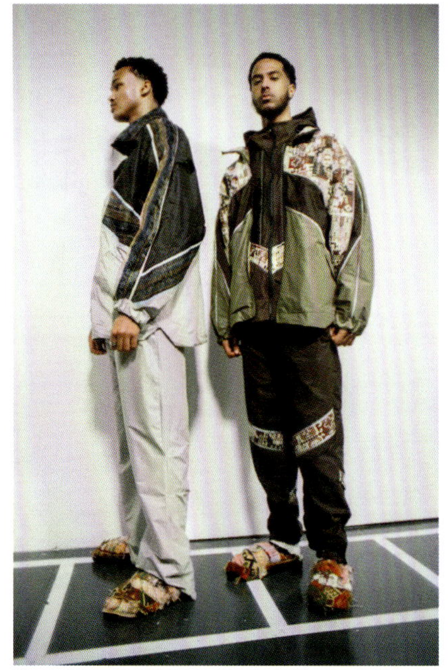

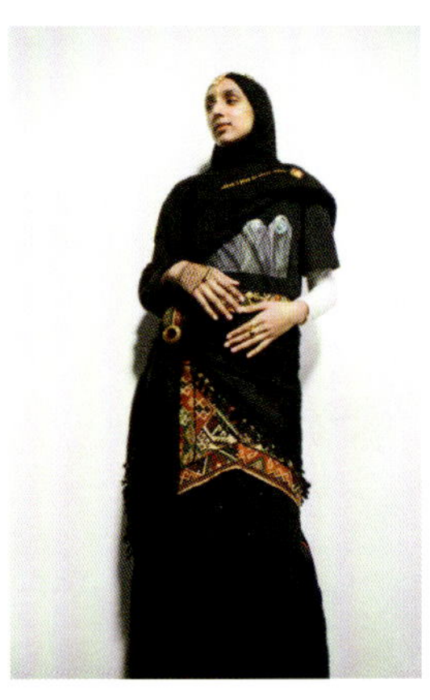

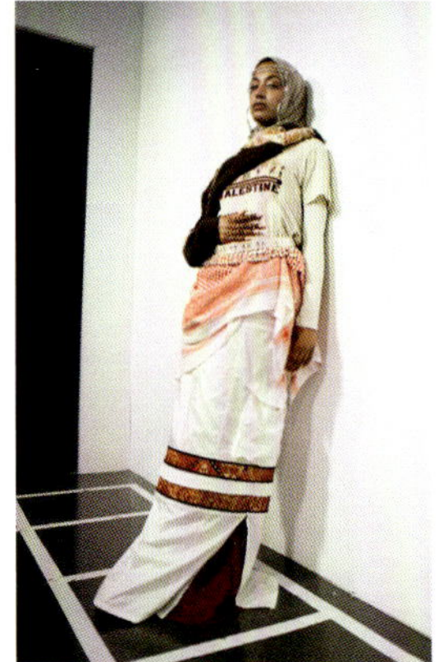

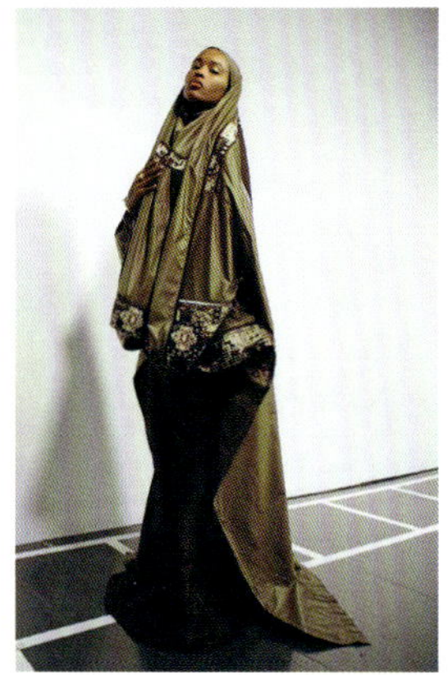

"What are we fighting for?"
Collection by Kazna Askker.
Images courtesy of Jameela Elfaki

Conclusion

To conclude, fashion has played a major role in influencing culture and identity in the past and present. Although fashion is commonly only associated with clothes, it is important to note that it is a form of self-expression through many vehicles, such as textiles, henna, tattoos, and behavior. The use of self-expression has always been influential on society, as it allows communities to wear their morals and beliefs, consequently directly impacting cultures and identities. For example, the use of sportswear and traditional fabrics in my own collection represents the history of our heritage, our families' journeys, being part of a diaspora and therefore creating our own culture. Like many tribes across the MENA region, we have used fashion as our tool to adapt to our circumstances and surroundings, influencing who we choose to identify as. This applies to the diaspora mentality of holding on to our history and embracing both worlds of culture, as well as to current tribes adapting to climates and regional dress codes.

Fashion is an ever-evolving platform that will constantly change as time progresses. As trends rise and fall and social media continues to act as a tool of fashion communication, it will create a sense of interconnectedness for cultural identities to act as a reference point to develop the fashion world even further. As a result, I believe the influence of fashion on culture and identities is interchangeable as the world develops.

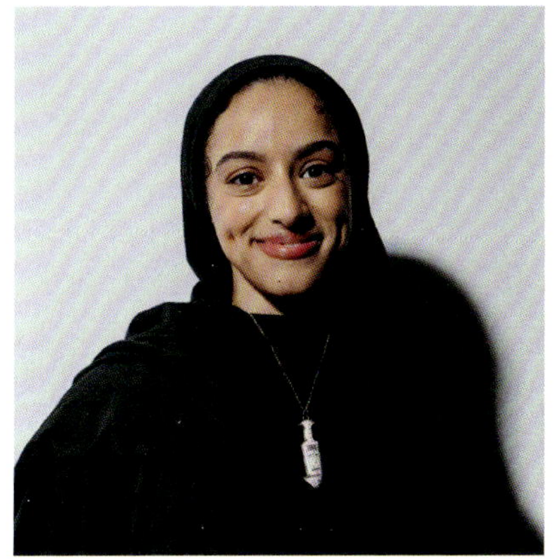

Kazna Asker is a fashion designer who has created a brand encompassing the values associated with community, activism, and charity. She won the Debut Talent prize at Fashion Trust Arabia, representing her home country, Yemen. She is currently part of BFC NEWGEN and has presented during London Fashion Week for two seasons. Her work combines traditional Middle Eastern fabrics with nylon tracksuits and outerwear. She is a graduate of Central Saint Martins.

1 McKinsey & Company and The Business of Fashion, *The State of Fashion 2017* (London: The Business of Fashion, 2017), 12, https://www.mckinsey.com/~/media/McKinsey/Industries/Retail/Our%20Insights/The%20state%20of%20fashion/The-state-of-fashion-2017-McK-BoF-report.pdf.
2 *Oxford Advanced Learner's Dictionaries*, 10th ed. (Oxford: Oxford University Press, 2020), s.v. "Fashion."
3 Amanda Ferguson, "The Berber People: Culture, Religion & History," Study.com, November 21, 2023, https://study.com/academy/lesson/the-berbers-origin-religion-culture.html.
4 *Oxford Advanced Learner's Dictionaries*, 10th ed. (Oxford: Oxford University Press, 2020), s.v. "Tribalism."
5 Clint Foster, "Islam in Africa: History & Timeline," Study.com, November 21, 2023, https://study.com/learn/lesson/islam-africa-history-timeline.html.
6 *Oxford Advanced Learner's Dictionaries*, 10th ed. (Oxford: Oxford University Press, 2020), s.v. "Culture."
7 "The Bedouin Costume Project," House Wild Rose, 2000, https://housewildrose.weebly.com/the-bedouin-costume-project.html.
8 Kevin Sampson, "What is Terrace Culture? And Who are Casuals?" National Museums Liverpool, July 3, 2023, https://www.liverpoolmuseums.org.uk/stories/what-terrace-culture.
9 Kevin Avruch, *Culture and Conflict Resolution* (Washington DC: United States Institute of Peace Press, 1998), 6.

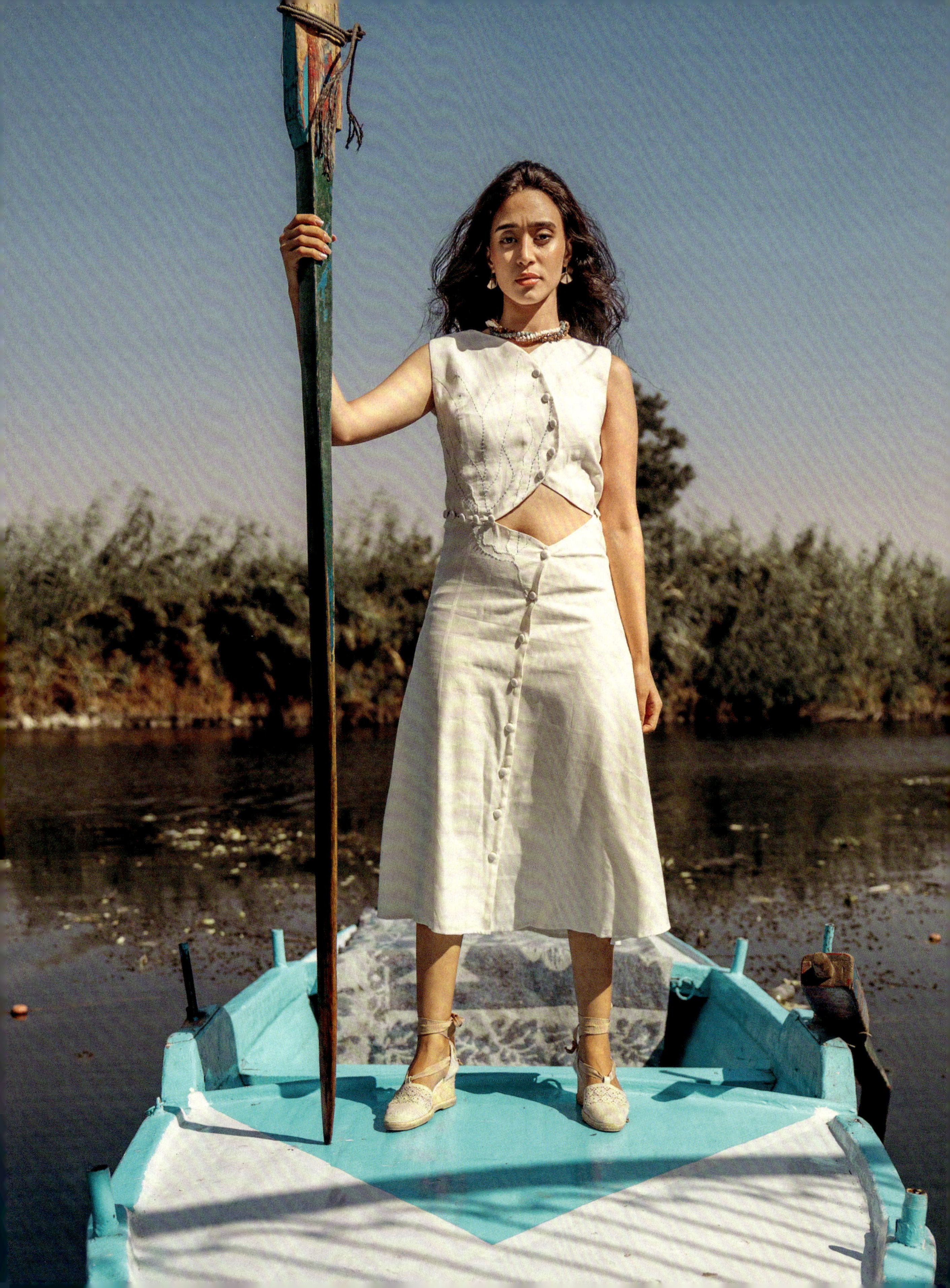

REDESIGNING EGYPTIAN HERITAGE

ON THE DECOLONIAL PRACTICE OF CULTURAL PRESERVATION THROUGH SLOW FASHION IN EGYPT

Norhan El Sakkout

With a globalized industrial fashion system dominated by "speed, volume and identical flawless products,"[1] the diversity of offering in fashion is slowly disappearing—and with it crafts heritage. In Egypt, a history of economic, political, and sociological events has affected its cultural heritage sector to a point where many of the crafts are on the verge of going extinct, affecting "the only viable forms of income for people, particularly women, living in rural areas."[2] Since crafts are not only representative of the physical output but are also a "cultural construct that evolves in response to changing mindsets and conditions of society,"[3] an erasure of identity, beliefs, and values also takes place similar to the effects of colonization on cultures.

This essay explores the relationship between globalization, post-colonial Egypt, and the erasure of crafts heritage and cultural identity, focusing on economic and sociological changes. With a special focus on Egypt's fashion design industry, the essay seeks to prove that increased use of heritage-based design is a viable approach to decolonizing the fashion design industry in Egypt, while reviving, documenting, and evolving with cultural heritage

Fast Fashion, Globalization, and Modern Colonization

Fast fashion has a notable impact on the environment and impedes social justice, while also contributing to the identity erasure of cultures with longstanding histories of colonization. The modern-day structure of a globalized fashion system, where fabrics are produced in China, sewn in Bangladesh, and exported to Europe, the UK, and the USA, has catapulted textiles into being the fourth environmentally pressuring industry, with synthetic fibers making up sixty percent of textiles used[4] and eighty-five percent of textile-based products ending up in landfills, roughly amounting to ninety-two million tons.[5] A hallmark event of the Rana Plaza collapse in 2013 marked the downfall of the fast-fashion facade of "democratizing fashion" at the expense of those working in it and the environment suffering from fabricated trend cycles.[6] These events can easily connect fast fashion to being a contemporary form of colonization. Traditional garments become less appealing to younger generations with the average consumer looking to "modernize" through "adopting a Western look"[7] and comply with the accelerated fashion trend cycle. This means that increasingly less traditional wear is sought after and with it the local handicrafts that organically developed through the environments, traditions, and natural pace of rich cultures with a vast historical heritage.

Not only does fast fashion contribute to the depletion of cultural heritage, but it paves the way for cultural appropriation. Fast fashion brands become synonymous with creating new, exciting, and exotic-looking designs pulled from the cultural heritage of countries of the southern hemisphere. Not only do the fast fashion labels draw inspiration from emerging countries' rich cultures,[8] but they replace the heritage-based work based on handicrafts taught through generational education with mechanized versions of the craft. Neglect of traditional handicrafts as a result of the cultural devaluation imposed by a globalized fashion system, combined with poorly credited inspiration drawn from emerging, formerly colonized cultures, leads to the stealing of the opportunity, income, and design innovation that Egypt can export and that can help to support its local economy, artisan community, and design industry to flourish.

An example of a culturally appropriating and fashion colonization incident is British singer's Adele dress worn in Glastonbury in 2016. Adele wore a dress by the global fashion brand Chloé, described by international news outlets as giving a "folky, 70s feel"[9] in 2016 and again in 2020.[10] Chloé's creative director at the time, Clare Waight Keller, then promoted the dress as a "bespoke beaded dress."[11] In contrast, local news outlets in Egypt were outraged at the promotion of the dress in international news sources, mentioning that "no official mention came from the creators at Chloé on any inspiration Siwa may have given in the design"[12] and that the "misleading assumptions describe the gown as '70's-inspired', the truth is that it actually copies the traditional embroidered black wedding dress famous in the Egyptian oasis Siwa. Locally known as 'asherah hawak azdhaf', the embroidered silk dress is traditionally worn on the seventh-day party of the week-long Siwan wedding celebrations, and is considered one of several items Siwan women usually wear during their wedding celebrations."[13] While the dress could have been only inspired by Amazigh Siwan and North African culture and executed in Chloé's

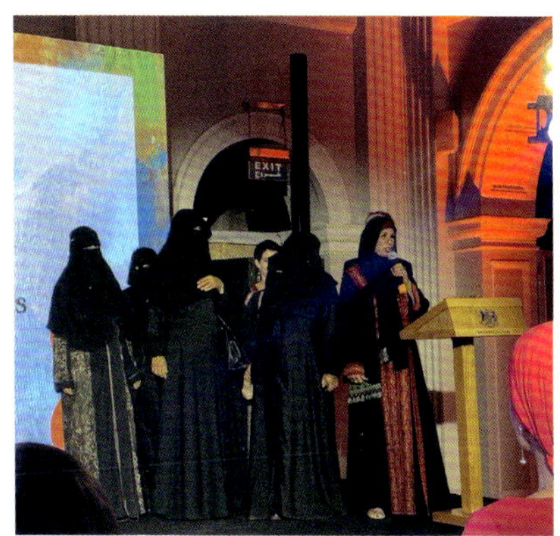

Fig. 1: Selema El Gabaly presenting the Red Dress at the British Embassy in Cairo, 2022. Photo by Norhan El Sakkout

atelier, it not being properly credited deems it a culturally appropriating incident that could have been avoided by sharing the cultural ties Chloé's founder Gabrielle Aghion has to Egypt, namely her being "born to a wealthy family in Alexandria, Egypt, in 1921."[14]

Whereas Chloé failed to adequately credit the inspiration or source of work of its dress, another example begs the question of monetary compensation of artisan groups, namely the Red Dress Project by British designer Kirstie Macleod. "A 14-year, award-winning global, collaborative embroidery project" running between 2009 to 2023 shed light on the women working on the embroidery of the dress and "provides an artistic platform for individuals, particularly women, around communities around the world, many of whom are marginalized and/or live in poverty, to tell their stories through embroidery."[15] Information on where the monetary proceeds derived from the dress being exhibited around the world until today, and the end point donations collected through the project's website, remains vague. A transparent, more impactful approach would have been to report if a portion of the monetary proceeds of the project's sponsors, donors, and exhibition are given back to the artisan groups (fig. 1).

With demand for traditional garments waning across the southern hemisphere, along with the identity erasure of younger generations, local designers turn to Western design ideals for their inspiration. This further reinforces the erasure of their identities, along with the local crafts sectors, and sinks their communities deeper into poor design and crafts dynamics, which gravely impact the income generation potential and long-term sustainability of artisan employment. Consumers, on the other hand, succumb to contemporary cultural colonization by lacking the awareness of the white savior complex that they have fostered by valuing imported, mass-produced brands over local alternatives, regarding local brands as lower value in terms of price and symbolic status. Most local consumers still believe that local brands should be cheap, and from a design, making, and quality perspective are not of the same value as imported alternatives. However, socio-economic events—including currency devaluation, local campaigns on valuing local products over mass-produced imports, along with political events in the region and the push towards sustainability, have triggered a movement towards supporting local brands that symbolize Egyptian identity and heritage.

The public audience on social media platforms questions local brands' value. A post on a major independent designer local market organizer, L.A Market, by an audience member asked: "Why are local brand prices higher than large-scale brands?" The market organizer responded, "I didn't find any more concise responses than the following: first I want to pay my respect to any local brand that is still surviving and is resilient given the economic recession we are experiencing, you are heroes." She went on to include four different posts promoting local brands, some of which stated the followng:

> Zara produces around 450 million garments a year.
> How can you compare small local designers with Zara?
> Show some mercy and grace to the hustling local brands.
>
> I really get irritated at this topic, in all industries, not just clothing, local businesses don't have the same amount of funding, resources, brand names, or the exploitation that large-scale chains can cut costs through. I believe small brands are likely less evil and more ethical, so if we can afford it we can support them.[16]

Whereas the overwhelming opinion still questions the value of local design, increasingly it has been noted that a fraction of the community is starting to prefer slower, more culturally-influenced, local products.

Reclaiming Narratives through Slow Fashion

To counteract the impact of globalization and fast fashion on artisan communities, the decolonial approach to heritage reclamation is imperative towards halting the depletion of crafts, identity, and culture. Such reclamation can occur by implementing new systems that integrate craftsmanship in the design and manufacturing process.

Kirsi Niinimäki coined one such method in her book *Sustainable Fashion: New Approaches.* Niinimäki believes that slow fashion can revive, grow, and imbed crafts and traditional techniques in a way that can result in high quality, durability, lower environmental impact, and ethically sound production.[17] Niinimäki's approach is aligned with Egyptian local designers' method of working with artisan groups to help revive and foster its cultural heritage and crafts innovation. This helps cement a clear value proposition among local fashion brands, while celebrating and telling stories of Egyptian culture and heritage.

Examples of brands that work on local handicrafts and the documentation of Egyptian storytelling through fashion are Saqhoute and Bulga. "Saqhoute (pronounced 'saqoot') is a slow fashion brand offering women's ready-to-wear built on the sustainable pillars of circularity artisanship and zero-waste. The brand tells stories of Egyptian heritage through intricate design and use of hand embroidery."[18] The brand launches a "series of capsule collections, each one telling a hidden story about Egyptian heritage to commemorate the beautiful culture, document [...] local stories and make them known all while honoring the artisanry behind it all."[19] Saqhoute's approach includes the revival and continuation of Egyptian storytelling through heritage, historical documentation, and hand embroidery based in Cairo. The brand incorporates traditional and handcraft methods, fusing them with the modern-day needs of its local and global audience, to ensure that there is demand, desire for, interest in, and conti-

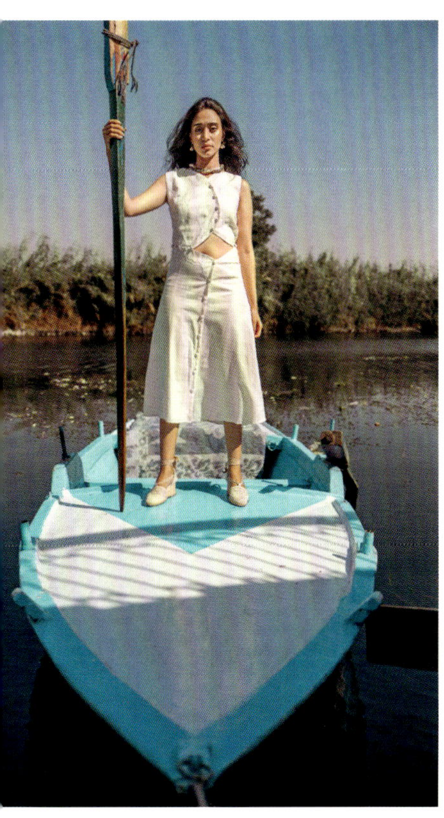

Fig. 2: Hand-embroidered and detachable multi-wear L'Eau Du Nil Set depicting the Nile Delta as an embroidery design by Saqhoute, Qursaya Island in Giza, 2024. L'Eau Du Nil Set of AMAN Capsule Collection by Saqhoute, photo by Mohamed El Maandi

nuity of having hand-embroidered garments with a traditional storytelling component. Not only does this open up room for sustainable income generation for the hand embroiderers Saqhoute works with, but it also popularizes the Egyptian story on a local and global level in a gentle form of decolonial practice[20] (fig. 2).

Bulga, in contrast, aims to revive "traditional footwear workshops in historic Cairo by using the oldest techniques in shoe-making to make vibrant, modern slippers that still hold the spirit of Egyptian heritage with an edge. Through adopting slow-fashion principles, [Bulga] hope[s] to make an impact in the industry one Bulga at a time, while providing jobs to women and marginalized artisans all over Egypt."[21] Bulga "works with Abadba women artisans from Shalateen to incorporate their heritage into footwear, while providing them with a steady income and preserving the craft using sustainable material coming from nature, like palm trees." Additionally, they incorporate the embroidery of the Siwa oasis on leather in order to revive a disappearing craft. "Siwa was known for special embroidery on leather, but this craft is now dying since most artisans in Siwa embroider on fabric." Bulga "brought back this to life by introducing [their] take on an ancient Egyptian collection all with Siwa embroidery on natural sheep leather." And finally, Bulga works with a third artisan group in Kerdasa, Giza, the home of"Abu Eissa's workshop in Kerdasa ... of ten men working on looms every day to create ... traditional fabrics sold in Libya and Siwa, amongst Amazigh culture. Handmade out of 100% cotton yarn and woven thread by thread with the looms by Abu Eissa and his artisans on this traditional technique that takes weeks to complete just a few meters" (fig. 3).

Having designers with knowledge of the unique culture of artisan groups, their heritage, and crafts bridging the gap between artisanry and the global consumer base is a gateway to not only keeping the various crafts clusters of Egypt alive, but also paving the way for the crafts and artisans to remain relevant, generate, and grow their income—a move towards economic, social, and creative liberation from the prevalent global fashion system.

Conclusion

Fletcher and Tham's "Earth Logic Fashion Action Plan" proposes a new system of fashion that honors cultures who are the main cornerstone of artistic creation. Their Action Plan advocates for multiple fashion centers, interdependence, diverse ways of knowing, co-creation, action research, grounded imagination, care of the world, and finally care of self. An alternative framework that is in alignment with cultural preservation and artisan community support. And designers' roles come into play with a more holistic approach not limited to just designing but rather across the entire fashion supply chain.[22]

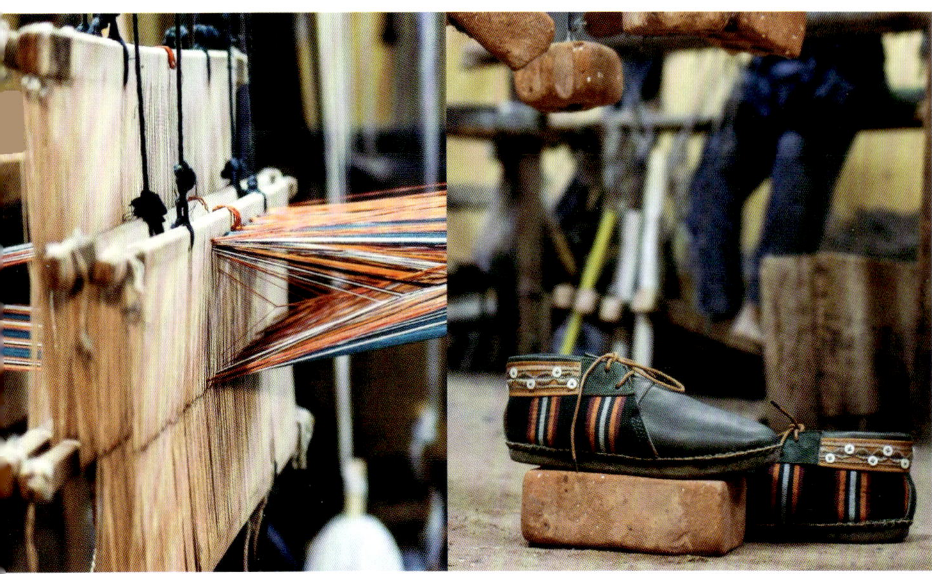

Fig. 3: Bulga's footwear using traditional techniques. Amazigh Simple Boots by Bulga. Photo by Jihan Ibrahim

The designer's role in slow fashion and heritage revival is not only limited to creating new visual languages utilizing crafts. Roles would include trust building with artisan communities, integrating with them, understanding and respecting their culture, mediating in terms of timeliness of production given the limitations marginalized groups have in terms of electricity, transportation, and freedom of movement, and finally forging an autonomous relationship where the craftsperson is able to manage their own workflow given the above-mentioned constraints.

Designers' advocacy, decolonial storytelling, adaptation to market dynamics, cementing a version of creation and a production supply chain that considers the unique community values and cultural characteristics artisans abide by, in order to ensure continuity, documentation, and sustainable development of culture, heritage, and the preservation of identity through fashion, design, and slow manufacturing, would all be new roles for designers working towards the support of artisan groups. It would enable the growth, revival, and, above all, decolonization of local fashion systems.

Norhan El Sakkout launched her brand Saqhoute in 2018 as a women's ready-to-wear brand that emphasizes sustainability and Egyptian heritage.

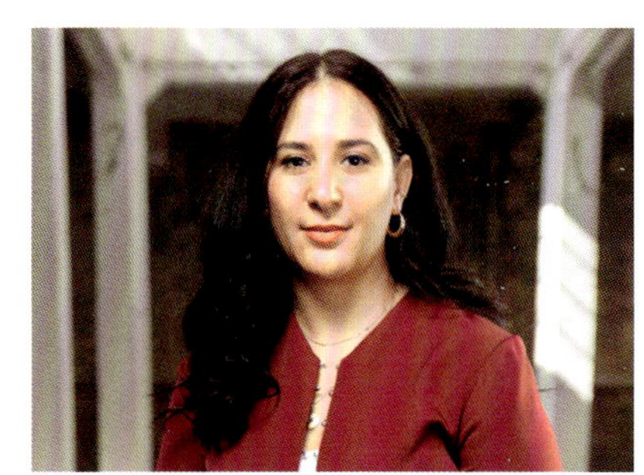

1 Tamsin Blanchard, ed., *Fashion Craft Revolution* (London: Fashion Revolution, 2019), 64–73.
2 Ibid., 73.
3 Peter Korn, *Why We Make Things and Why It Matters: The Education of a Craftsman* (New York: Vintage, 2017), 31.
4 European Environment Agency, *Private Consumption: Textiles EU's Fourth Largest Cause of Environmental Pressures after Food, Housing, Transport,* 2020, https://www.eea.europa.eu/highlights/private-consumption-textiles-eus-fourth-1.
5 Xuandong Chen, et al., "Circular Economy and Sustainability of the Clothing and Textile Industry," *Materials Circular Economy 3*, no. 12 (2021), https://doi.org/10.1007/s42824-021-00026-2.
6 *The True Cost*, directed by Andrew Morgan (Untold Creative, Life Is My Movie Entertainment, 2015), film.
7 Mona Abaza, "Shifting Landscapes of Fashion in Contemporary Egypt," *Fashion Theory: The Journal of Dress, Body and Culture* 11, no. 2–3, (2007), 287.
8 Jessica Ouano, "Cultural Sustainability: Colonialism, Appropriation, and What Justice Looks Like," *Good on You*, October 6, 2024, https://goodonyou.eco/cultural-sustainability/.
9 Amy De Klerk, "Adele's Glastonbury dress took over 200 hours to make," *Harper's Bazaar*, June 27, 2016, https://www.harpersbazaar.com/uk/fashion/fashion-news/a37488/adeles-glastonbury-dress-chloe/.
10 For pictures of the dress see https://www.instagram.com/p/BHK-Ip9jGfg/ and https://www.instagram.com/p/CB8nZOJg2u5/.
11 Clare Waight Keller (@clairewaightkeller), "So proud - the incredible amazing @adele live at #Glastonburyfestival in @chloe green bespoke beaded dress," Instagram, June 25, 2016, https://www.instagram.com/p/BHGGPOfAkRd/?utm_source=ig_embed&ig_rid=b3d1eb39-d0d7-4fb2-a370-872cc8d3ba60.
12 "Adele's dress by Chloé sparks Siwa comparisons on social media in Egypt," *Ahbram Online*, July 2, 2016, https://english.ahram.org.eg/News/232330.aspx.
13 Enas El Masry, "Adele's Egypt-Inspired Dress Sparks Cultural Appropriation Controversy," *Egyptian Streets*, July 1, 2016, https://egyptianstreets.com/2016/07/01/adeles-egypt-inspired-dress-sparks-cultural-appropriation-controversy/.
14 Ann Binlot, "The Story of Chloé Founder Gaby Aghion's 'Ready to Wear' Revolution," *CNN*, October 24, 2023, https://edition.cnn.com/style/chloe-gaby-aghion-exhibition-jewish-museum/index.html.
15 "A 14-year, award winning global, collaborative embroidery project 2009 to 2023," *The Red Dress*, 2024, https://reddressembroidery.com/.
16 L.A Market Summer Breeze, "Why are local brand prices higher than large-scale brands?" Facebook, June 2, 2022, https://www.facebook.com/events/708975010300199/?active_tab=discussion.
17 Kirsi Niinimäki, *Sustainable Fashion: New Approaches* (Helsinki: Aalto University, 2013), *62-66*.
18 "The Brand," saqhoute, https://saqhoute.com/en-us/pages/the-brand.
19 Ibid.
20 Sarah Corbett, *How To Be A Craftivist: the Art of Gentle Protest* (London: Unbound, 2017), 1-10.
21 "About Us," Bulga, https://bulga.co/pages/about-us.
22 Kate Fletcher and Matihlde Tham, *Earth Logic: Fashion Action Research Plan* (London: JJ Charitable Trust, 2019), 19–20, https://katefletcher.com/wp-content/uploads/2019/10/Earth-Logic-plan-FINAL.pdf.

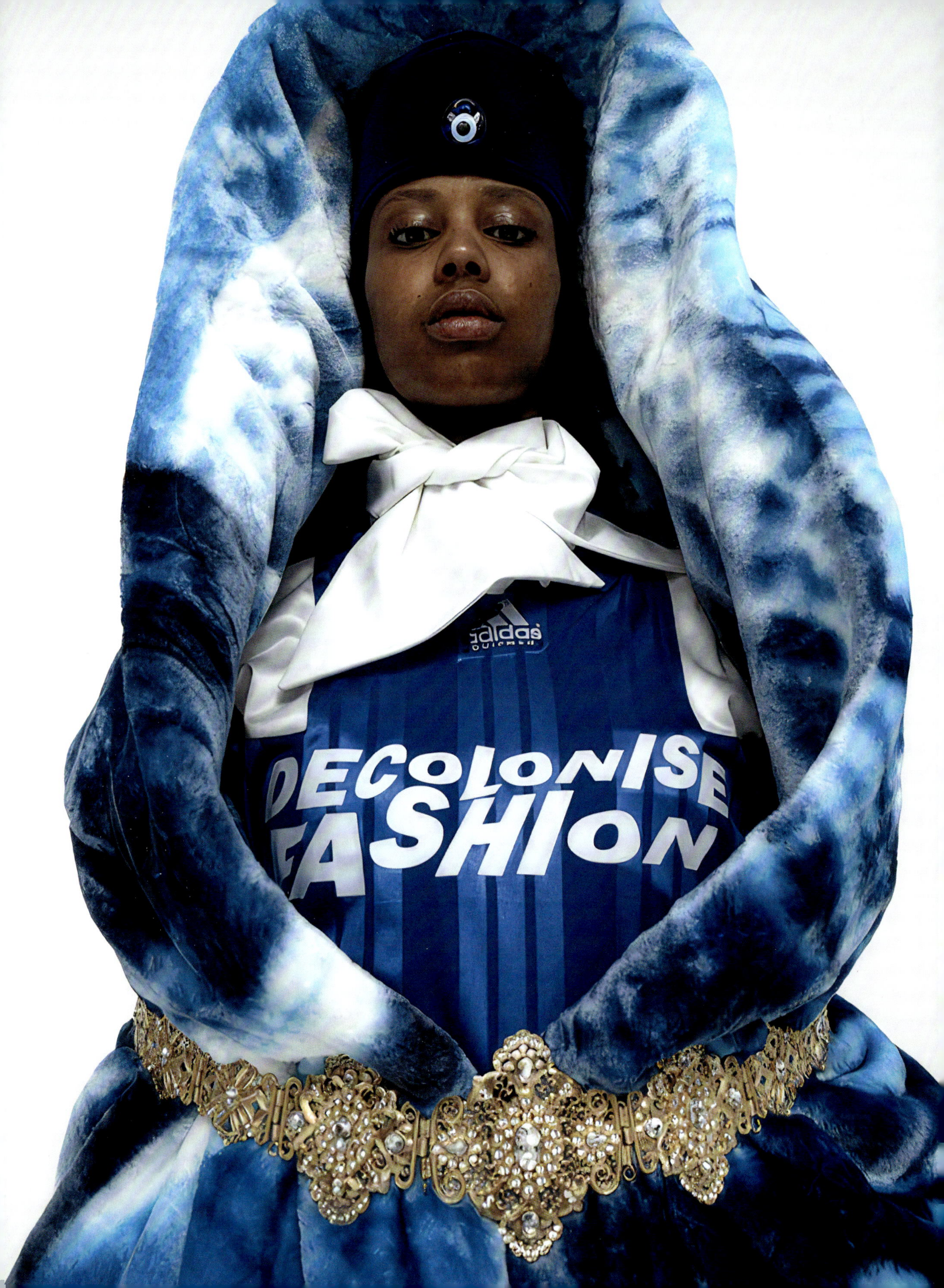
adidas
DECOLONISE
FASHION

FROM ALGERIAN PRIDE TO DECOLONIALITY IN FASHION

THE CASE OF KASBAH KOSMIC

Kenza Vandeput-Taleb

Fashion has always been a space where culture and politics meet—a way for people to express identity, resist norms, and create new stories. But let's be real: fashion has also been part of power structures, with its roots in colonial exploitation and cultural theft. This duality makes the landscape of fashion a space of unstable equilibrium where this tension is sometimes also magic.

In 2021, I (Kenza Vandeput, founder of Kasbah Kosmic) launched my independent fashion label in Brussels with the goal of shaking things up. I wanted to explore how fashion could open up new narratives. Kasbah Kosmic celebrates cultural identity, sustainable fashion, and creative collaboration, offering a hopeful vision for what fashion could become. This essay illustrates how my work engages with decolonial ideas through fabric prints that empower North African women, playful nods to fake luxury logos, and nostalgia as a way to stay connected to home (fig. 1).

Cultural Identity as Resistance

Colonial powers like France used visual media—especially photography—to dominate and erase local cultures. In Algeria, indigenous women were often photographed in staged, exploitative ways, highlighting nudity or exotic appearances. These photos, turned into postcards, became tools to spread colonial narratives, reducing women to stereotypes of the "exotic other" (fig. 2).

Reclaiming Power Through Radical Patchwork

In my collection "Radical Patchwork: A New Narrative," I flipped these colonial images into something empowering. I used high-quality scans of colonial postcards from my mom's personal collection and printed

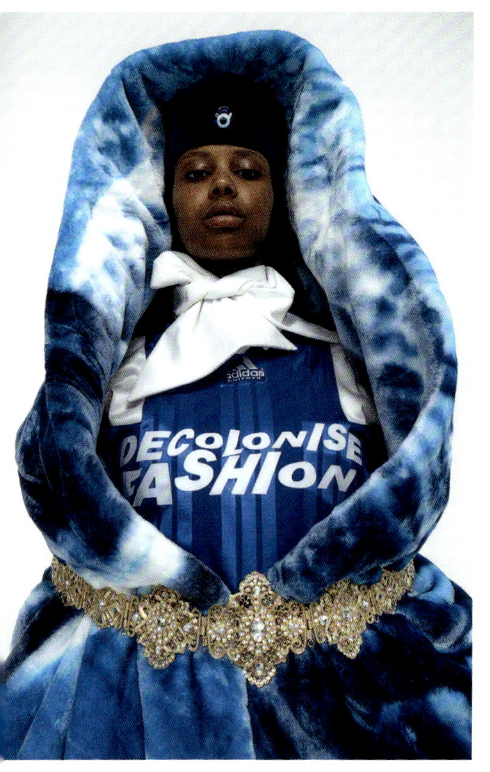

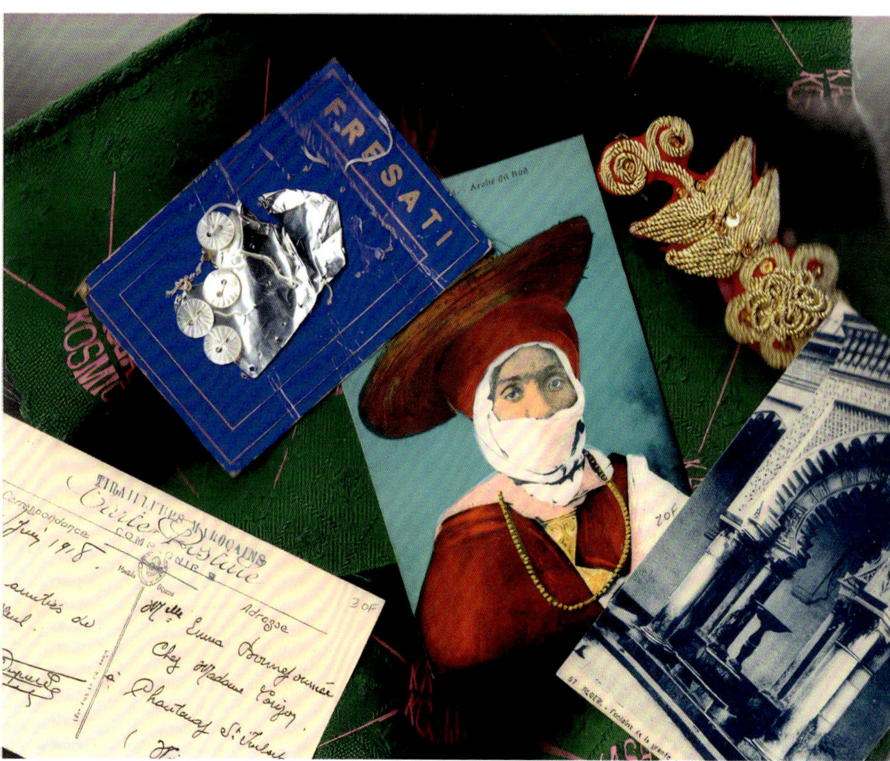

them onto fabric. These images, once tools of oppression, became symbols of pride and resistance.

The postcards feature traditional Algerian clothing, which I highlighted to reclaim the narrative. Instead of seeing these women through a colonial gaze, my designs center them as proud subjects. By wearing these pieces, people carry a message of resistance—an act of reclaiming agency for those whose stories were erased.

Edward Said's *Orientalism* helps explain the way that colonial imagery shaped how the West viewed non-Western cultures.[1] The postcards I use are classic examples of exoticism, portraying Algerian women as mysterious and passive. My designs aim to break this narrative, showing North African culture as a source of strength.

Fig. 1: Image courtesy of Mous Lamrabat, 2023

Fig: 2: Kenza Vandeput, 2023, scan

Exoticism and Orientalism

Said's *Orientalism* provides a framework for understanding how Western perceptions of non-Western cultures have historically been shaped by power dynamics. Colonial imagery often depicted "the Orient" as exotic, mysterious, and inferior—a constructed "other" that justified Western dominance. The postcards are a prime example of this, as they exoticized Algerian women, stripping them of individuality and agency to fit a narrative that served colonial interests. They focused on the depictions of "Oriental" women, particularly in

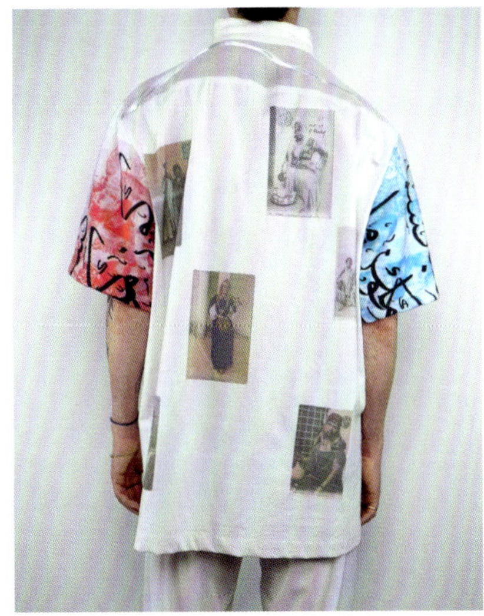

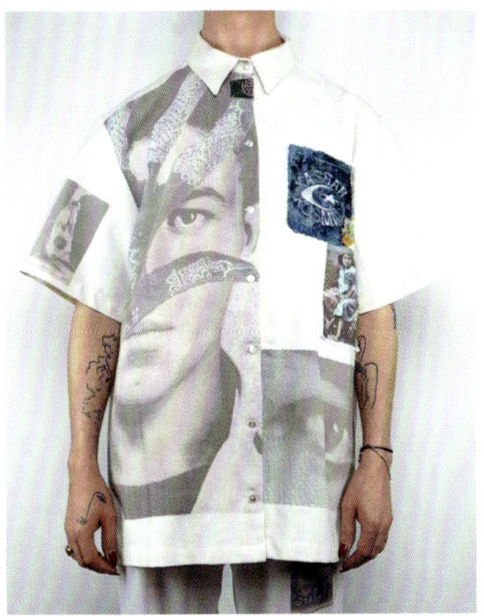

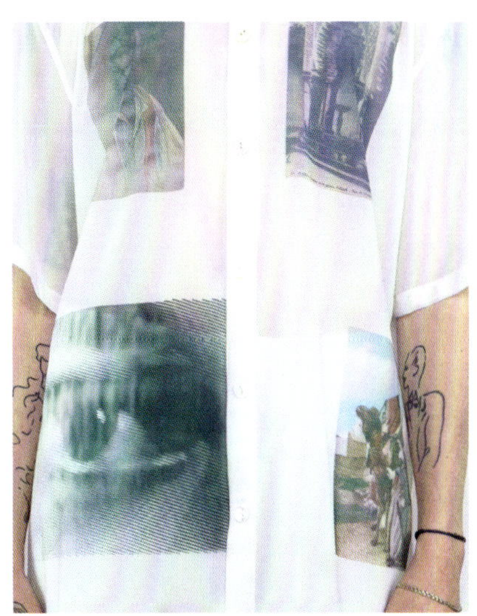

Fig. 3–7: Peter Emmanuelov, 2023, Packshot Up-cycled shirt and trouser made from vintage tablecloths

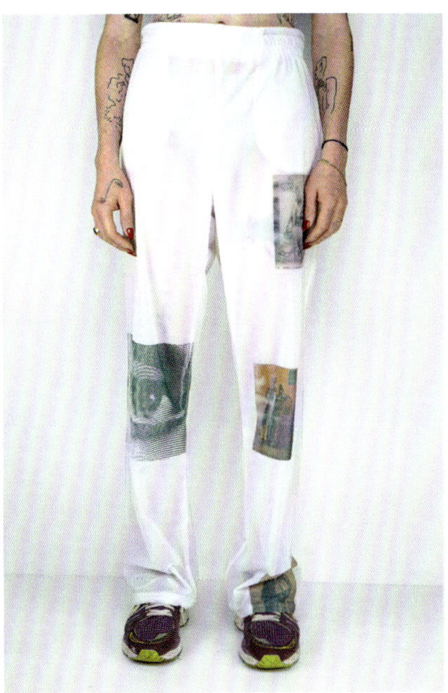

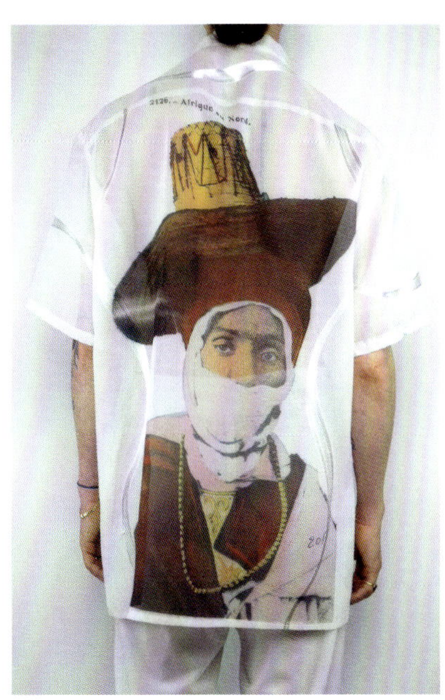

literature and visual culture, portraying them as passive, mysterious, and eroticized.

To disrupt this framework, I re-center these women as subjects, not objects. Through the re-appropriation of those images, the collection challenges the exoticization of North African culture, reframing it as a source of strength and giving back the power. I place these women in a garment like they are heroes. It is a way of empowering them after their souls have been taken by the colonial forces. I hope in a much bigger picture that they transcend reality—that this work is a part of the healing journey of the ancestors (figs. 3–7).

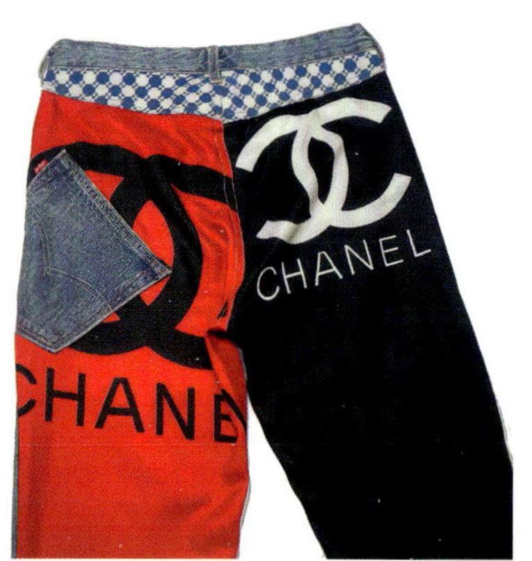

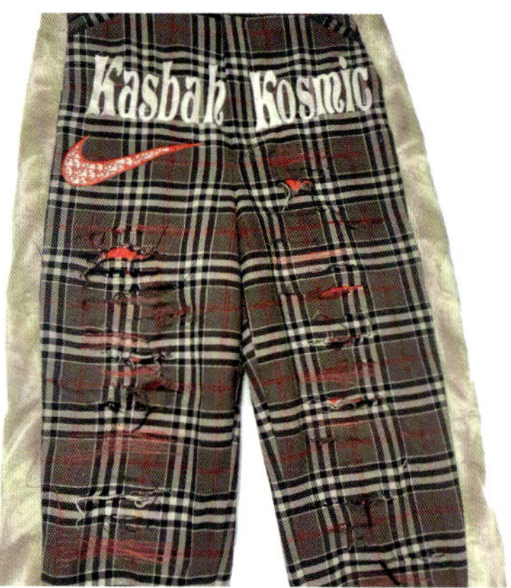

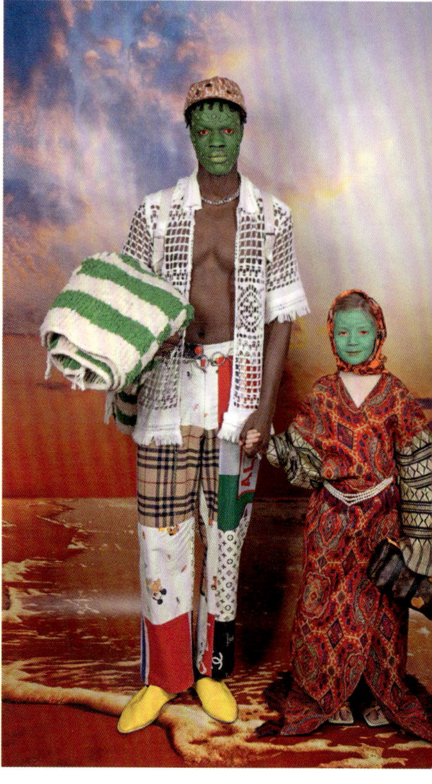

Fig. 8–9: Kenza Vandeput 2022
Fig. 10: Jan Hoek, *Fucking Young* magazine Green Issue, 2022. Image courtesy of Jan Hoek

Bootlegs and Consumerism

If you have ever been to North Africa, you know bootlegs are everywhere. Louis Vuitton, Gucci, Nike—you name it, there is a fake version on the market. From socks to scarves to plates, these logos have become part of the landscape. It is almost a tradition to bring back fake Nike TNs or a Louis Vuitton wallet after visiting Algeria.

In my designs, I use fake monograms as a playful way to critique consumerism and cultural appropriation by luxury brands. For years, these brands have taken cultural elements from the Global South, made them trendy, and sold them at sky-high prices without giving credit. My work questions these dynamics.

Aja Barber's *Consumed* talks about how the fashion industry exploits the Global South while promoting wealth and exclusivity in the Global North. The use of bootlegs aligns with her call to dismantle colonial systems in fashion and create a fairer, more sustainable industry (figs. 8–10).[2]

Decolonial Heroes

Fashion is more than just clothes; it is a tool for telling stories and imagining new realities. By taking figures from my heritage and making them wearable, I turn them into symbols of resistance. One of the key figures I have honored is Ali la Pointe, a revolutionary hero from the Algerian War of Independence. Born in 1930, Ali la Pointe was a street kid who became a key leader in the National Liberation Front (FLN). He played a major role in the Battle of Algiers and became a symbol of resistance against French colonial rule. He was killed in 1957 during a standoff with the French army, becoming a martyr for Algerian independence.[3] In my designs, Ali la Pointe represents strength and resil-

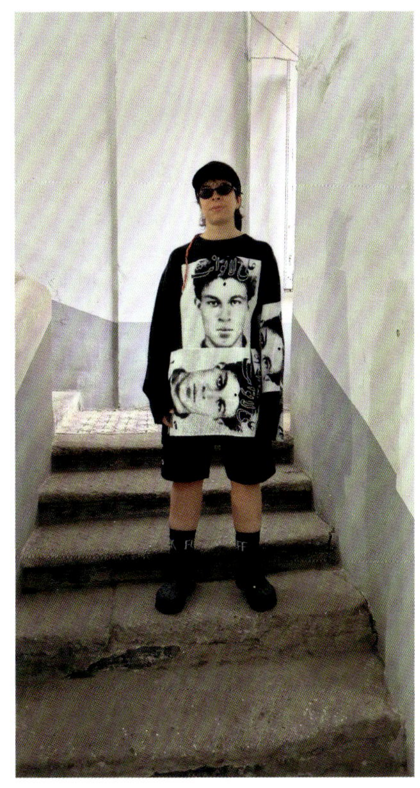

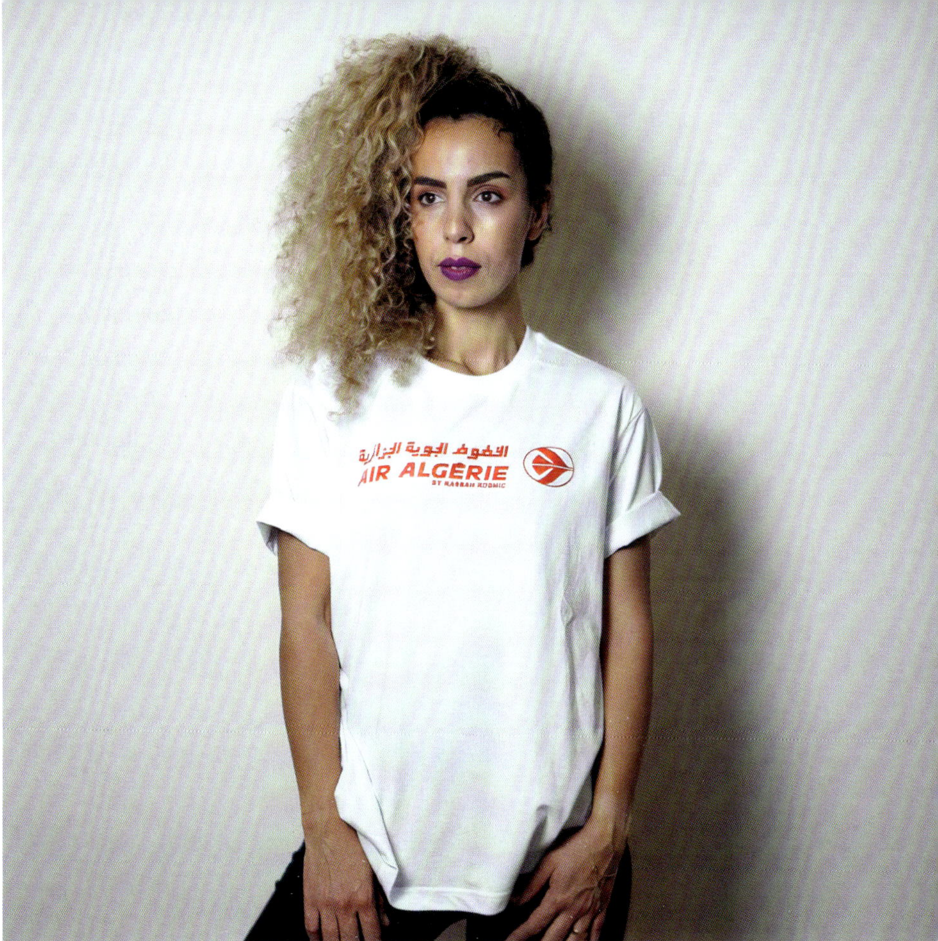

Fig. 11: Sarra Ryma, 2024
Fig. 12: Kenza Vandeput, 2020

ience. I aim to make people feel like they are wearing their own story of resistance and pride—a wearable tribute to our ancestors (fig. 11).

Nostalgia as a Form of Resistance: "LE BLED"

When coloniality wants us to be disconnected from our community and from the land. When you live in the diaspora, nostalgia hits differently. Holding onto memories, brands, and symbols of home becomes a way to stay connected. It's also a way to resist assimilation into the dominant culture. Clinging to airlines like Air Algérie or local snacks is like saying, "I still belong to my roots."

In my work, nostalgia is huge. In 2020, I launched a series of T-shirts featuring the iconic Air Algérie logo. Why? Because this logo has emotional power. It has not changed in years, and that vintage look makes it even more nostalgic. Air Algérie's unchanged branding makes it a legacy symbol—it is part of the "bled starter pack" (fig. 12)

Getting on an Air Algérie flight feels like being in Algeria already. People switch to Derija, they chat about the *bled* (village), and it feels like home. In 2021, I worked with Sarah Ryma on a short film called *Air Kasbah*, which explores this nostalgia of exile. It's a visual love letter to the *bled*, capturing that longing to reconnect with home.

Miles magazine: AIR KASBAH, the short movie invites you to embark on the nostalgia of exile by exploring some of the cultural codes we are dearly missing.

From the fits, looks, and aura of the film, the conceptual project encapsulates what we would all like to relive in the times to come: a trip back home. (fig. 13; https://www.youtube.com/watch?v=cv4S1QxSFR0)

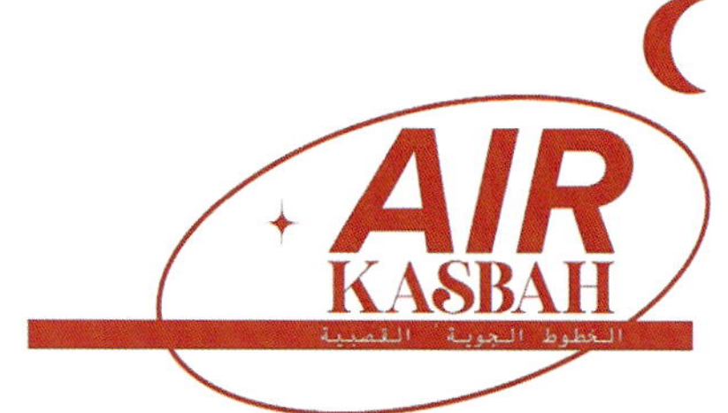

Conclusion

Kasbah Kosmic is a playground to experiment, explore, and create hybrid identities. I try to implement emotion and feelings so people can question their connection with clothes. When I see my clothes, I see memories, stories, and fragments of cultural identity that have traveled through time and space.

My decolonial journey has only just begun, and I'm happy to open this conversation within the world of fashion. There is so much to discuss on this topic, and I feel deeply called to do this work. Decoloniality is a process—a call to repair, to give back, and to be more mindful of the land, our eco-systems, and the histories that were stolen or erased. It's about embracing the complexity of identity and reclaiming narratives that have been shaped by colonial powers.

I hope that in this historic moment we are living in, there is space to rethink fashion and the way we dress—to move towards more meaningful, conscious connections with what we wear. It's about acknowledging the mistakes of the past.

Fashion can be a powerful tool to reclaim identity, challenge systems of oppression, and imagine new possibilities for the future. With Kasbah Kosmic, I aim to create a space that celebrates pride, connection, and storytelling, and embraces playfullness (fig. 14).

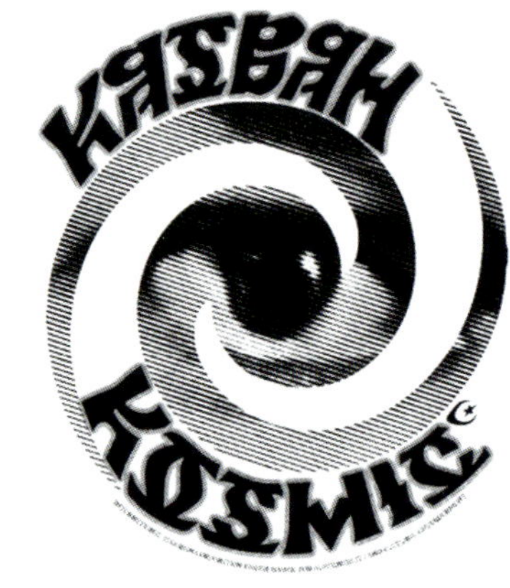

13 Kenza Vandeput, 2021

Kenza Vandeput-Taleb is the founder of the Brussels-based fashion label Kasbah Kosmic (p. 84)

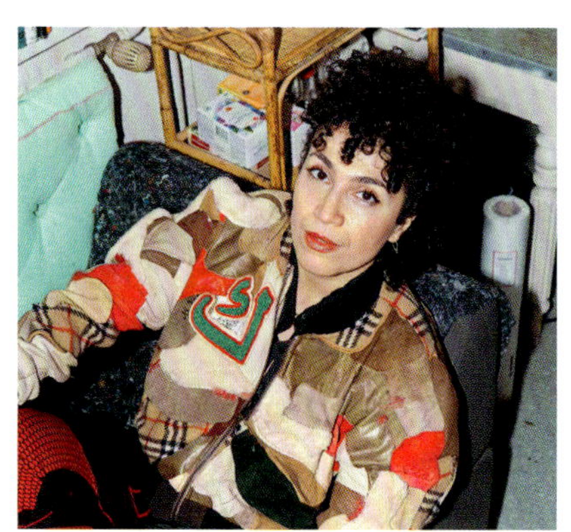

1 Edward Said, *Orientalism* (New York: Pantheon Books, 1978), 118–121.
2 Aja Barber, *Consumed: The Need for Collective Change: Colonialism, Climate Change, and Consumerism* (London: Penguin, 2021).
3 Martin Evans and John Phillips, *Algeria: Anger of the Dispossessed*

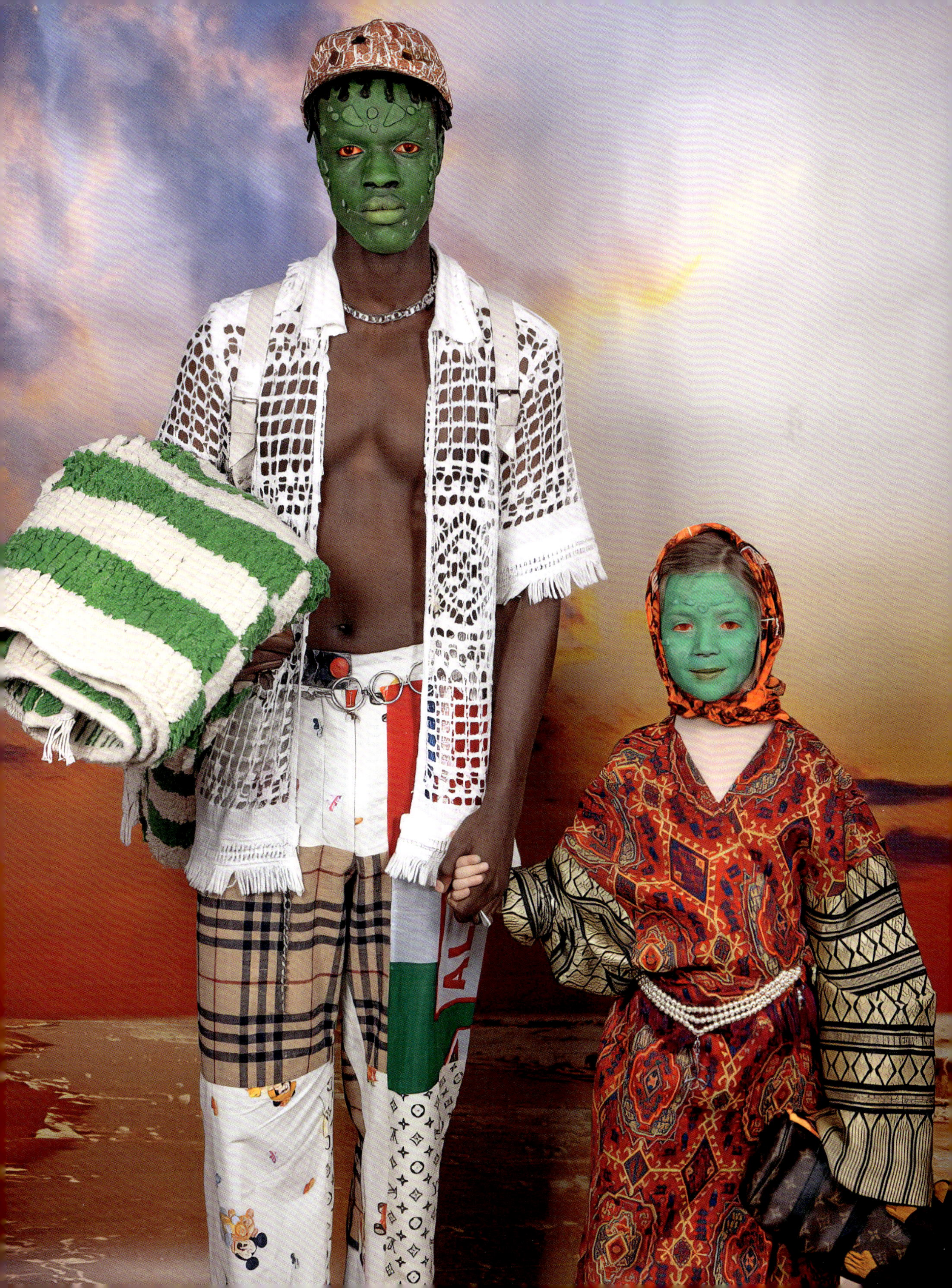

DISRUPTORS

المقاومون

Timeless. Unchanging. Dress styles in North Africa are often considered to be bound by tradition and thus fixed by centuries of custom. The designers we have designated as "Disruptors" force a rethinking of the notion that the region's dress is staid and conservative. Fashion is by its very nature a balance between new and old. Designers introduce new aesthetics that iterate previous styles. But in some cases, young designers present work that demands a rethinking of established cultural patterns. Many North African designers are challenging the conventional roles of men and women by presenting unisex garments. While the attitude of these designers borders on iconoclasm, they still see themselves as bearers of North African culture. The Instagram handle of Karim Chater, "Style Beldi," epitomizes the integration of cultural heritage with the new and modern. *Beldi* is a word in the Moroccan dialect of Arabic which signifies authentic and traditional. The aesthetic of Chater's account reflects his love of vintage style while also taking as a backdrop the urban setting of Casablanca. Just as globalization does not lead to homogenization, local styles do not need to be either fixed or historic.

BERBERISM

HAYET KAMINSKY

Berberism is a line of jewelry and accessories launched by Hayet Kaminsky, who adopted the name of the brand as her artistic name. The name comes from the political-cultural movement supporting the interest of the Amazigh communities (also known as Berbers). Berberism was born in Paris in an Amazigh family and moved to Algeria when she was fourteen. She learned to sew from her mother starting at the age of seven. In making pieces using different techniques, including crochet, embroidery, and knitting her mother demonstrated both curiosity and dexterity.

Berberism is now a visual artist who works with leather and metal as her primary media, exploring both their rigidity and flexibility. A passionate collector of beads from across Africa and an avid researcher of African artisanal techniques, she studies their craftsmanship and rhythms to interconnect them. Each of her masks serves as a map of Africa. She created the crown featured on the poster of the 2022 Dakar Biennale of Contemporary African Art, a piece paying tribute to Senegalese blacksmiths. This crown is part of Algeria's Berber jewelry heritage. She represented Algeria at the She Designs African Women Designers Salon in Sharm El-Sheikh, Egypt, in 2018. In 2024 she exhibited in collaboration with the artist Rocé at the Dakar Biennale of Contemporary African Art with a piece featured in the Kandinsky Review of the Centre Pompidou.

The designer uses her multi-national identity in her designs, which blend tradition and modernity in pieces that pay homage to the Amazigh culture. The two pieces shown here epitomize the way Berberism honors Amazigh and African culture. Kahina Crown represents the story of La Kahina, the daughter of an Amazigh ruler who resisted the Arab invaders. The Makeba Headphones is a tribute to the artistic and political work of revolutionary Myriam Makeba.

Kahina Crown, image courtesy of Berberism
→

Makeba Headphones, image courtesy of Berberism
↓

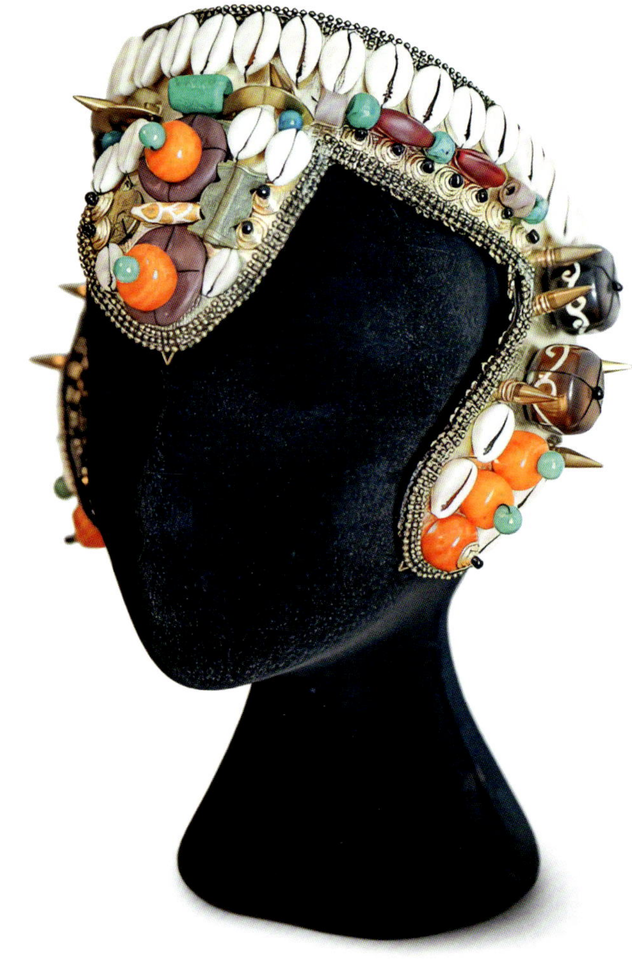

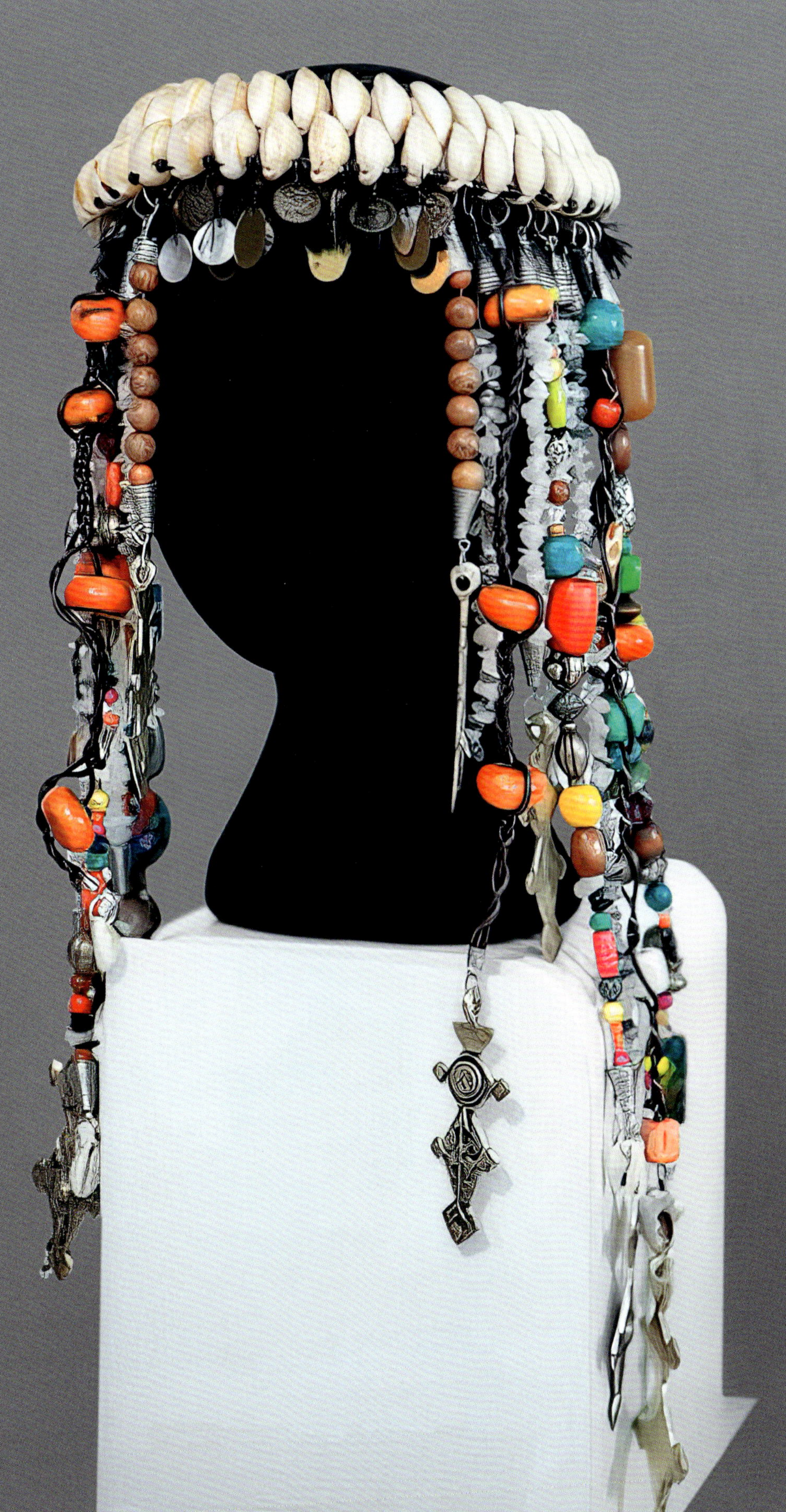

BOAUNA

EMNA BOUAOUN CARRASCO

Photographer: Hamza Ben Nour
stylist: Emna Bouaoun

Emna Bouaoun Carrasco is a stylist and fashion designer in Tunisia. She studied fashion design in Barcelona and continued training in styling, design, and upcycling. Early in her professional career, Bouaoun started Boauna as a streetwear clothing brand that launched in 2021, while also working on film, theater, and television productions. She also used her dual Spanish-Tunisian nationality, as well as her experience working in Tunisia, Algeria, Spain, and Dubai, to incorporate different ways of working according to different cultures. Boauna's style is unisex and oversized. The inspiration for the materials and colors come from trades, working, and uniforms. Bouaoun had the idea for the brand when her unemployment conflicted with her desire to feel productive. She began experimenting and creating designs that express her concerns over modern culture's obsession with being useful and constantly productive. As the founder and director of Boauna, she is in charge of the identity and artistic direction of the brand. She is responsible for aesthetics, visual narrative, conceptualization, garment design, choice of color and fabrics, and content creation, which includes casting models and searching for locations. Prototyping, production management, and quality control of garments are also a part of her responsibilities.

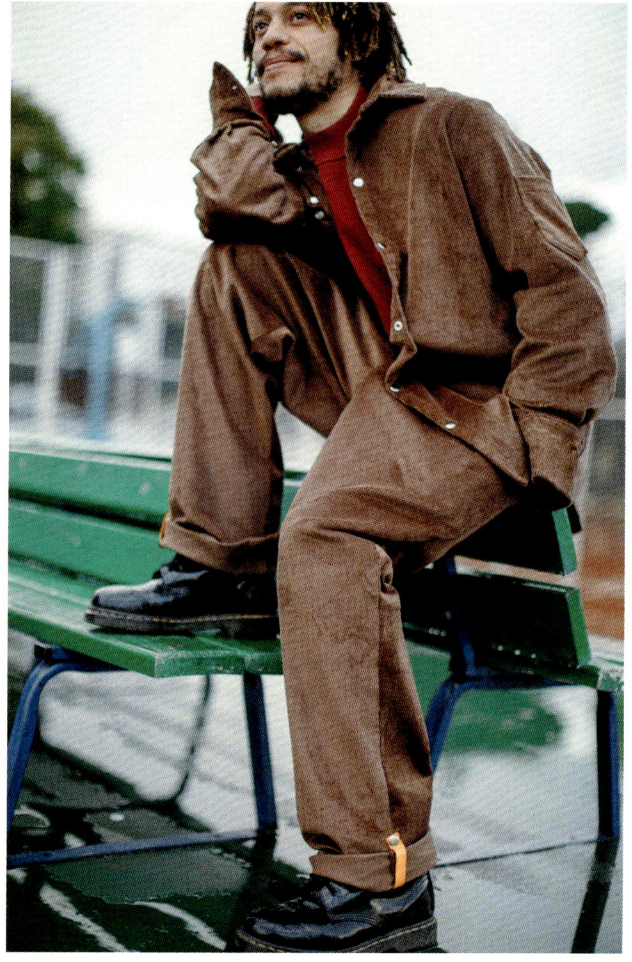

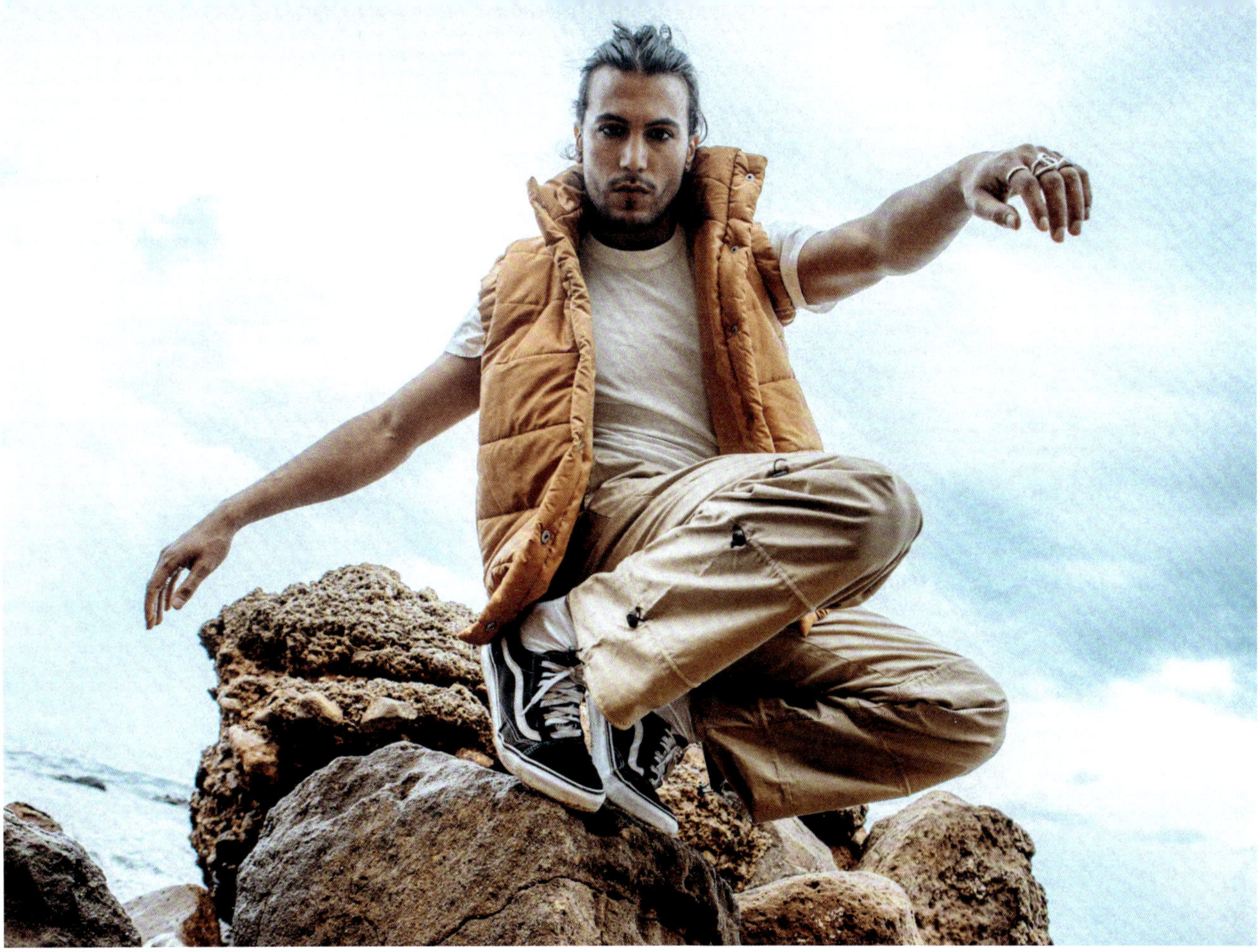

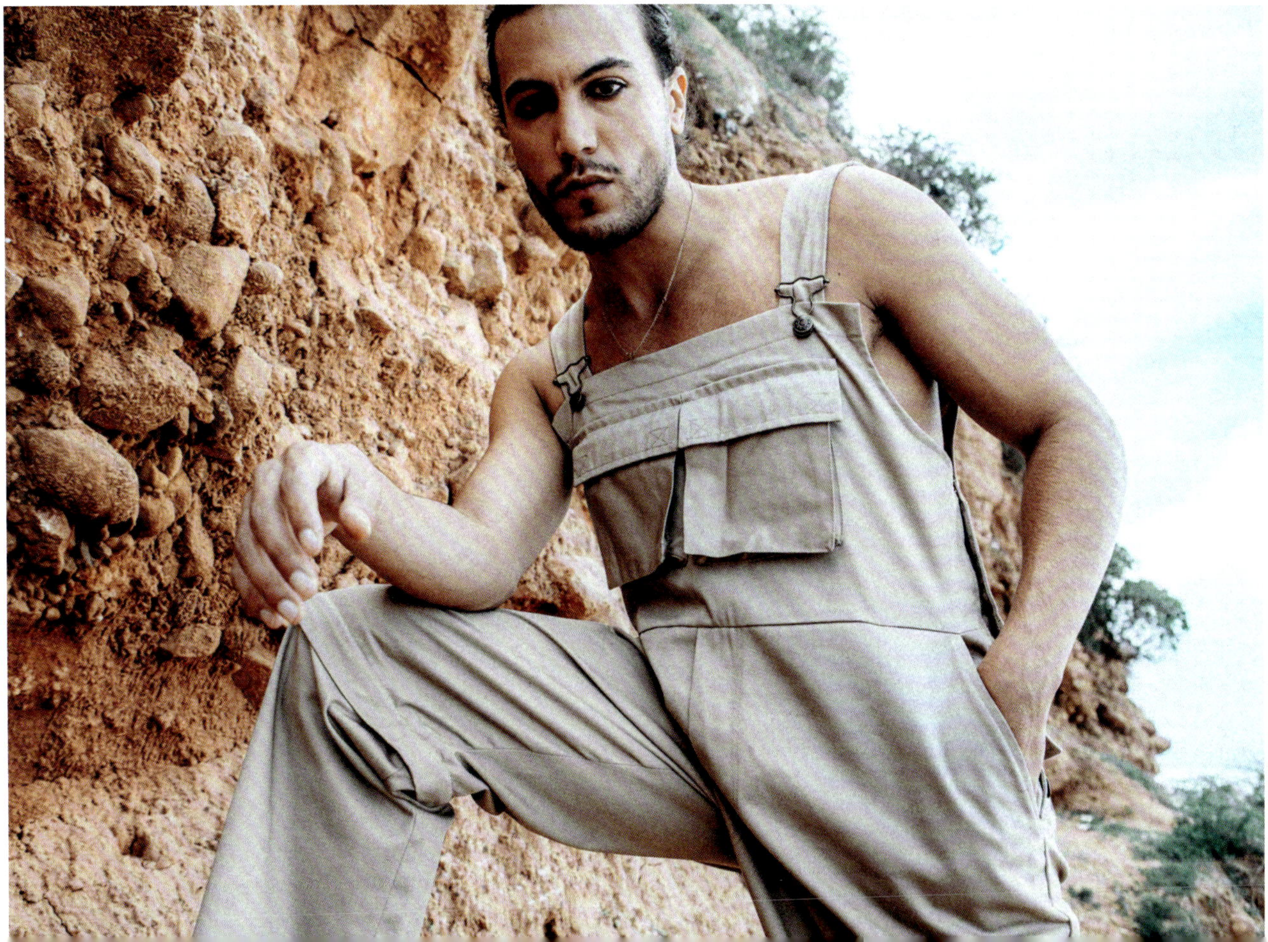

BOPHONYSSE

BADRA CHERFI

Bophonysse aims to be ahead of the curve with designs that are trendsetting and sustainable. Style and functionality work in tandem to create pieces that are fashionable but still cater to practical needs. Bophonysse, which is based in London, puts craftsmanship first, with high quality items that are produced with eco-friendly materials, ethical production practices, and a minimal carbon footprint. The founder of Bophonysse, Badra Cherfi, is an Algerian woman born in France who grew up near the Mediterranean. She has degrees in languages, literature, and teaching and worked for TikTok before leaving to start her brand. The name Bophonysse was inspired by Sophonisbe, a Numidian queen known for her bravery and sacrifice and an important figure in North African and Berber history. Cherfi wanted to pay tribute to the queen and to revive her story and the history of North Africa that predates the Islamic period with her collections. Cherfi did not grow up in Amazigh culture, but feels connected to it and that it is a vital part of her identity. She also draws from poetry and art for inspiration, especially the poet Lord Byron and the painter Eugène Delacroix. Cherfi is passionate about eco-friendly production. All of her garments are made to order to prevent pollution and overconsumption, and her zero-waste policy means that all fabric scraps are reused to make decorative elements.

Her Wild-Winged Butterfly ensemble is inspired by the Algerian *karakou*, a traditional ensemble composed of a velvet jacket embroidered with gold or silver paired with sirwal or loose-fitting pants. The second ensemble entitled Out of a Silver Shell is inspired by a wedding dress and burnoose, in which the cape is made of silk and hand painted.

Wild-Winged Butterfly, image courtesy of Bophonysse
→

Out of a Silver Shell, image courtesy of Bophonysse
↓

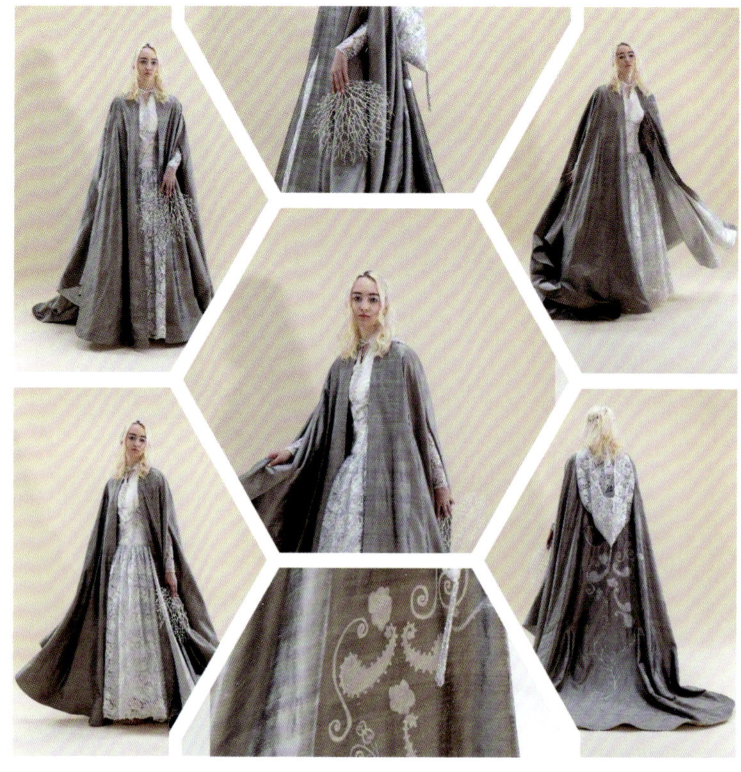

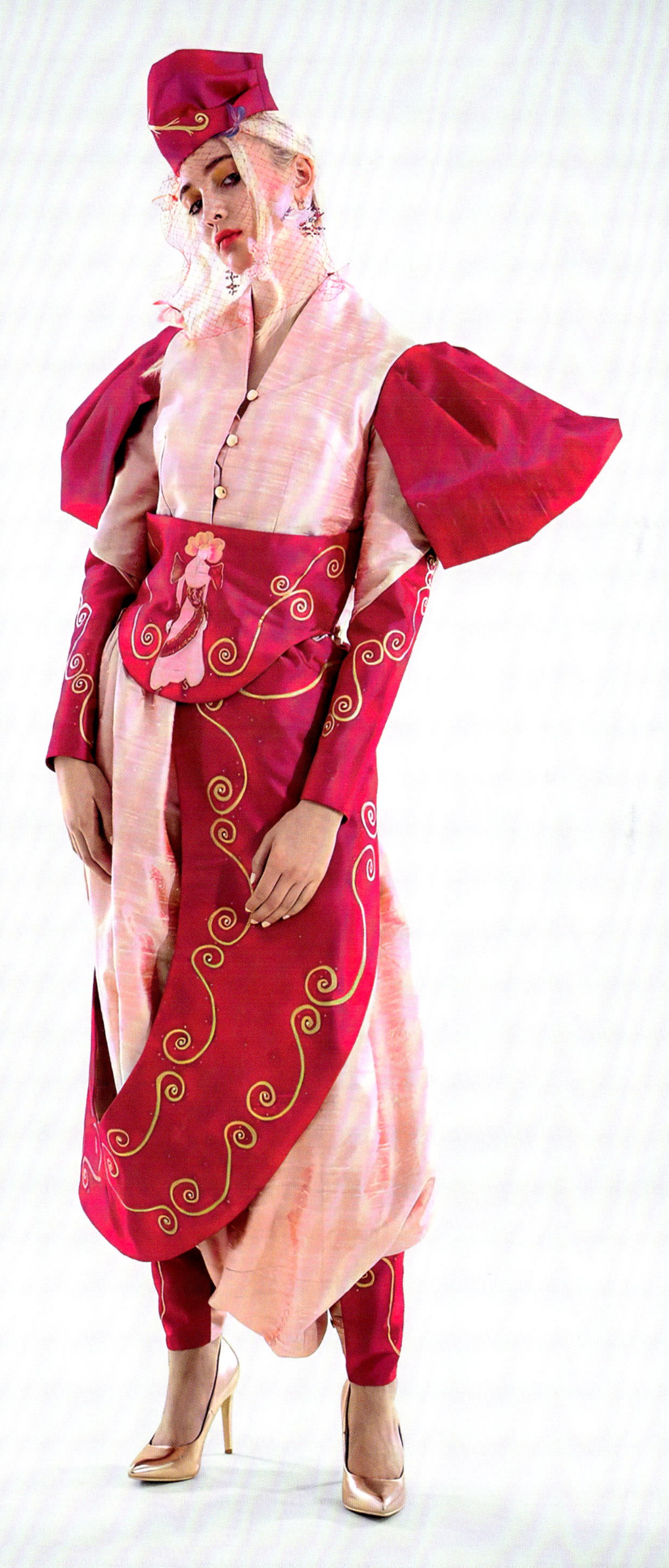

BORN IN EXILE
IBRAHIM SHEBANI

Ibrahim Shebani's brand Born in Exile takes inspiration from Libya and all its beautiful complexities. Shebani was born in Germany and grew up between Egypt and Libya. He studied architecture at the African University of Benghazi and later worked in marketing, before fulfilling his childhood dream of launching a clothing brand inspired by Libya. His identity is reflected in his approach to design, which not only portrays Libya through its culture and traditions but also through its politics and Western influences. Shebani aims to show all sides of Libya through his designs: not only its beauty but also its complexities. He says that instead of traditional clothes, he and many others often wore European clothes, his designs drawing both from Libya and from those foreign countries that influenced Libyan clothing.

His first collection, he explains, has a feeling inspired by the rock music popular in Libya in the 1990s, because Libya did not produce a large amount of its own music and people instead listened to music from abroad. This collection features traditional embroidery on modern garments, a unique style that Shebani implements often and that his brand has become known for. His other collections have been inspired by the traditional Libyan horse track, immigration, Greek mythology, and Gaddafi's propaganda machine. The pieces in the exhibition come from his Fall/Winter 2021 collection Blood, Sweat, and Oil, intended to capture the hopes, fears, and uncertainties of Libya's oil boom, which radically changed the economic and social landscape of the country. Shebani hopes to one day turn his brand into a lifestyle with an atelier, a team of designers and producers, selling internationally, and expanding into accessories, shoes, perfume, and menswear.

COA shirt and skirt, photo: Bachir Tayachi →

Libya Leather Biker Jacket, photo: Joanna Ben Souissi ↓

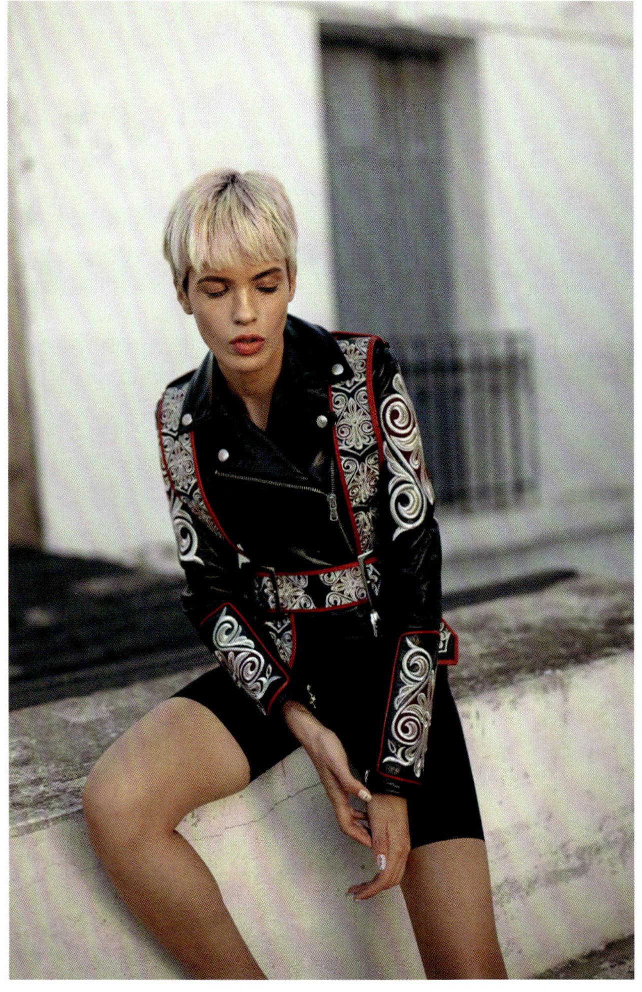

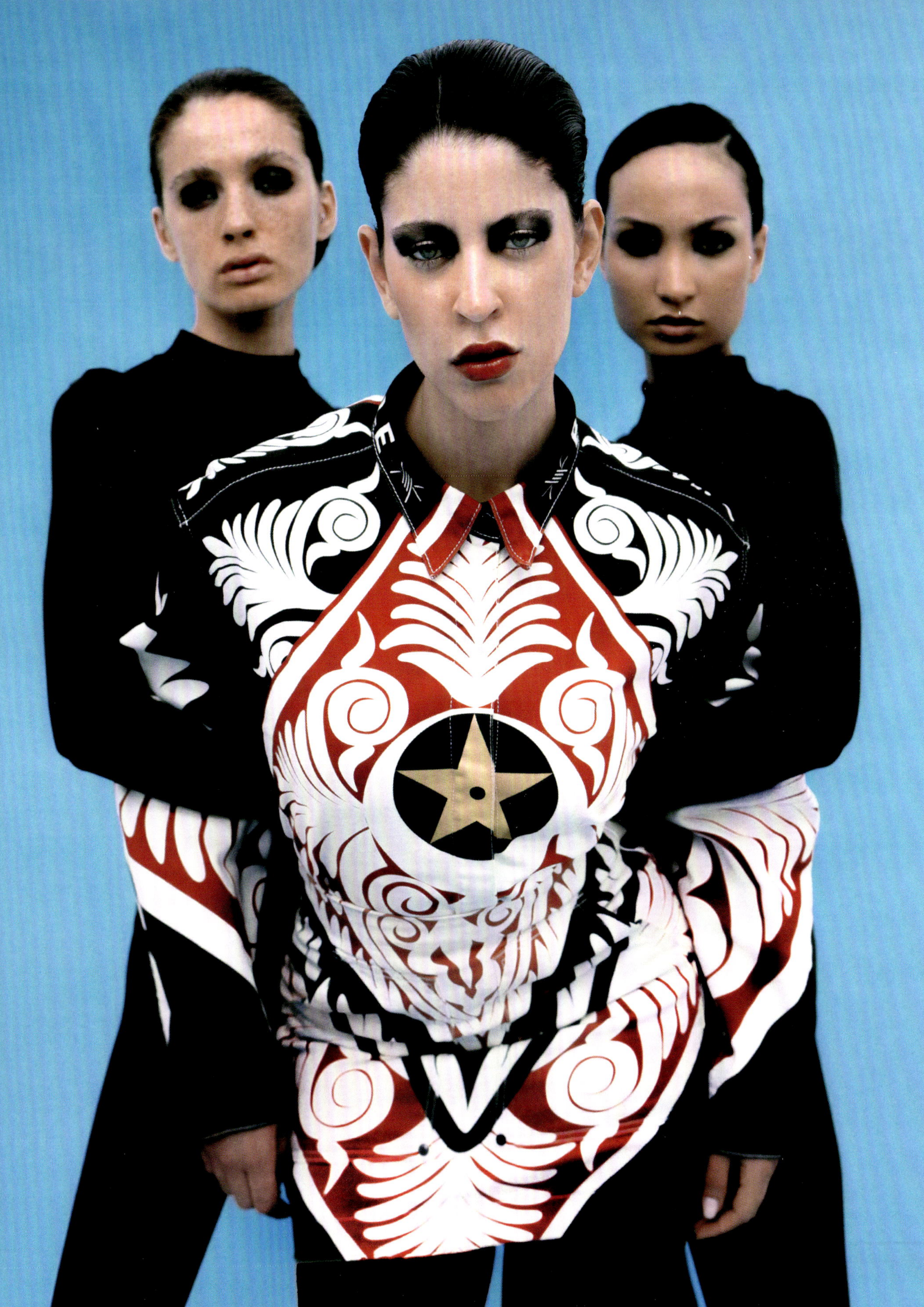

KARIM CHATER

Karim Chater is the Casablanca-based artist, stylist, model, videographer, and photographer behind the social media account @style_beldi. His unique style combines traditional Moroccan dress with vintage and modern Western styles. While Chater incorporates vintage pieces into his style, especially those that remind him of his parents' style in the 70s, he always keeps a Moroccan flare in his looks. He hopes to inspire other artists with his hybrid style and to help the growth of Moroccan style and influence in the world of fashion. His popular Instagram account has over 170,000 followers, including most of the designers and artists represented in this exhibition. The name behind his platform comes from the word *beldi*, meaning traditional, local, or authentic in Moroccan Arabic. The term used to refer to things seen as old fashioned, but today is seen as representing the best aspects of Morocco, especially those associated with its past. This is part of a search for authenticity that drives people to connect with tradition and an idealized past. Chater uses this association to support his platform's style of incorporating older styles into modern ones. This use of bringing traditional and vintage styles, production practices, and arts into the modern-day characterizes both *beldi* and Karim Chater's Style Beldi.

L7atta originale,
image courtesy of Karim Chater
→

Steady Clear Vision,
image courtesy of Karim Chater
↓

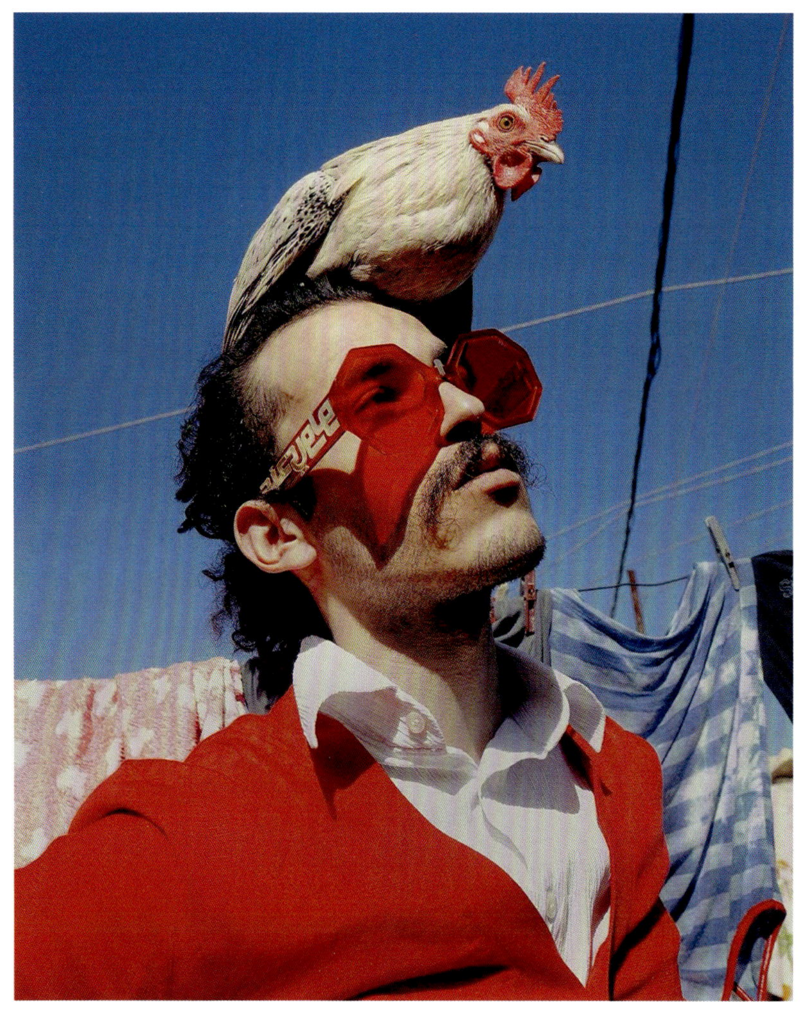

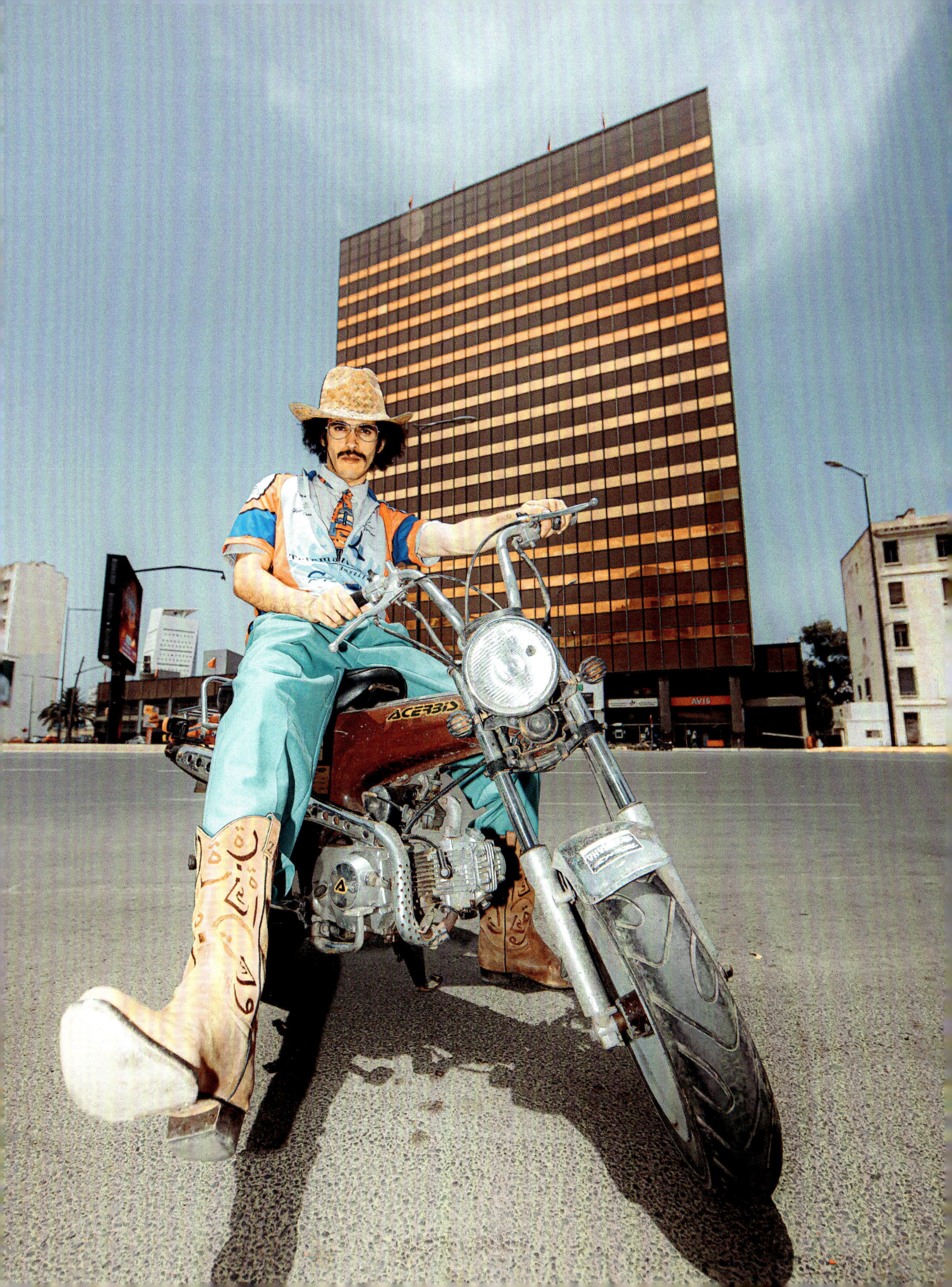
ACERBIS
AVIS

KEGHAM DJEGHALIAN

Kegham Djeghalian is an art director, visual artist, fashion stylist, and educator based in Paris and Cairo. He is a Professor of Fashion Studies, Image and Design, and the Artistic Director of the Fashion Design Department at the German International University (GIU). Djeghalian has been a faculty member at Paris College of Art (PCA) since 2016 and is one of the faculty members who premiered the Master of Arts program in Fashion Film and Photography in 2016. He was the Acting Pedagogic Director of the Master of Image Design in fashion at the Institut Français de la Mode (IFM) in 2018 and 2019. He has consulted and collaborated with many fashion houses and designers such as Dior, Kenzo, Louboutin, and Hermès. In 2014, his short film "To Schiap with Love" was selected and shown at Diane Pernet's "A Shaded View on Fashion Film 7" at the Centre Pompidou in Paris. In 2020, he was appointed as the Creative Director of the Egyptian footwear brand Zee with a mission to revamp and restructure its identity, image, and product.

Djeghalian is represented in the exhibition by his video and installation *ToGather*, a contemplation inspired by Farid al-Din Attar's poem *Conference of the Birds*. The cube was constructed of upcycled clothing items in collaboration with the Egyptian Clothing Bank and its upcycling fashion brand Almah. As he described it, "I deconstruct the wholeness of these individual garments into flat pieces of fabric, into mere pattern blocks which I reconstruct into another hybrid entity, 'the Cube.' The second skin of the body becomes a spatial second skin; a humble edifice with a new potential of possibilities."

Construction of the Cube, image courtesy of Kegham Djeghalian
→

ToGather, video installation, image courtesy of Kegham Djeghalian
↓

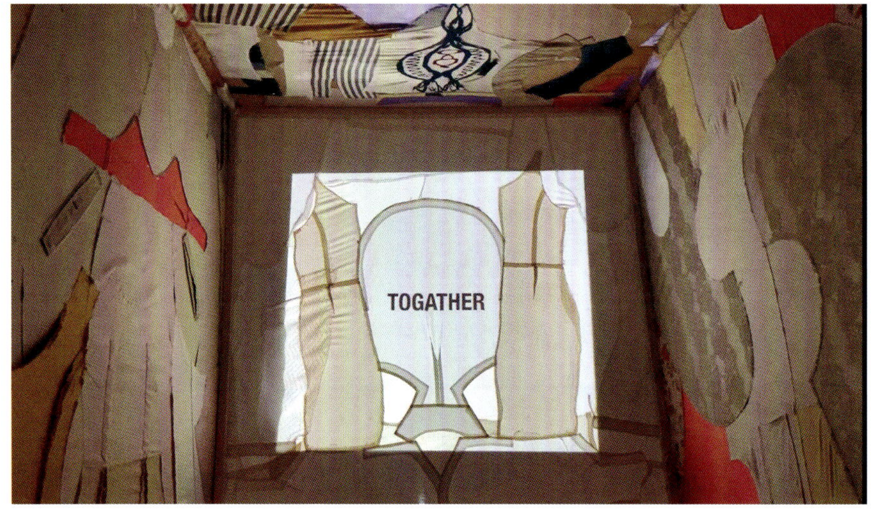

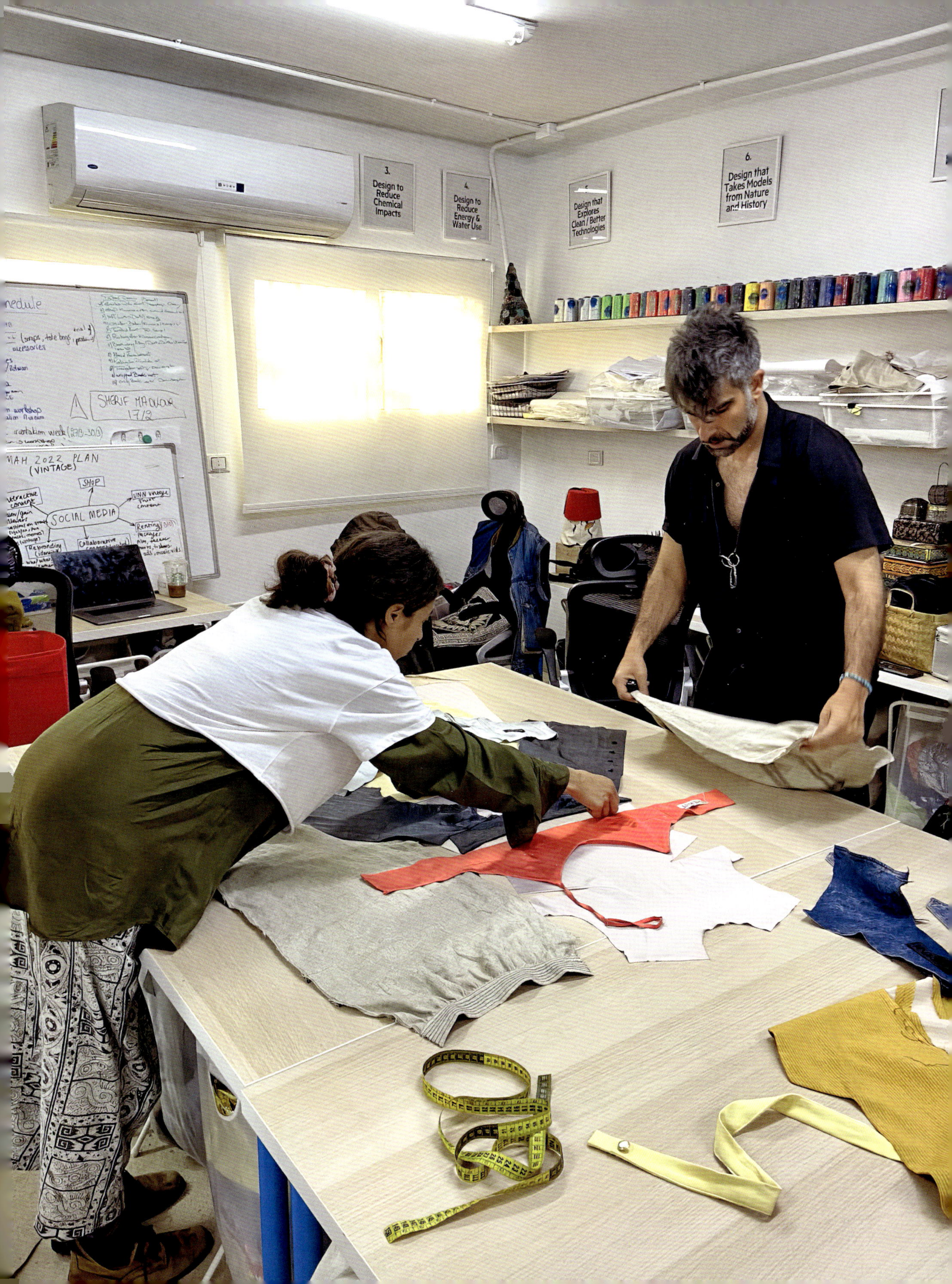
3.
Design to Reduce Chemical Impacts
4.
Design to Reduce Energy & Water Use
Design that Explores Clean / Better Technologies
6.
Design that Takes Models from Nature and History
SOCIAL MEDIA

FFORFARAH

FARAH ABDELHAMID

Farah Abdelhamid is the artist behind FforFarah, a jewelry brand based in Cairo. She moved around frequently starting at a young age. She has lived in nine countries and attended more than thirteen schools. Abdelhamid graduated from the Rhode Island School of Design with a BFA in Jewelry and Metalsmithing and has just received her MA in Design in Germany. Despite this, Cairo is where she considers home. Her brand focuses on the relationship jewelry has with the body, which was inspired by her studies in psychology and social research. She is specifically interested in what a person goes through in the moments before deciding to wear a piece of jewelry. Abdelhamid explores this through design, form, and material. She replaces conventional design elements that suggest how the piece should be worn with unexpected elements and materials, allowing the wearer to explore the piece and have a more engaging and personal experience with the jewelry. In this way the experience of wearing jewelry becomes the art form rather than the jewelry itself being the art. Farah also has over ten years of experience teaching at the community and university levels, including being the assistant director and project manager at The Design Studio by Azza Fahmy. During her time there, she developed curriculum and classes while aiming to empower students through practical techniques. For the future of the brand, Farah hopes to continue to be a small business with all of the products handmade by her, as well as to teach in the studio and collaborate with others on projects to expand her creativity and outreach.

The examples of FforFarah's work shown here are hand-fabricated and raised from one sheet of copper. These bi-forms are inspired by the Hollow Vessels in Ancient Egypt which preserved, protected, and honored the body. With their ergonomic forms and silhouettes, they invite the human body to hold, experience, and contemplate their relationship to the object itself, and then the maker and how these objects came into being. The blown-glass is a reflection of the maker's breath, the hollow space that is empty but filled with another material, the ephemeral beauty of the intangible experience of the body. They are invitations, they are also statements of what is, what you do not see, and what you can feel if you honor the body, the maker, and material—as the Ancient Egyptians did so well.

Bi-Form 2: copper, glass, linen, image courtesy of FforFarah
→

Bi-Form 1: silver galvanized copper, image courtesy of FforFarah
↓

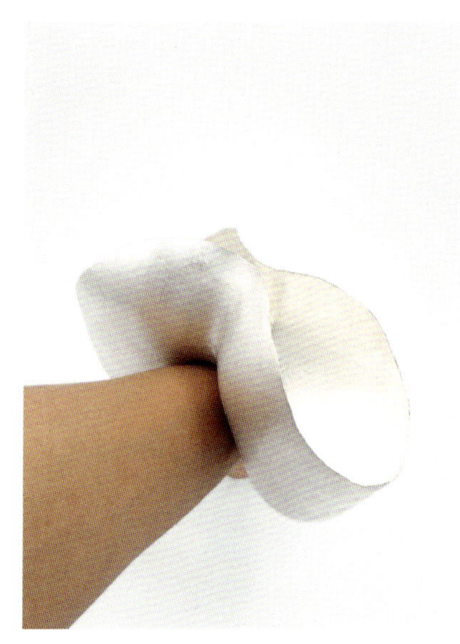

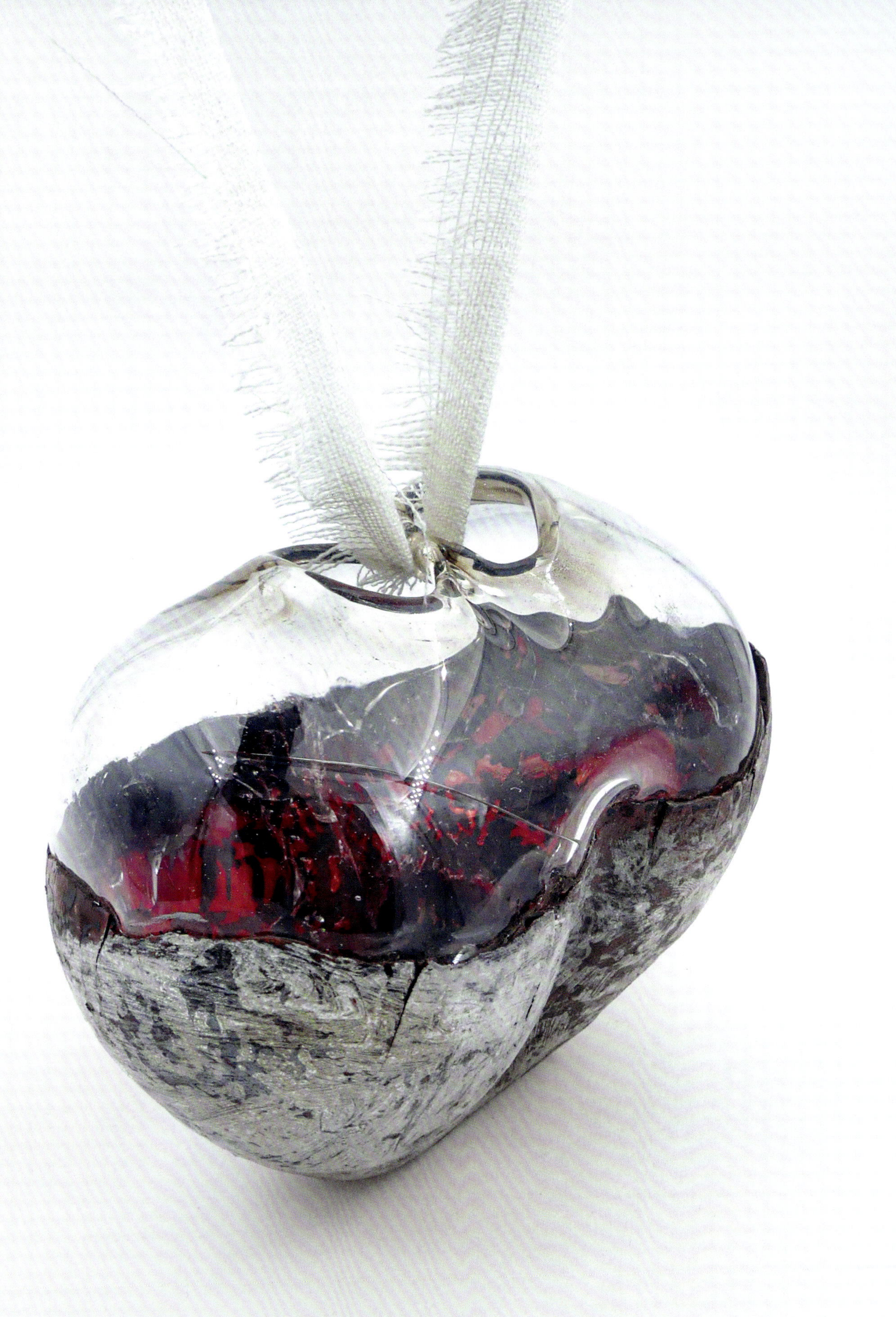

IBRAHIM GAMAL

Ibrahim Gamal is a photographer and creative director who narrates garments through stills. He aims to give the viewer a powerful insight into his subjects' lives. As he describes it, he "expresses the fashionable and beyond, anchoring universes through shots."

Fashion by Shahira Lasheen; art direction: Sara Lasheen; photography: Ibrahim Gamal
→

Fashion by Amina Galal; art direction: Ibrahim Gamal and Amina Galal; photography: Ibrahim Gamal
↙

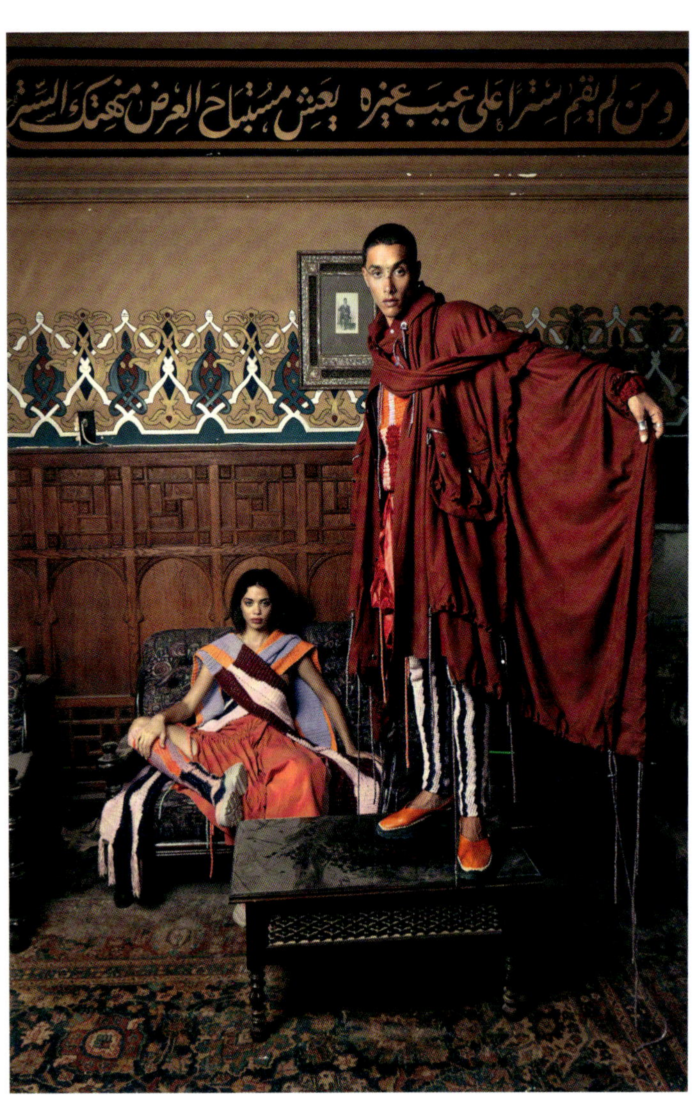

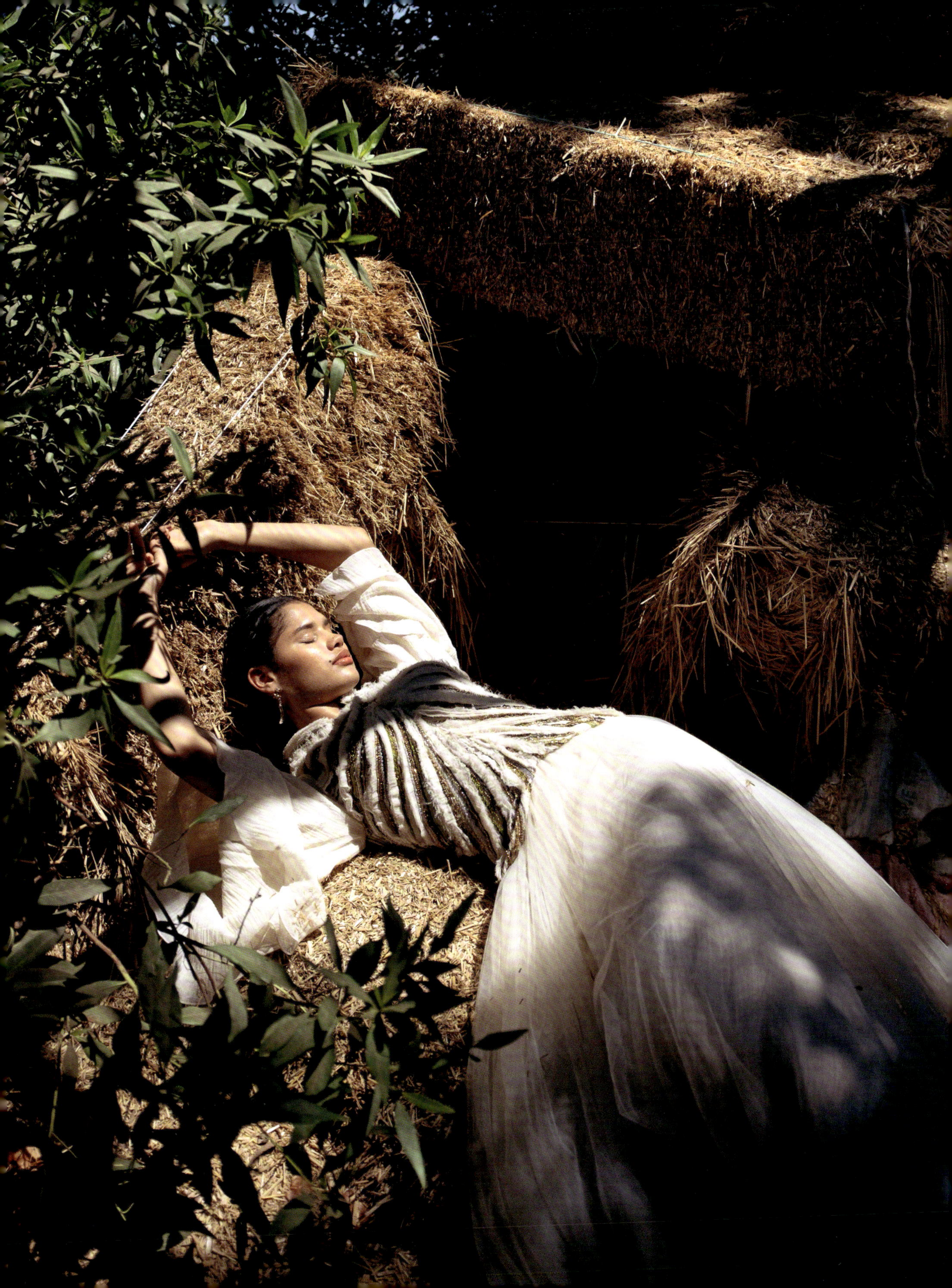

KASBAH KOSMIC

KENZA VANDEPUT-TALEB

Kasbah Kosmic is an independent fashion label created by Kenza Vandeput-Taleb in Brussels, Belgium, in 2019. The name of the brand comes from the word *kasbah* in Arabic, which refers to the center of a city, and "kosmic," which refers to the ideal of clothing being of infinite use and reuse and is a nod to her father, who was fascinated with space travel. At its core, the label is characterized by its dedication to sustainability, slow fashion, and the authentic expression of cultural identity inspired by Vandeput-Taleb's dual Belgian-Algerian identity. Growing up, her exposure to the two cultures created a fusion of identities within her personal style. During her childhood she began appreciating second-hand clothing, often shopping for them with her mother. This inspired her to use vintage pieces as a key element in her designs, shaping her philosophy while studying at the Royal Academy of Fine Arts in Antwerp, and set the tone for her future brand.

Her label offers a style that is a mix of North African and Western fashions with upcycled creations, linking different cultures by combining heritage with contemporary symbols and aesthetics. Sports clothing is a notable part of the label's style, including a collaboration with the MIMA Museum in Brussels. The collection was inspired by a fusion of clothing worn by boxers with traditional North African dress, such as *kachabia* and the robes worn by spiritual healers. Another collaboration that she participated in was with artists with Down syndrome, as part of an exploration into social art practices and as a commitment to inclusivity and liberation. The brand has also been featured in pop-up events around the world and several other collaborations during its residency at the MAD incubator in Brussels.

Images courtesy of Kasbah Kosmic

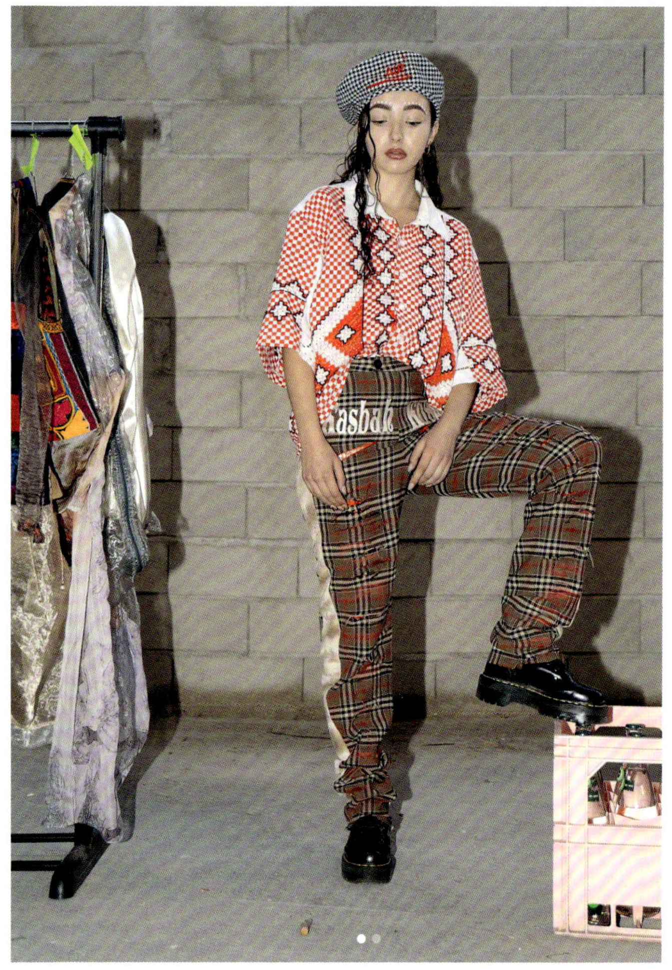

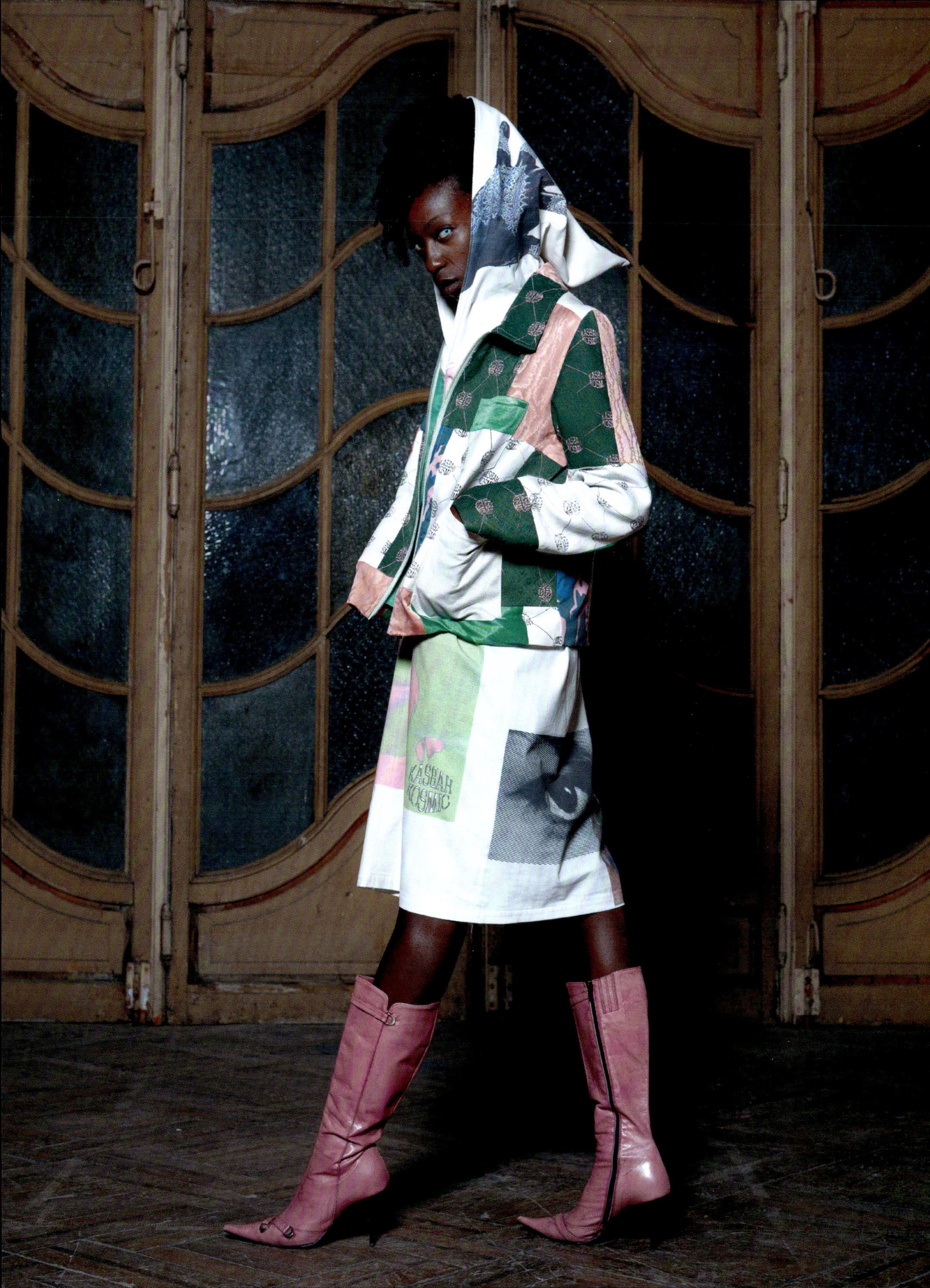
KASBAH
KOSMIC

OUR LAND

أرضنا

From the Atlas Mountains in the west to the Nile in the east, North Africa boasts myriad dramatic and varied landscapes. The sun as it glimmers off the Mediterranean offers a distinctive quality of light which has inspired generations of artists from near and far. Designers have taken inspiration from the region's unique landscape. The architecture which has historically developed alongside the natural setting has also shaped the aesthetic identity of the region. A color palatte of bright pastels, clear white, and striking blues distinguishes both fashion designs and photography. Designers such as Samia Ben Abdallah of AwA and Anissa Meddeb of Anissa Aida actually trained in architecture; it informs not only the aesthetics of their work but also its structural underpinnings. Anissa Aida creates designs from repetitive geometric units which echo the shapes of ceramic tile. Other designers pay their respect to their cultural heritage by maintaining traditional elements in their design. Drawing inspiration from garments and accessories such as *babouches, badroun, djellaba,* and *karakou,* these designers create contemporary fashions with respect for their past.

ANISSA AIDA
ANISSA MEDDEB

Anissa Meddeb's brand Anissa Aida is a slow fashion line that combines influences from Tunisia and Japan. These inspirations lean into the brand's goal of preserving cultural heritage and traditional craftsmanship while putting a modern spin on ancestral garments. Meddeb takes traditional garments such as caftans and kimonos and combines them with Western tailoring to create new, modern forms. Reinterpreting tradition is just one of Meddeb's goals, who also aims to have an environmentally conscious approach to production with a focus on traditional techniques by carefully choosing materials, collaborating with artisans, and creating timeless pieces meant to last. Her ultimate mission is to spread the beauty of Tunisia on a global scale, while preserving its traditions and creating stepping stones for its future. Meddeb excels in designs that are minimalist, Mediterranean, and architectural, bringing traditional silhouettes into modern style. She grew up in Tunisia and Paris and attended Parsons, the New School, participating in an exchange program with Central Saint Martins in London and receiving her BA with a focus on women's wear. She went on to study at the Fashion Institute of Technology, where she attended the Design Entrepreneur program. Before launching her label, she gained experience working at A.P.C., Marc Jacobs, threeASFOUR, and Outdoor Voices.

The first ensemble from Anissa Aida features a burnoose, which is the long, hooded cape for men of Amazigh origin. This particular example draws from similarities between the North African garment and Japanese men's kimonos. The cape is worn over a tunic made of hand-woven silk called *stacrouda*, from the Italian *seta cruda*, unbleached silk. The tunic is inspired by the traditional *kamis*, which gave its name to the French word *chemise*. Completing the outfit are *sirwal*, Arabic for pants, characterized by a low crotch, again similar to trousers worn by Japanese samurai, paired with a crisscrossed skirt, opening to reveal the *sirwal* underneath. The second ensemble from the Fall/Winter 2023–24 collection is called *Ailes d'Hirondelle* or "Swallow Wings." The inspiration came from traditional Tunisian architecture, particularly the *Jnah Khoutifa* or small triangular tiles. Meddeb responded to this source material by manipulating the fabric through laser cuts or folds. She also worked with color blocking with angles and changes of direction.

Africa Burnoose, photograph by Hamza Bennour
→

Architectural knit top, architectural pants and origami coat, photograph by Photokolach
↓

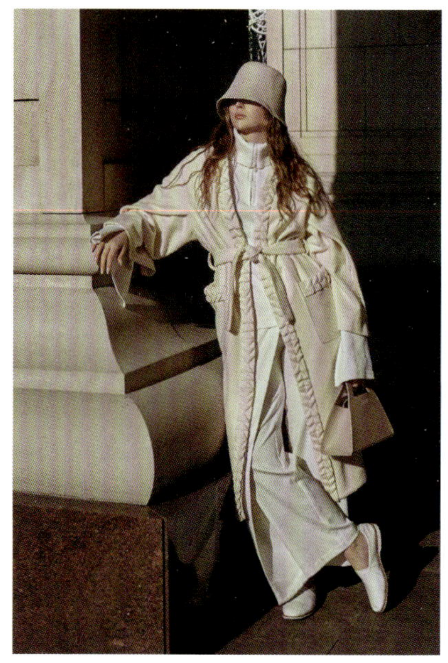

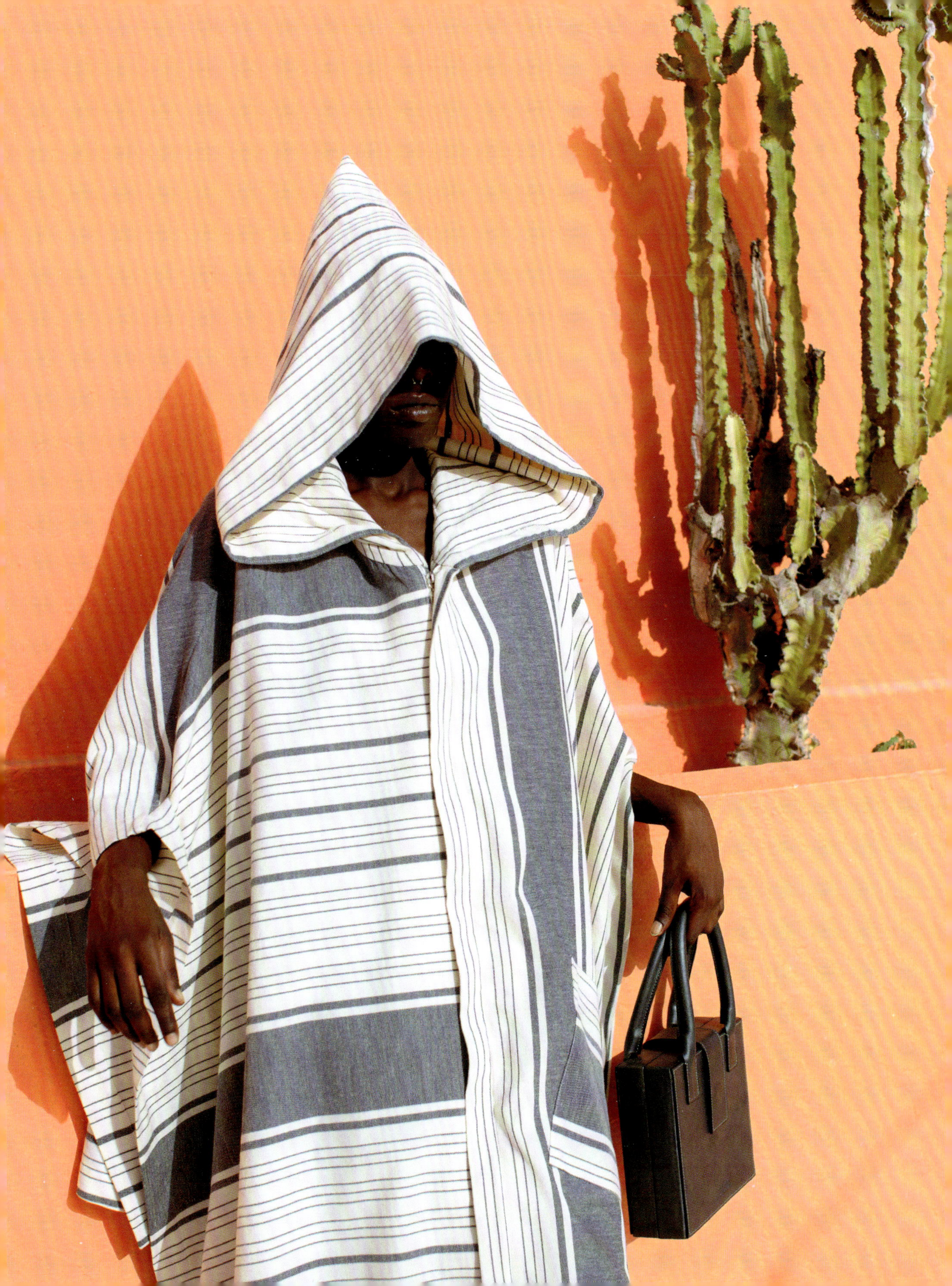

REEM ATOUT

Two ensembles from the Teta Chic collection by Reem Atout, image by Baiba Photography
→

Behind the scenes; photography: Sara Merey; assisted by: Hagar Merey
↓

Reem Atout is a recent 2022 graduate of Virginia Commonwealth University's School of Arts in Qatar. That same year, her inaugural collection "Teta Chic" (*teta* meaning grandmother in Arabic), an homage to her grandmothers, won the Cairo Design Award for Fashion Design. Atout blended tradition, innovation, and sustainability by taking her grandmothers' old *jalabeyas* to create new pieces that preserved their authenticity. She created cutouts that allowed the garments to retain their modesty and classic silhouette while layering them with athletic streetwear elements. This merged the worlds, personalities, stories, and memories of Atout with those of her grandmothers in garments that both revive and preserve tradition. As an Egyptian who has lived abroad for most of her life, she has been able to connect with her grandmothers by adding to her few memories of them from afar. As a designer, Atout experiments with upcycling techniques that focus on print, color, and texture in order to transform traditional and vintage garments into modern wear while still preserving their stories and memories. Sustainability and upcycling are important to her both for environmental purposes and because she believes that clothes represent stories and memories. She favors using strategies that decrease the environmental impact of the fashion industry while encouraging others to further appreciate fashion. One of Atout's goals as a designer is to direct people to shift their focus to topics that are ignored or overlooked. This is reflected in her desire to take that which is unconventional or of bad taste and turn it into fashion.

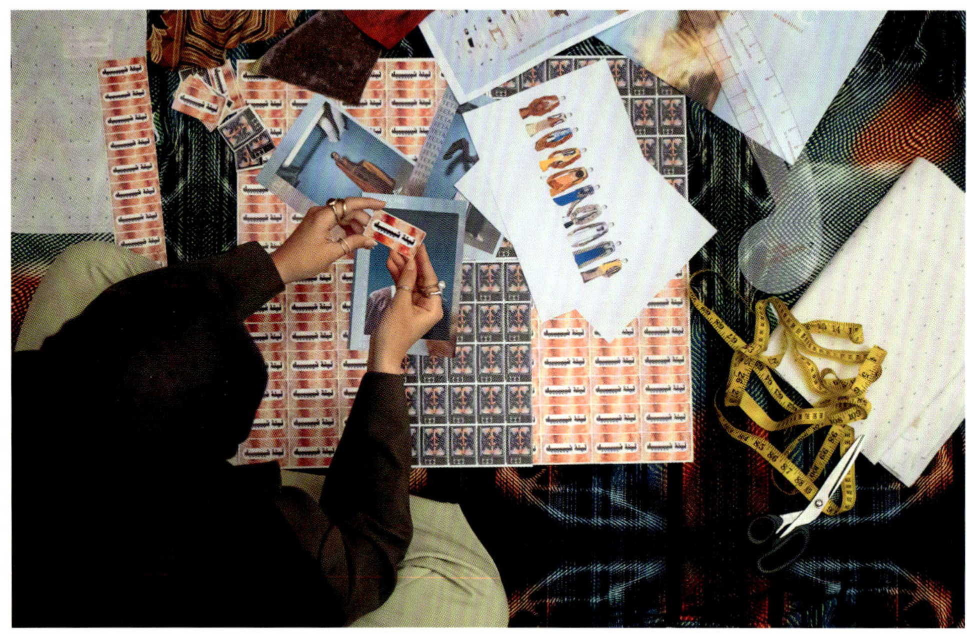

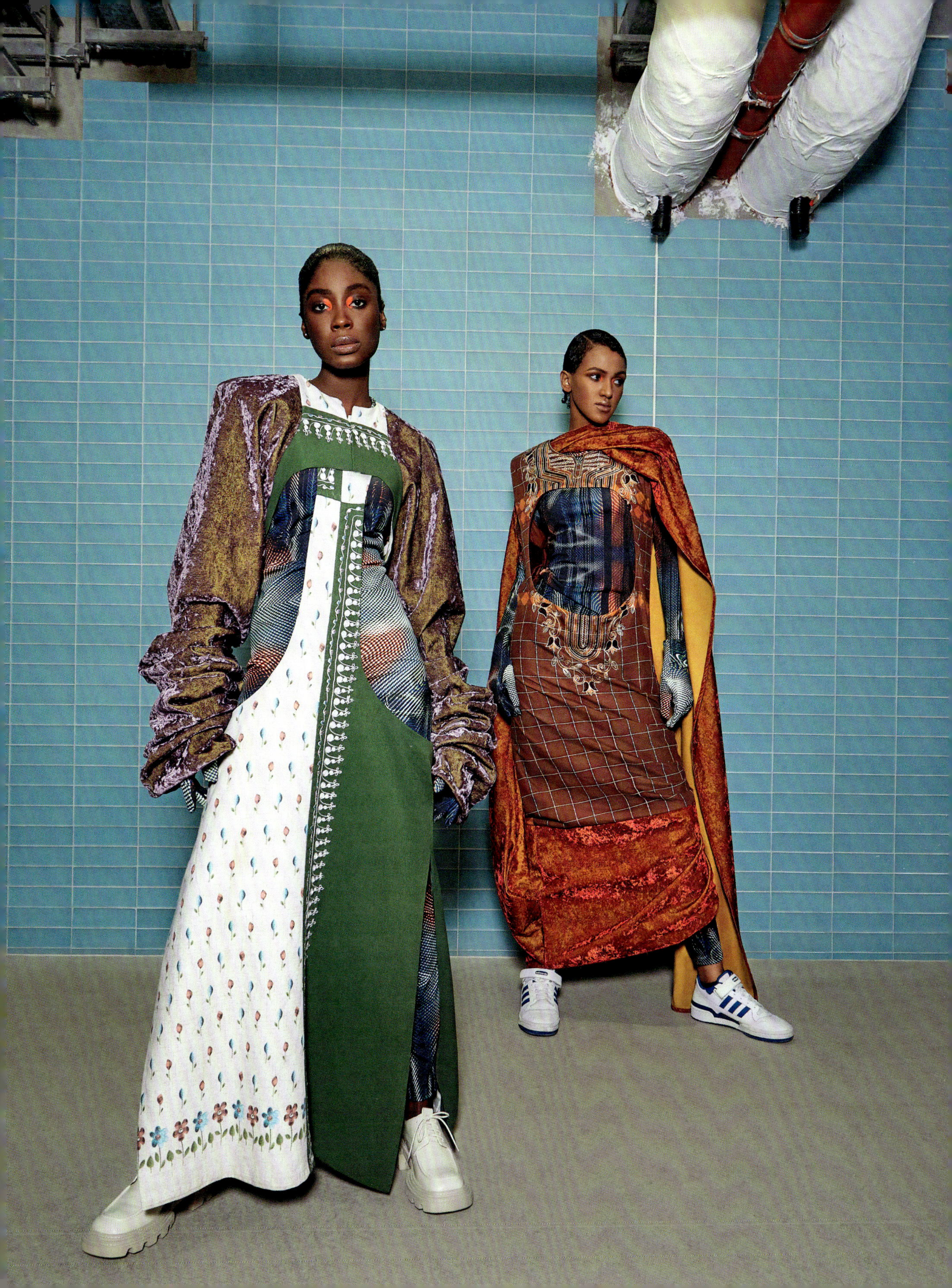

AWA

SAMIA BEN ABDALLAH

AwA, which stands for "Architect with Artisan," was launched in 2017 by Samia Ben Abdallah and mixes leather goods and accessories with architectural craftsmanship. Ben Abdallah received her formal training in architecture at the National School of Architecture and Urbanism in Tunis before completing an internship in Paris at Architecture Studio. She went on to found her own architecture agency. In 2019 she was selected to travel to the United States through the International Visitor Leadership Program sponsored by the United States Department of State. She serves as a consultant with a program supported by the WTO and the UN to mentor female entrepreneurs in e-commerce.

Her background as an architect prepared her for designing pieces that adopt architectural styles and heritage while still reflecting inspiration from film, music, and other art forms. The results are chic modernity with classic lines and shapes that make this brand stand out. The products are made locally by Tunisian artisans using sustainable materials such as offcuts from leading luxury brands. The mirror bag showcases the inspiration drawn from the lines and forms of Tunisian architecture. The hard, reflective surface captures the modern aspect of the design. Similarly, the Medina necklace repeats the shapes of the Tunis skyline brightened with an array of colors.

Mirror bag; photographer: Mohsen Bencheikh; stylist: Samia Ben Abdallah →

Medina necklace, double ring, and wallet; photographer: Mohsen Bencheikh; stylist: Samia Ben Abdallah ↓

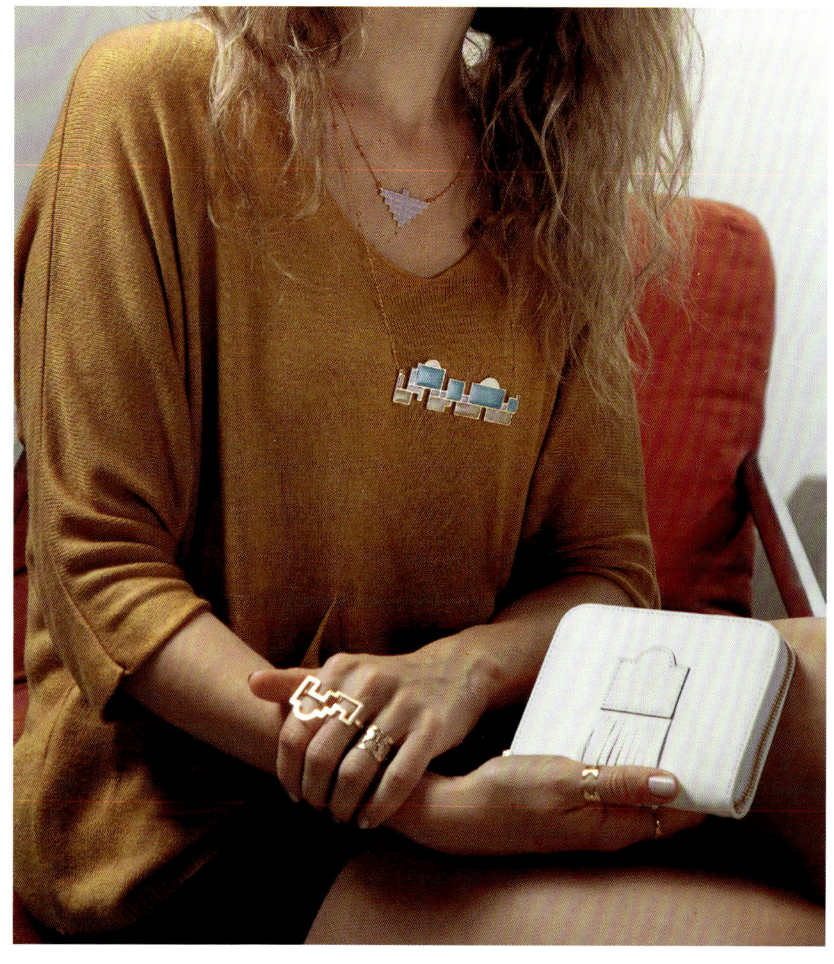

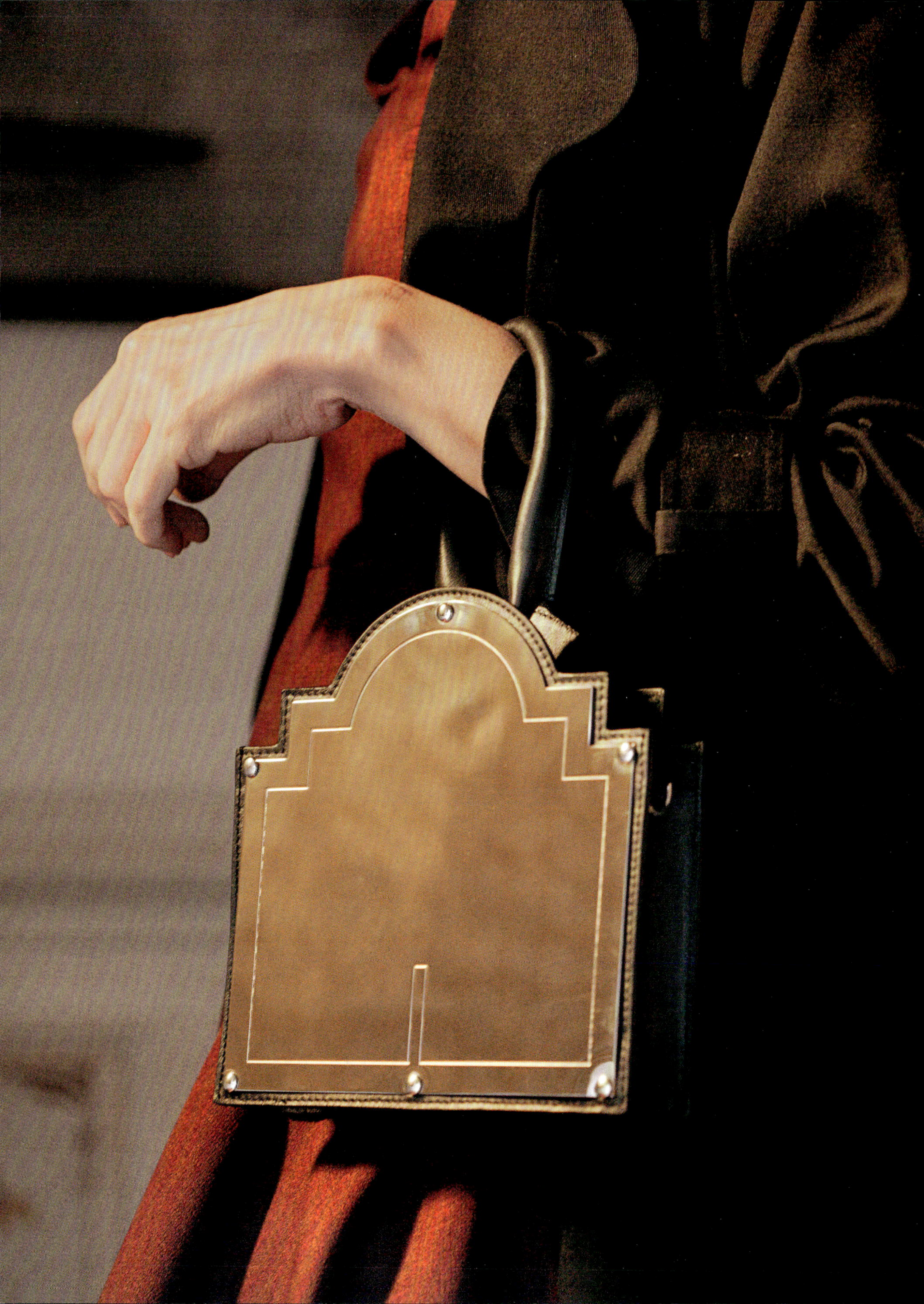

BADROUN'Y

213 CONCEPT-STORE SALIMA, MANEL, AND SARAH MESSAL

Salima Messal, an Algerian stylist based in Paris, runs 213 Concept Store with her daughters, Sarah and Manel. The name of the store comes from the telephone code for Algeria. The business brings products from Algerian creators to Paris to showcase the creativity, tradition, and modernity present in Algerian arts and design. This not only spreads Algerian arts and culture to the younger generations in the West, but also brings a piece of home to Algerians who live abroad.

While Salima has dedicated the basement of the store to the creation of traditional Algerian ensembles, Sarah Messal also established a brand of contemporary Algerian streetwear called Badroun'y offering contemporary outfits inspired by the Algerian *badroun*. She worked for months to adapt the *sirwal*, a distinctive style of pants with a very low strip of fabric passing between the ankles, for the modern woman. Essentially, the brand offers a new vision of a typically Algerian garment. The garments are designed and produced in Paris.

The ensemble shown here represents a collaboration between Badroun'y and Katoushti, the milliner who created the hat. Katoushti is a brand founded by Katia Katouche, who studied in Paris at a vocational high school dedicated to fashion where she specialized in millinery. She is committed to the idea that hats should not be reserved for high society but can be worn by anyone who has a head.

The elements of the ensemble each represent a modern interpretation of traditional Algerian garments. The shirt is developed from the *haïk,* a large piece of white cloth made from wool or silk which covered Algerian women from head to toe as a symbol of modesty and respect. The blouse is combined with a *sirwal chalka*, the traditional Algerian pants open at each side. The choice of faux-leather for the material adds a modern touch to a traditional garment. The hat is inspired by the fringed shawl, *m'harmete el ftoul,* that women traditionally wore wrapped around their head.

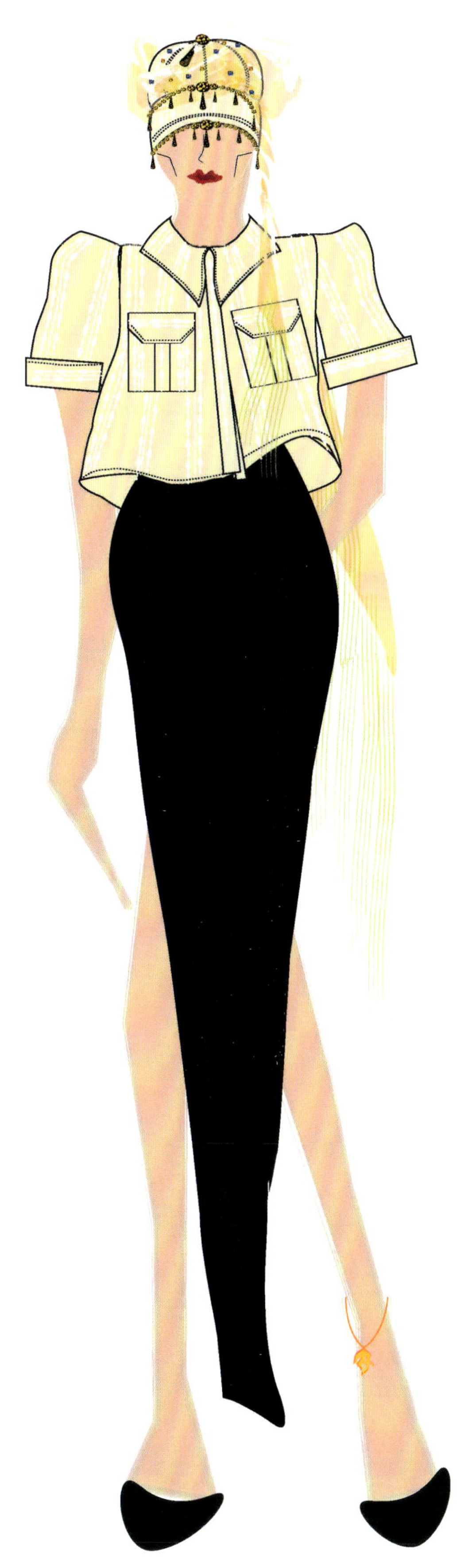

JOANNA BEN SOUISSI

Joanna Ben Souissi, born in 1988 in France, is a Tunisian-Irish photographer and producer. Her role in her visuals often includes artistic direction and styling. After completing her studies in history, French literature, and fashion design, Ben Souissi was offered her first job as an artistic director and producer in 2012. In a pre-Instagram Tunisia, where very few fashion campaigns and editorials were produced, she collaborated with local photographers to shape the visual identity of young designers' brands. In 2014, she began taking on the actual shooting role as well, and co-founded her own audiovisual production company: Empiriq. Today, her activities range from video producing to collaborating with global print media such as *Vogue Arabia*, commercial and celebrity photography, as well as personal projects.

The images shown here were created by Ben Souissi for a campaign for a small curated thrift shop in La Marsa, Filupo. One image is from their first campaign, which they named *Audace* in French. The artistic direction was to showcase the diverse and original selection of second-hand clothing and their identity by taking intensely Tunisian references and turning them into scenes of rebellious behavior. The second image, "The Last Supper," draws on the idea of a Ramadan table arranged to resemble Jesus's last meal. Each photo from this series depicts a fun take on the dinner concept, here you can see a young lady "stealing" *bricks* (a traditional dish with a runny egg and garnish in a flaky pastry, always present at a Ramadan table), along with *chorba*, a red broth.

The Last Supper; photograph by Joanna Ben Souissi
→

Audace; photograph by Joanna Ben Souissi
↓

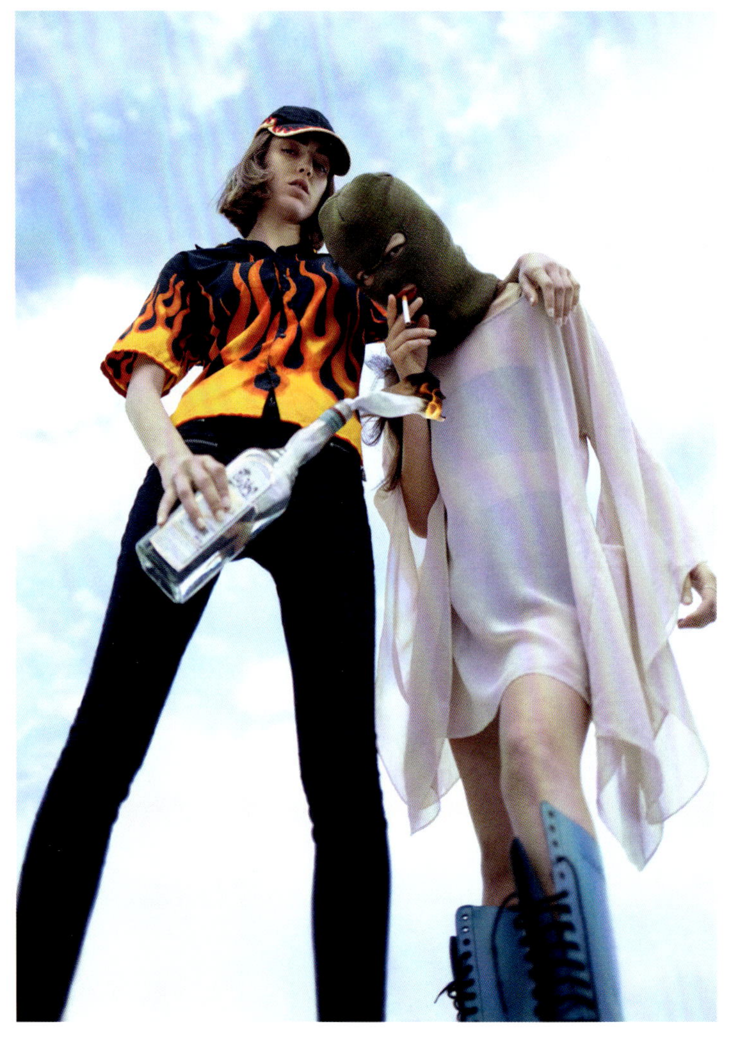

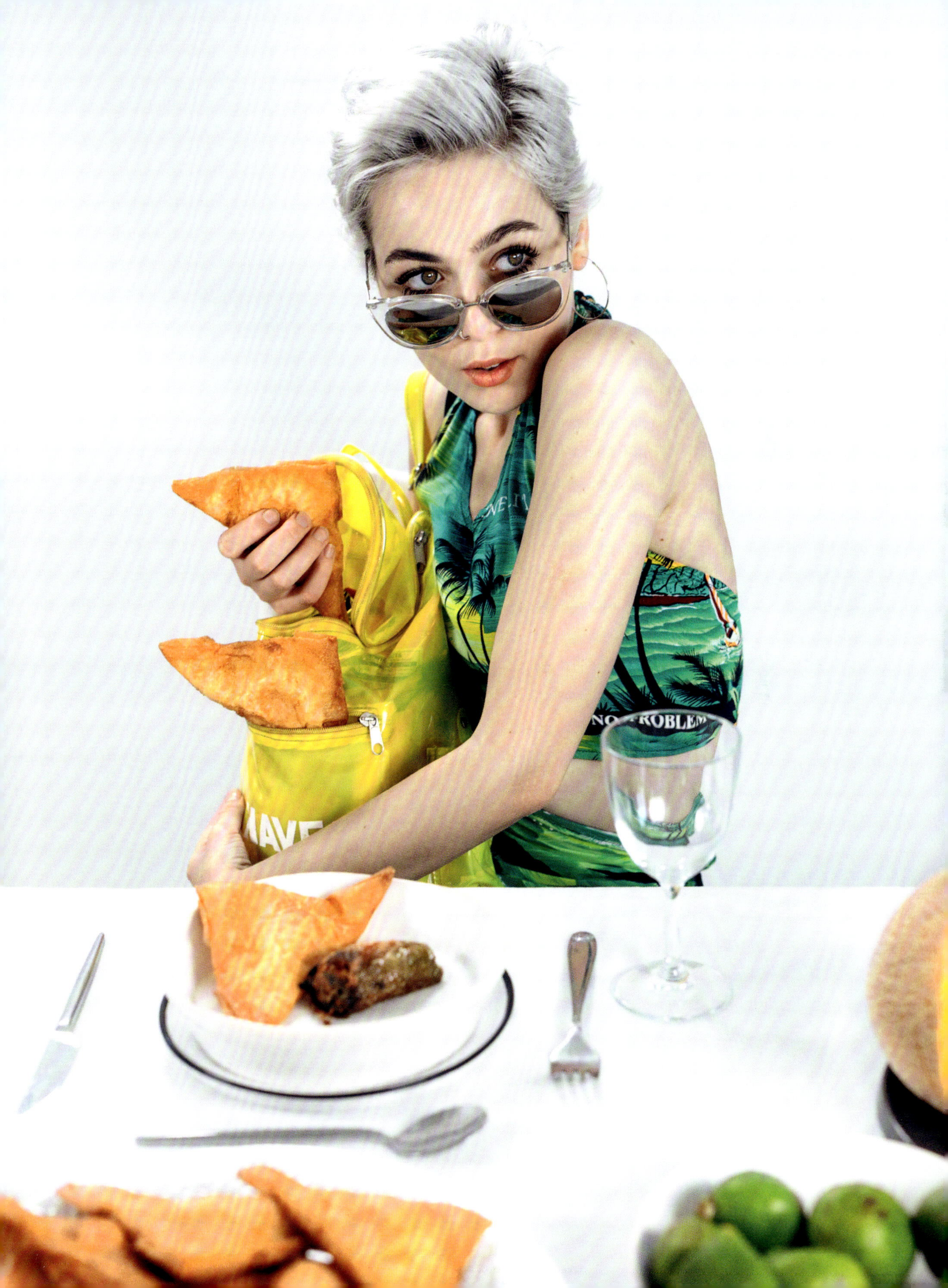

BULGA

GIGI IBRAHIM AND MUNA SOUROUR

Bulga is a handcrafted footwear brand founded by two Egyptian women, Gigi Ibrahim and Muna Sourour, based in downtown Cairo. By adopting slow fashion and fair trade principles, the brand incorporates Egyptian heritage and traditional techniques into everyday, comfortable, unisex footwear with a strong focus on its environmental, social, and cultural footprint.
Bulga controls 100% of its supply chain, starting by locally sourcing all their raw materials to employing artisans across Egypt to create handcrafted shoes with the soul of Egyptian heritage in every step and stitch. This new form of slow fashion retail focus on sustainability, usability, and after-purchase services to create timeless pieces that last more than one season.
The aim of Bulga is to revive the sector of traditional shoe workshops in Cairo through using the oldest techniques in shoemaking, in order to make vibrant modern slippers and shoes that still embody the spirit of Egyptian heritage. The hope is that every customer feels like they have something that is not only beautiful and comfortable but tells a story everywhere they go and positively impacts the local community.

The Shalateen Khof shoes are made from all-natural Egyptian camel leather outsoles and sheep and goat leather tops hand-braided by Ababda women artisans in Shalateen. The Siwa Nut shoes are made from Egyptian camel leather. They use a special embroidery technique developed in the Siwa Oasis and honor the Goddess of the Sky, Nut.

Shalateen Khof; image courtesy of Bulga →

Siwa Nut; image courtesy of Bulga ↓

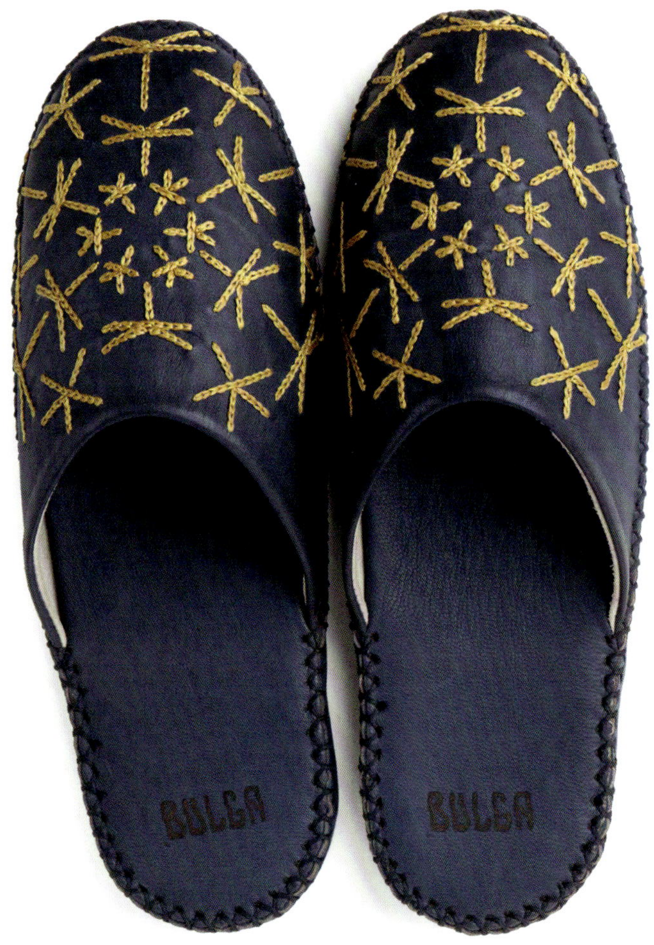

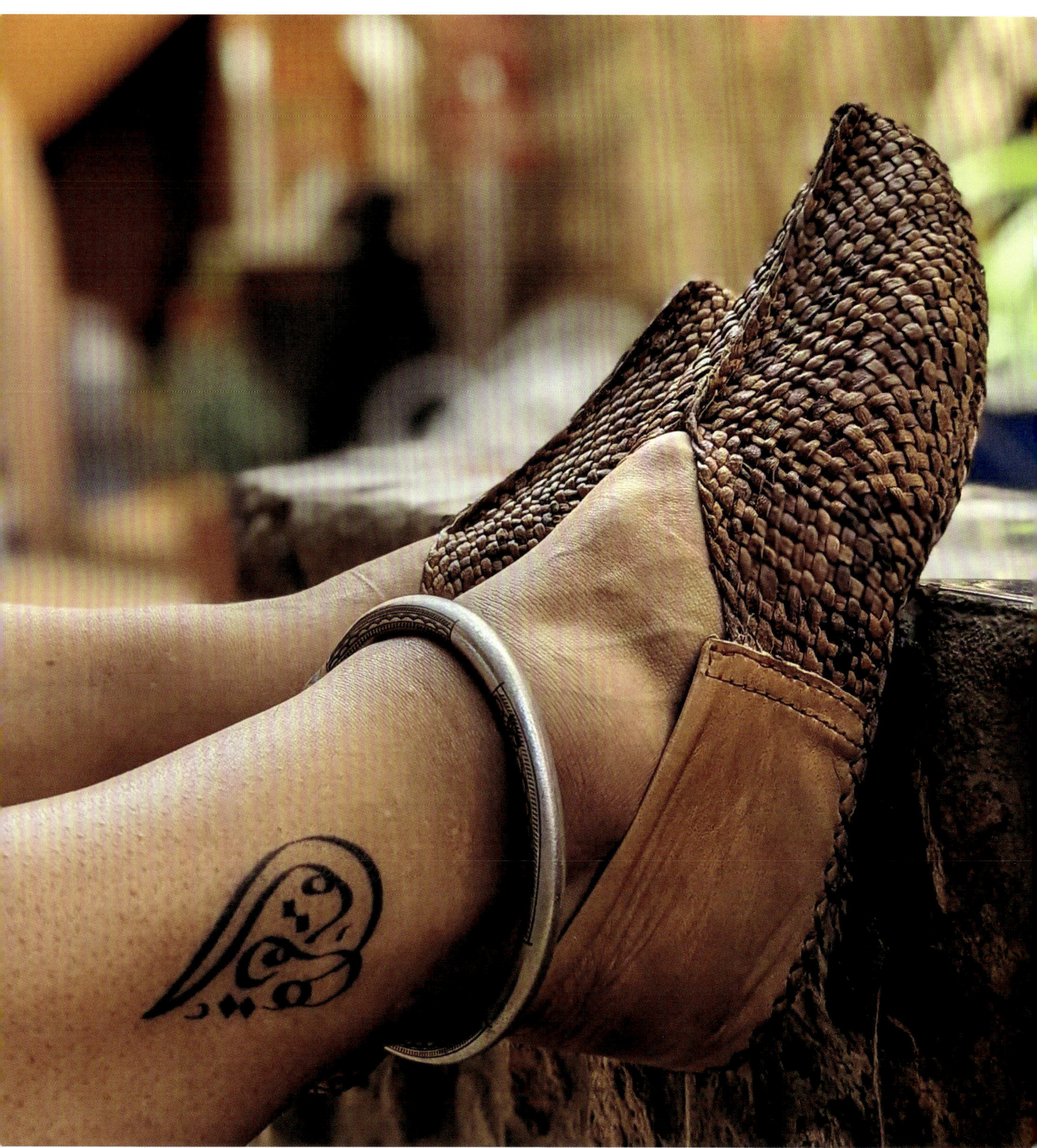

FARES

FARES BENABDESLAM

Fares Benabdeslam acquired a fascination with materials and sewing at a young age from his father, a textile merchant. When he began sewing he experimented with integrating traditional elements into decidedly modern designs. His social media presence allowed him to achieve a wide audience attracted to his unique capacity for interpreting cultural heritage with his distinctly contemporary creativity. Fashion designer, stylist, and content creator, Fares Benabdeslam was a finalist on the Algerian version of Project Runway in 2023. For the works included in the exhibition, Fares has upcycled traditional Algerian rugs into brightly colored garments.

Image courtesy
of Fares Benabdeslam

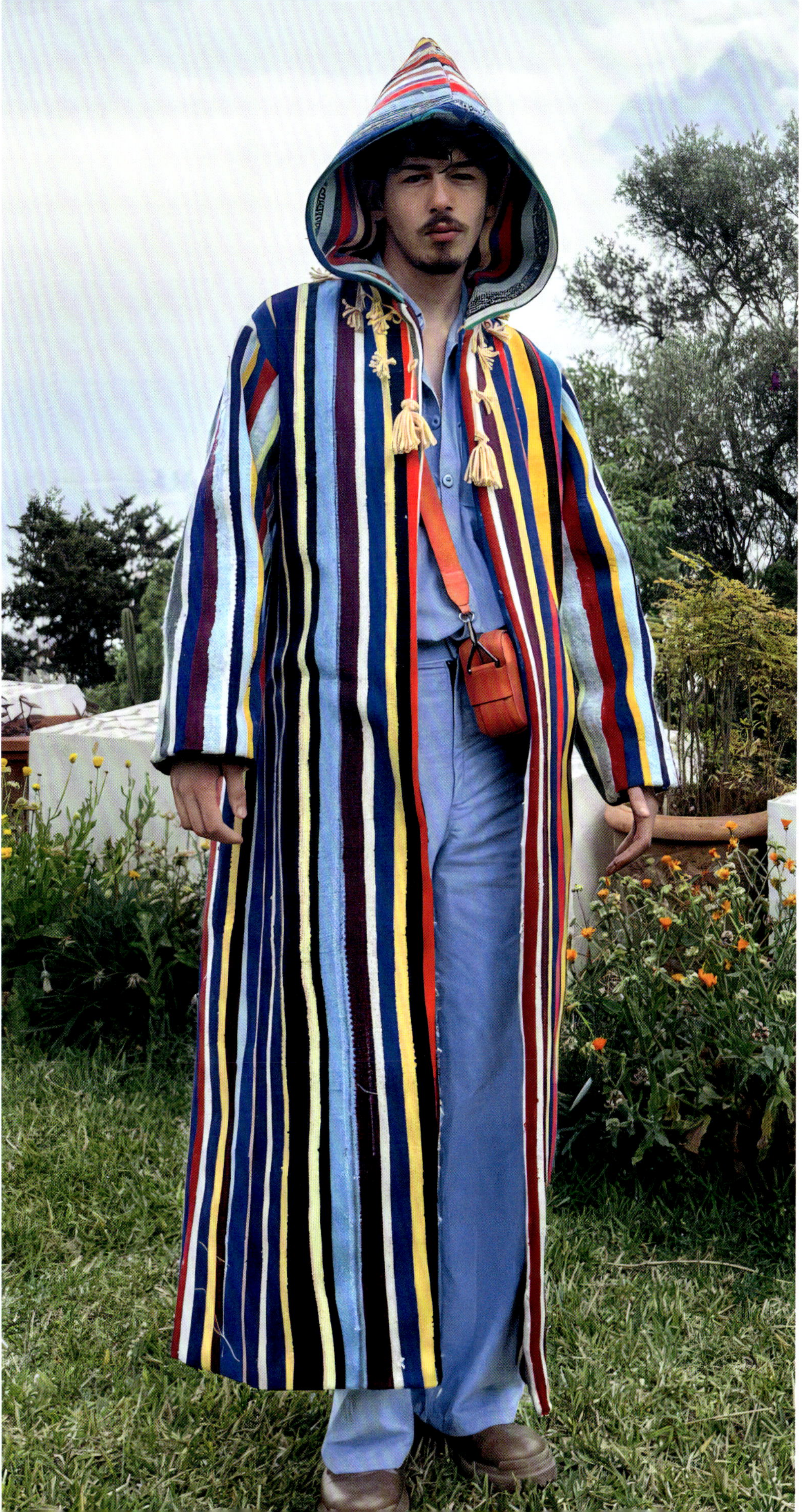

INTIQUE

NOUR CHEKIRI

Nour Chekiri is the founder and designer behind Intique, a brand rooted in the rich traditions of the Mediterranean. Born and raised in Algeria, her designs are a heartfelt tribute to the culture, identity, and stories that connect us. With Intique Nour transforms heritage into timeless creations, evoking a deep sense of belonging and pride in every piece.

Dzayer Oversized T-Shirt; image courtesy of Intique →

Palestina Oversized T-Shirt; image courtesy of Intique ↙

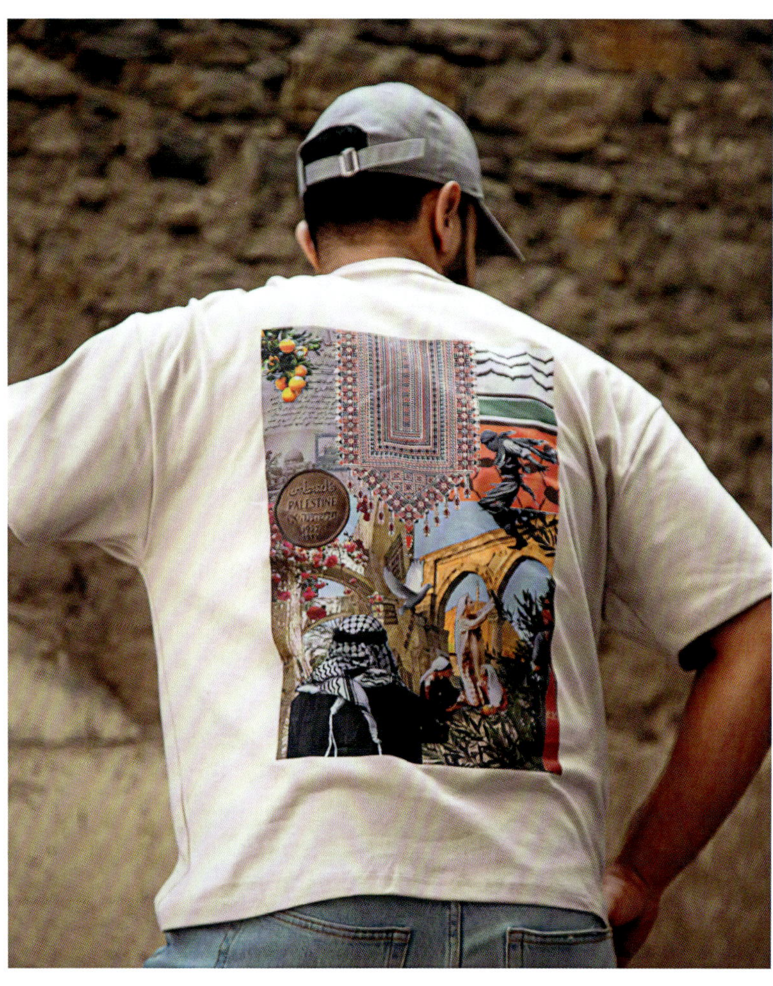

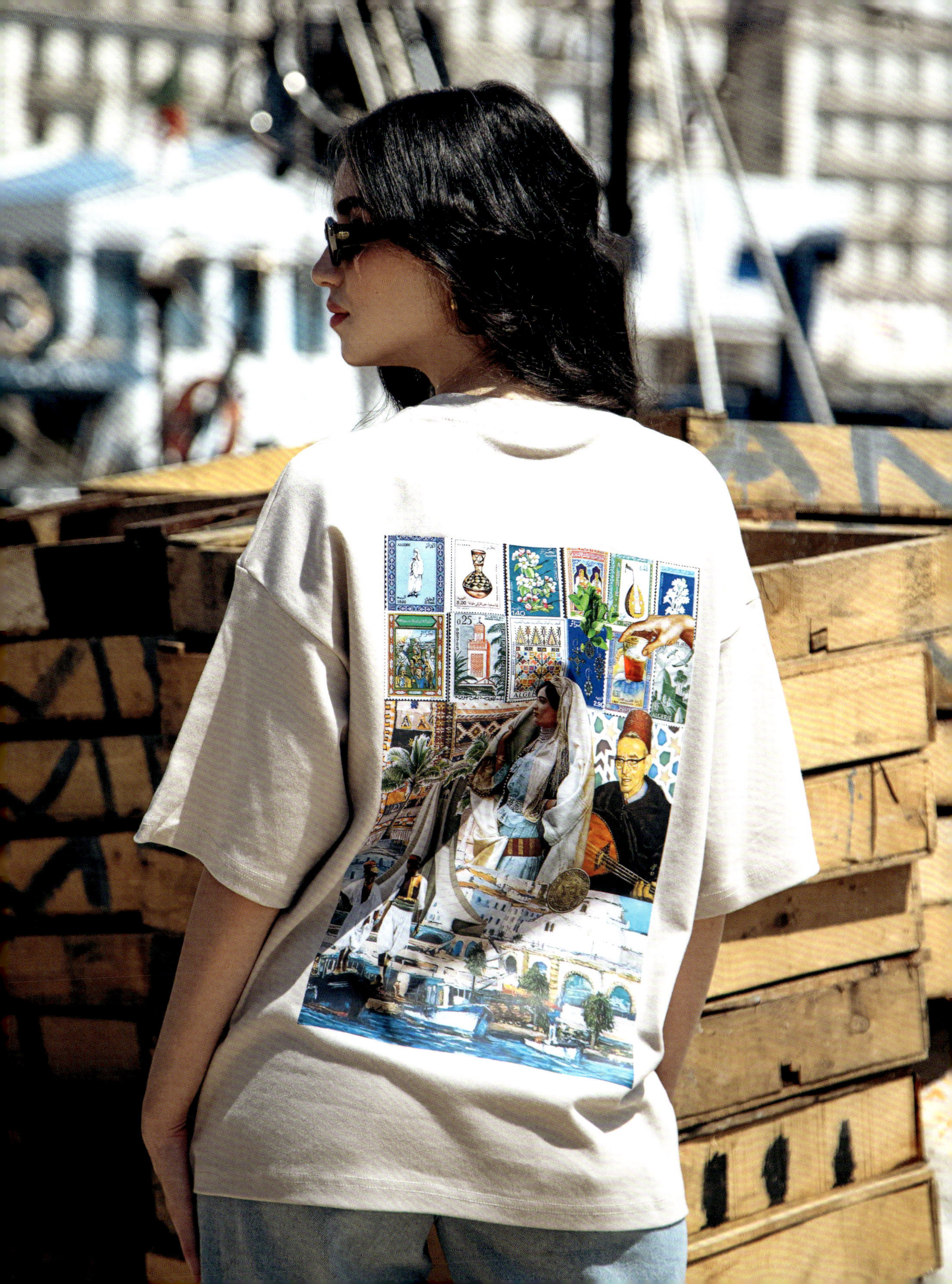

TÉNÉRÉ CONCEPT

NAWEL ATSFAHA

Ténéré Concept is an Algerian brand launched in 2022 by Nawel Atsfaha, who studied painting at the Ecole Supérieur des Beaux-Arts in Algiers. The brand offers pieces crafted by hand, including ready-to-wear garments as well as accessories, leather goods, household linens, customized furniture, ceramics, and beauty products. It prioritizes craftsmanship, creativity, and culture. Its goal is to create an experience with art and authenticity by taking inspiration from southern Algeria, as well as traditional cultures from around Africa. Ténéré Concept uses quality materials and geometric shapes to tell legends and stories, as well as colors to evoke emotions. It strives to create pieces that are easily portable for different occasions, whether in the city or desert.

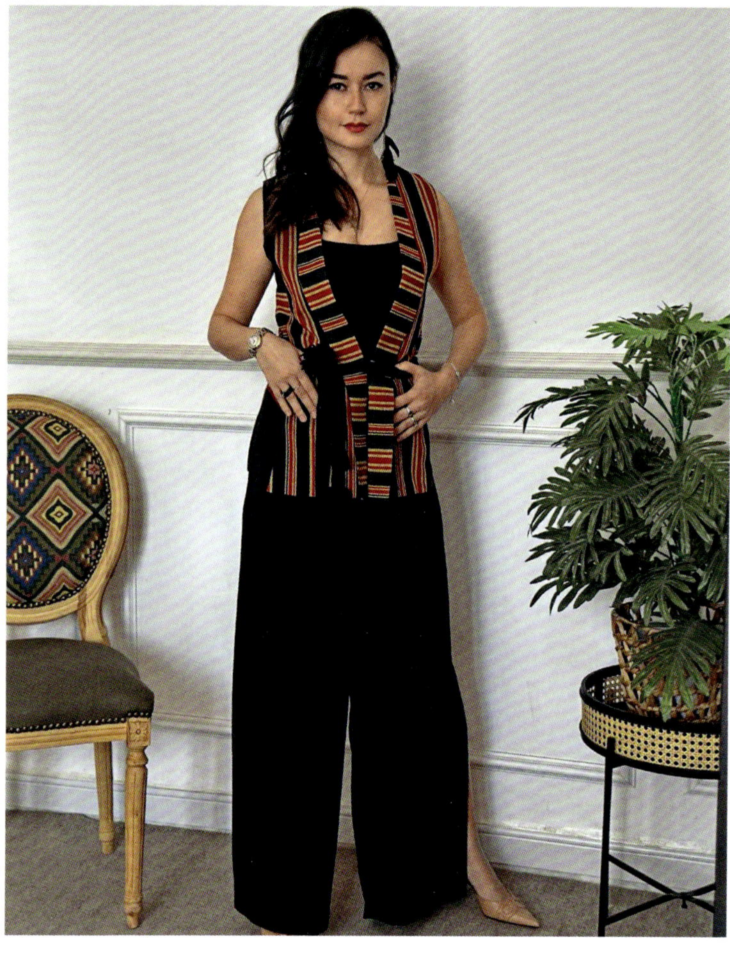

Ensemble by Ténéré Concept; stylist: Nawel Atsfaha; photographer: Lotfi Hichem Nabi; model: Nawel Atsfaha; image courtesy of Ténéré Concept ↗

Two ensembles by Ténéré Concept; stylist: Nawel Atsfaha; photographer: Lotfi Hichem Nabi; model: Nawel Atsfaha; image courtesy of Ténéré Concept →

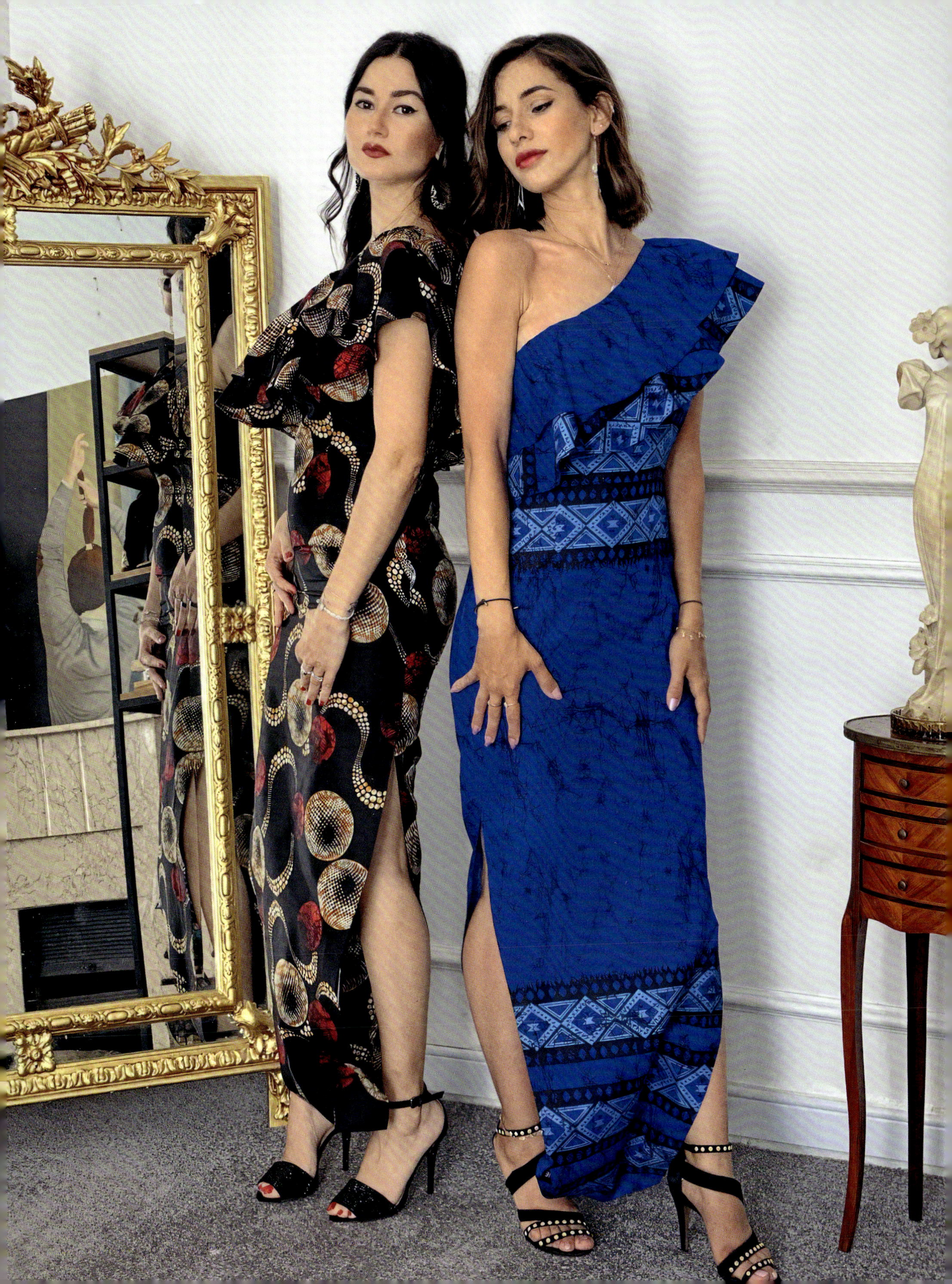

ZANNAD

EYA ZANNAD

Before studying fashion design at ESMOD in Tunis, Eya Zannad received a Master's degree in marketing. With her skills in fashion design and business she has established a successful women's wear brand, Zannad. For over a decade, the designer has developed an exclusive line based on precise construction, local sourcing of quality material, and respect for the environment, all while committing to premium finishing. The pieces are designed to offer a joyful and authentic style that takes its inspiration from the cultural and natural richness of Tunisia. In seeking out local material, Zannad has prioritized natural fibers and recycled material. By establishing collaborations with talented artisans from different regions of the country, Zannad has worked to perpetuate ancestral knowledge and refinement, while at the same time remaining up-to-date in style.

Zannad declares that her mission is to bring joy through her creations, to re-enchant the daily lives of people, especially women. She describes her culture as happy, where every event is an excuse to celebrate life. Zannad is committed to creating clothes that take her clients from day to evening. The looks shown here epitomize the effortless drape of her work and her attention to straddling the line between casual and formal attire.

Asymmetrical ankle pants with poplin blouse; photographer: Amel Guellaty; model: Lydia Lhote; image courtesy of Zannad
→

Asymmetrical dress of silk satin; photographer: Hend Jebali; model: Hiba Hkimi; location: Dar Traki in the Tunis medina; image courtesy of Zannad
↓

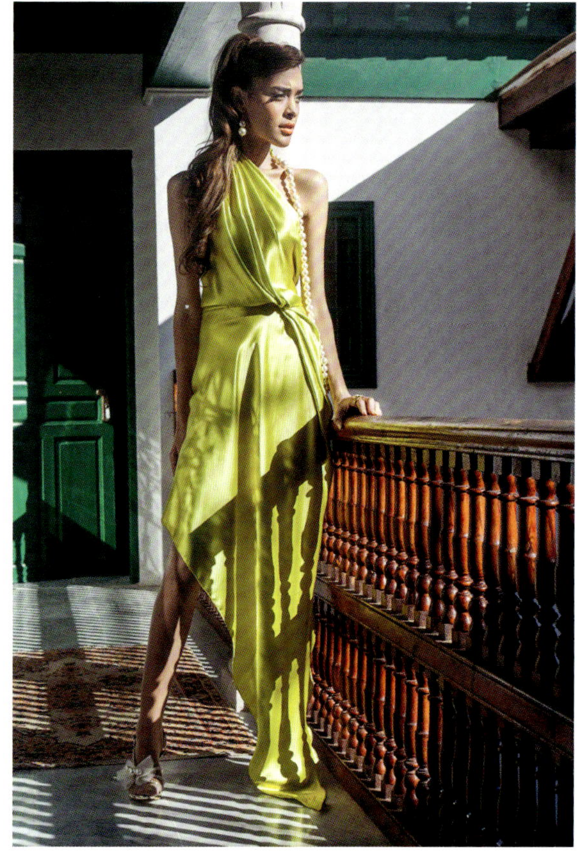

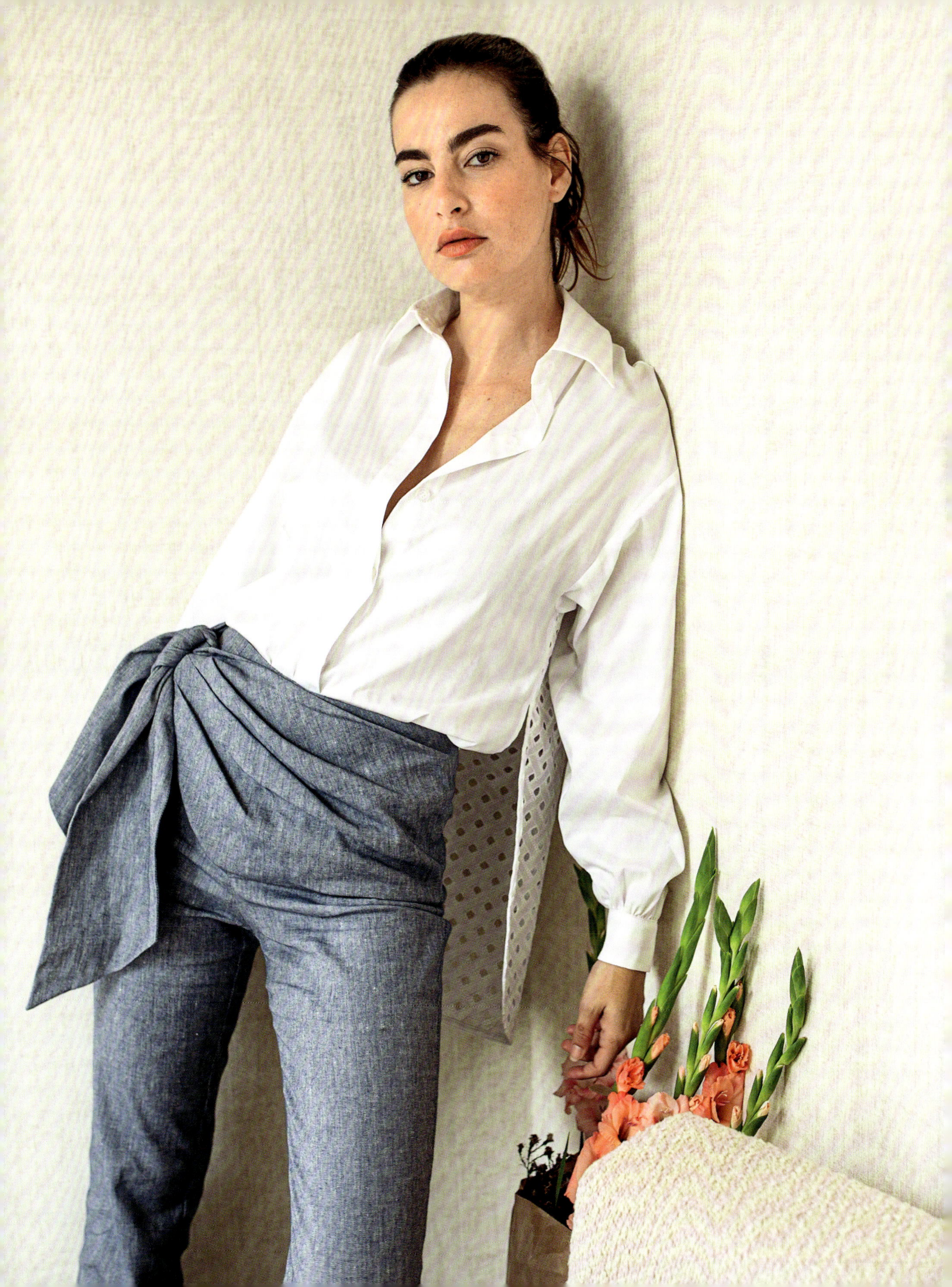

THREADS

الروابط

Industrialization was accompanied in the West by the rise of ready-to-wear clothing. First introduced to provide uniforms for men in the army, standardized sizes allowed a revolution in how clothing was made. Today, factory production occurs around the globe in quantities that far exceed what resources can support. Countries including Morocco, Tunisia, and Egypt are increasingly becoming manufacturing hubs for the clothing and textile industries. Global brands take advantage of low labor costs and a skilled workforce to create their products in North Africa. North African brands also exist, such as Marwa, which is Moroccan owned and operated, but creates low cost, trendy fashions similar to H&M or Old Navy. In deliberate resistance to the advance of industrial practices, many North African designers continue to operate small ateliers, where they meet individual clients for whom they fit each garment they sell. The designers in this section produce on a relatively small scale, but work hard to maintain local expertise. Men and women with years of experience continue a legacy passed down through generations. Not only are garments sewn in small workshops, but the materials are also locally sourced. Rather than a modern concept, sustainability has been integral to how clothing has been produced for generations. The distinctiveness of clothing from North Africa comes not only from the expertise which facilitates its creation, but also in the very materials that are employed. Vegetal fibers, goat leather, camel wool, or locally grown cotton are all drawn from the resource-rich region. Many designers pay careful attention to where they source the fibers and component parts of their designs. “Threads” focuses on the materials that designers use, which draw from the raw material long cultivated in the region.

SOMAIA ABOLEZZ

Illustrator and designer Somaia Abolezz established her brand in 2017; it is committed to telling stories in the form of doodles on modern fashion. The brand's mission and logo take inspiration from Bastet, the ancient Egyptian cat goddess. As the daughter of the sun god Re, Bastet exemplified a warrior deity, safeguarding homes, preserving women's secrets, and offering healing, particularly for women and children. Abolezz strongly believes in the butterfly effect, where every small act of goodness resonates throughout the world. She began by volunteering in Ezbt Khirallah with Dawar Art Space, aiming to empower women in underdeveloped areas to express themselves through art. Carrying her beliefs into her business, Abolezz dedicates five percent of her sales prices towards support for various special causes.

Anubis and the Cat tunic; image courtesy of Somaia Abolezz
→

Bird's Coat; model: Irina Krupneva, photographer Mostafa Titos venue: Nut Oraby
↓

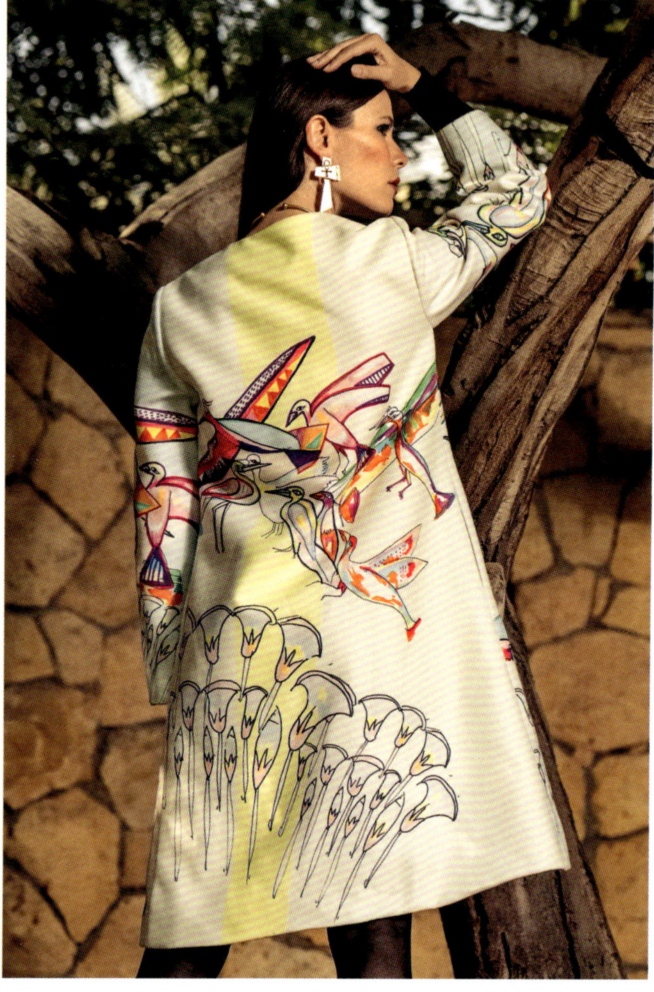

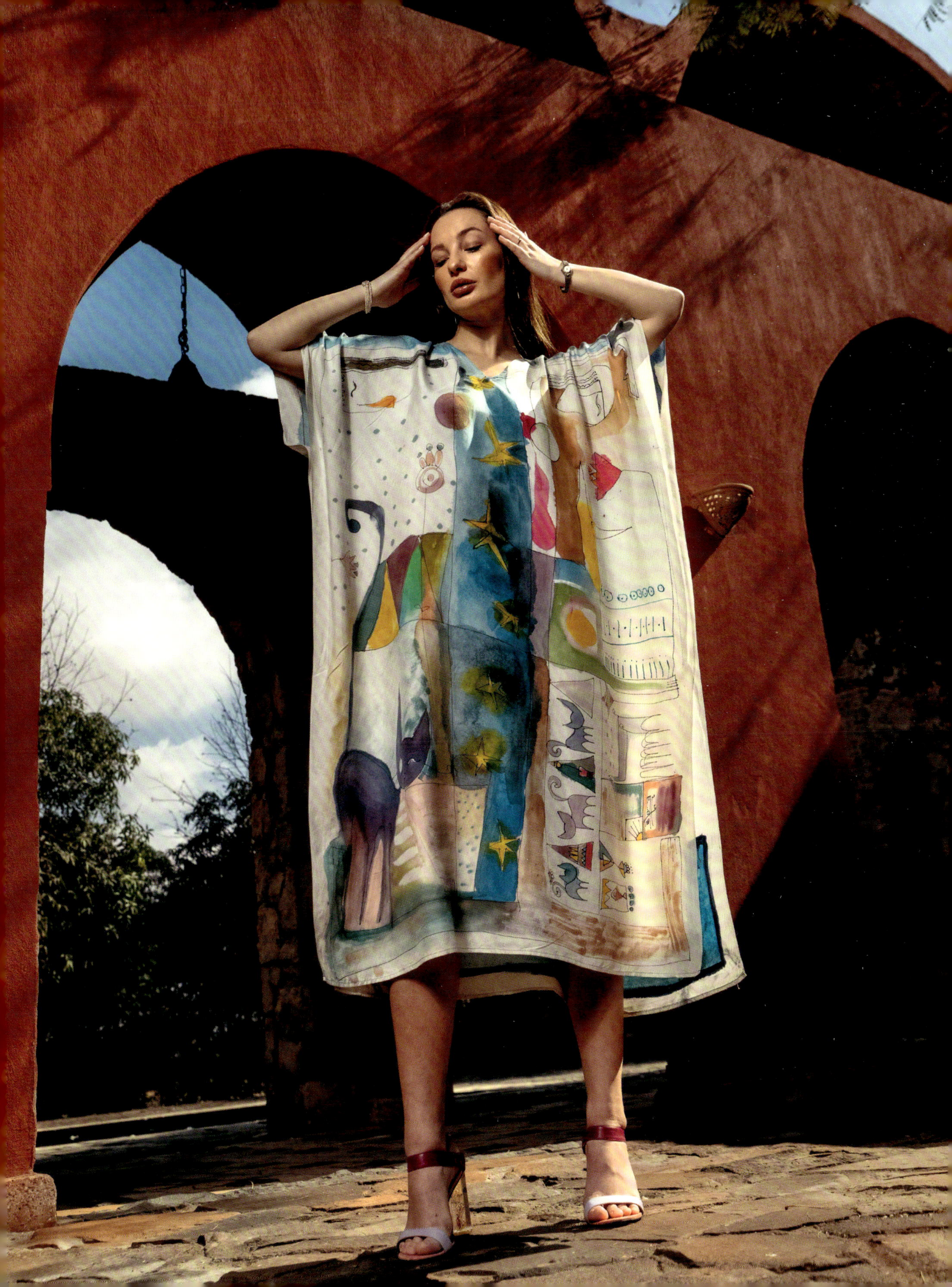

ALMAH

YOUSSRE ABDELKADER, CREATIVE DIRECTOR AND MANAL SALEH, FOUNDER

Almah was founded in 2020 with a foundational mission of sustainability. The brand was conceived to work alongside the Egyptian Clothing Bank (ECB) by preserving and repurposing donated garments. This idea started when the ECB noticed that a large amount of vintage clothing from the 1960s and '70s that was being donated was rare and unique. Not wanting these garments to go to waste, they began experimenting with upcycling. Each collection they design helps to raise awareness by focusing on a specific environmental crisis. The brand also raises awareness and inspires conscious consumerism and sustainable living through workshops, educational material, and research on alternatives to unsustainable materials. Their "Foe-Fur," for example, creates textures similar to those of animal fur by using slashing and brushing techniques on scrap fabrics in different combinations to achieve the desired color, shape, and form. Their debut collection consisted of cocktail party dresses made from high-quality silk ties that had been donated. The response to the collection was overwhelmingly positive, pushing the brand to continue with its production of repurposed garments.

Almah collaborated with Saqhoute on the installation "On Slowness," which is included in the exhibition. This piece represents an immersive experience revolving around handicrafts and sustainability in fashion and is made from upcycled fabric waste, embroidery thread, and various synthetic materials donated to the Egyptian Clothing Bank.

Coral Blues Collection; photography and art direction: Ismail Sabet; hair and make-up artist: Agnieszka Hoscilo; set design: Aleiyaldin Al Zayan; wardrobe, creative direction, and styling: Almah; model: Adhar Abiem
→

On Slowness; image courtesy of Saqhoute.
↓

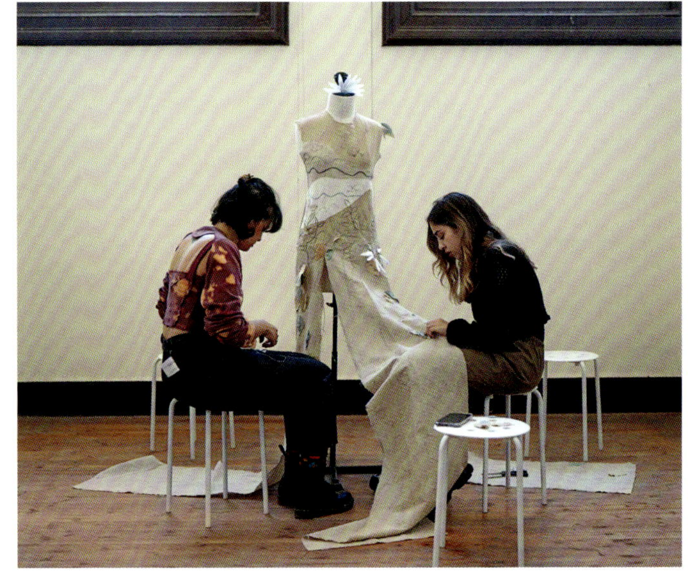

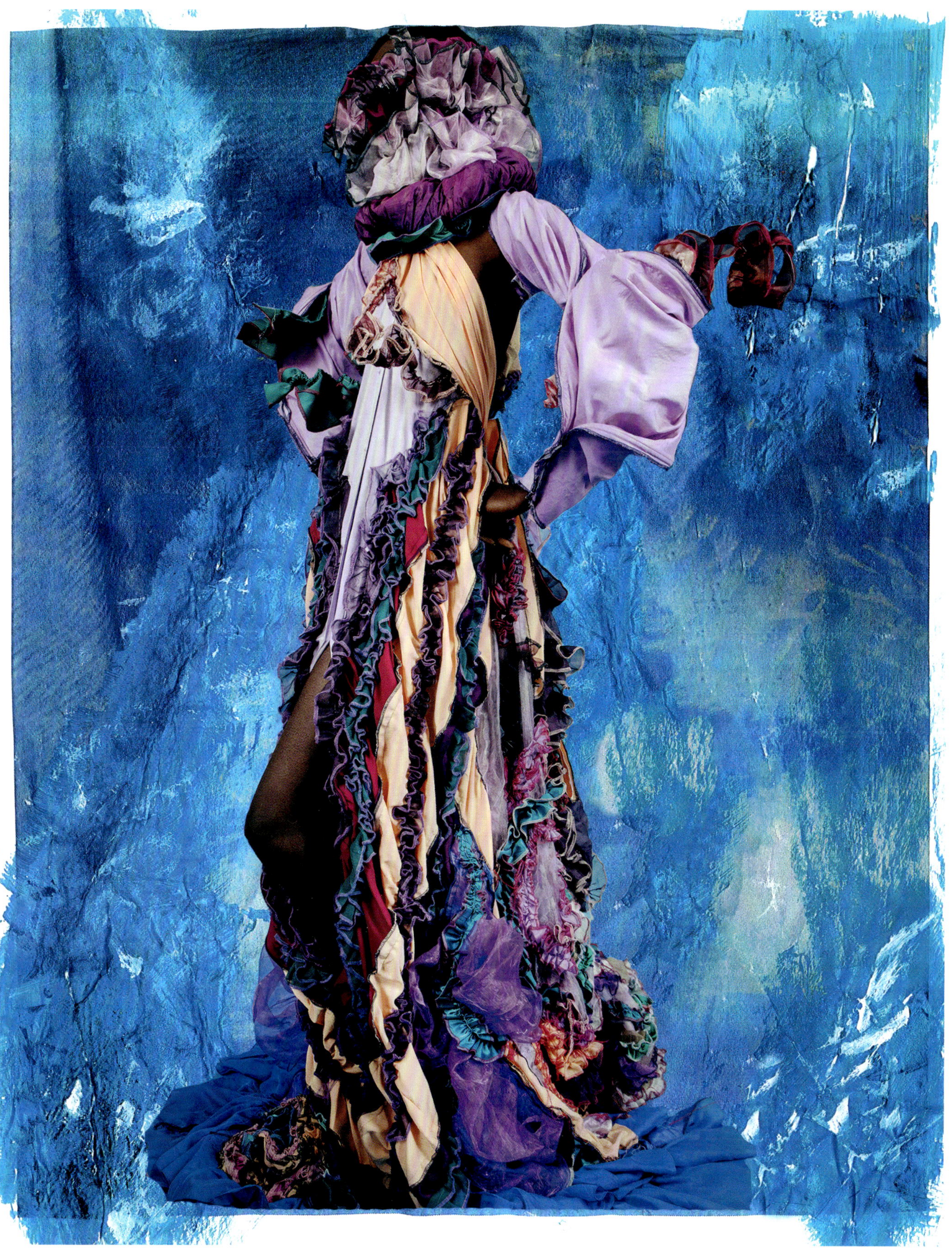

SALAH BARKA

Images courtesy of Salah Barka

Salah Barka creates pieces that fuse Tunisia's past and present. Barka's looks celebrate Tunisian cultural heritage and diversity by combining current local and international trends in streetwear with references to vintage and ancient styles and cultural motifs. Salah Barka was the youngest in a family of nine children and fashion played a part in his daily life with his four sisters. He started his career in fashion as a model at the age of fifteen, before switching to styling and costume design for film, theatre, and dance. In 2004 he launched his label Oshy and resumed work in the fashion industry, alongside his work in costumes. Barka pushed boundaries as an openly gay, black designer while also aiming to enrich the textile and garment industry in Tunisia by exclusively using locally sourced materials. In his work within the realm of responsible and sustainable fashion he has participated in Moodha Okhra, an educational project in Tunisia aimed at raising awareness about sustainable fashion.

The ensemble featured here is entited *el Arbi* that combines a *burnoose*, or ample cape, with bat wings, a *kamis* or shirt with an embroidered front panel, *sirwal* or pants, and a pair of *babouches* or slippers.

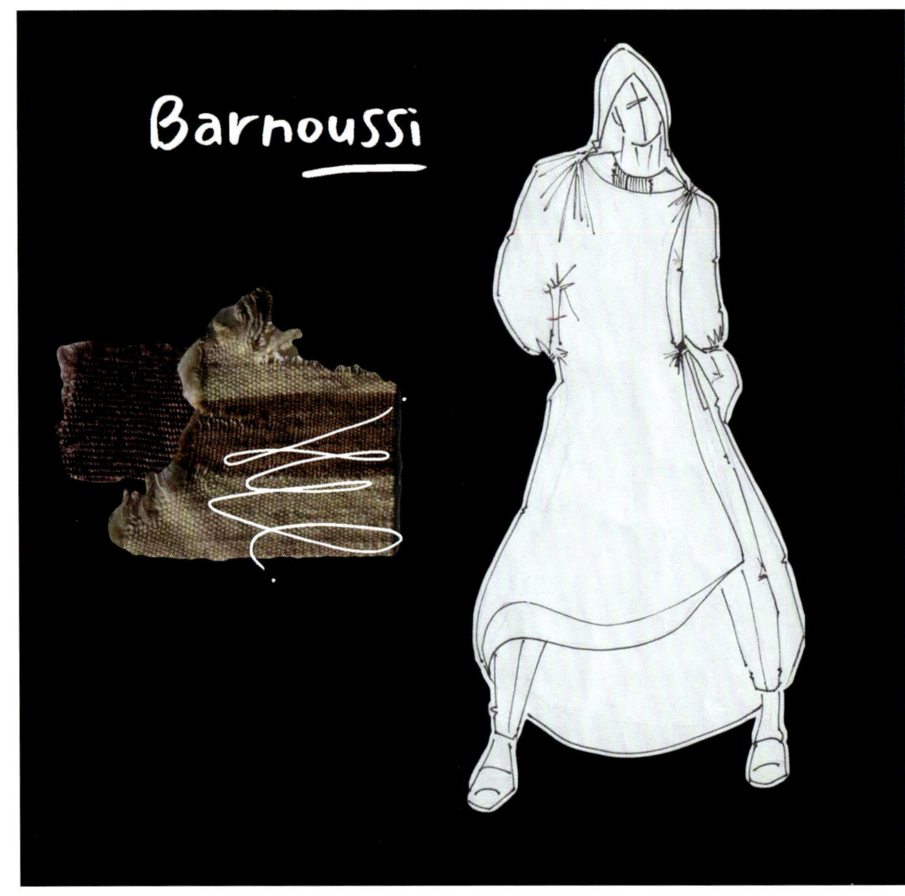

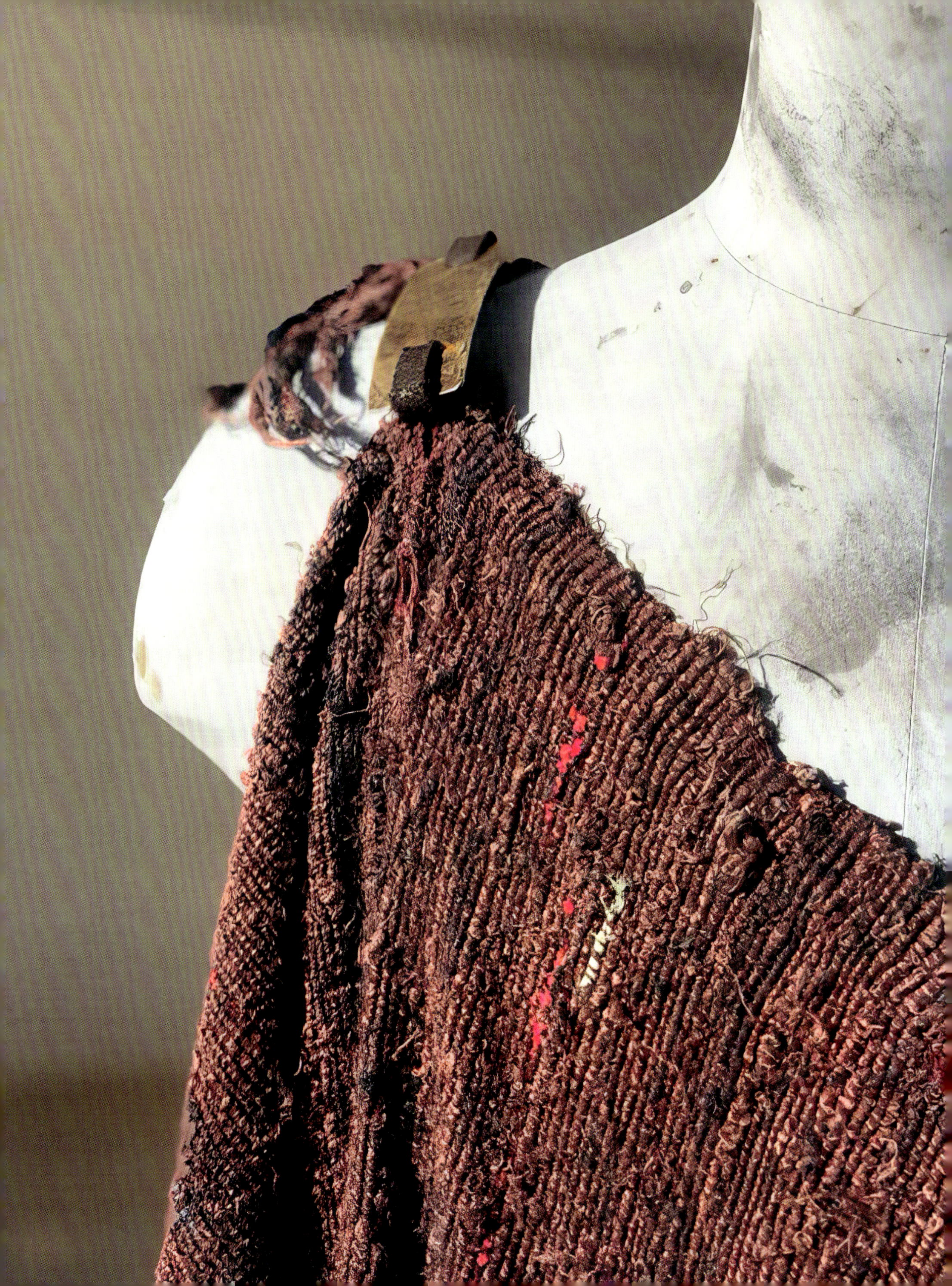

BENMA

HEDI BEN MAMI

Hedi Ben Mami is a Tunis-based designer who began studying engineering before switching to fashion design at ESMOD Tunis. He launched his label Benma in 2019, where he embraces the nature of the Mediterranean in his designs. Recently, he participated in the second edition of Moodha Okhra, which was centered around upcycling. Five Tunisian-based designers and creators were invited to participate in the project by combining their talents in a zero-waste approach to sustainable fashion practices. The project was centered around "Moodh'Up," a program focused on fashion upcycling, as well as awareness and support modules dedicated to styling, modeling, artistic direction, marketing, and business. Together, the designers created a marketable collection made with upcycling that had a laid-back aesthetic. Hedi Ben Mami's contribution was inspired by nature, including sand, greenery, and water. He also studied the shrinkage of fabrics and well-finished seaming in order to enhance his project. His completed outfit consisted of a plastron blouse made of two linen shirts, a skirt made by fusing gabardine pants and a linen skirt, and a bomber jacket made from an anorak, trousers, a corduroy skirt, and a leather skirt.

Benma's Mamia jumpsuit shown here takes its name from a feminine name widely used in his family, linked to his surname, Ben Mami, from which the label's name, Benma, is derived. The design of this outfit, with its bold shoulders and voluminous pants, evokes traditional Tunisian silhouettes, like the *marsaoui*, yet presents them through a more contemporary and minimalist lens. This outfit also draws inspiration from the Mediterranean, reflected in its color palette and materials, including plant fibers and white silk. Ben Mami is deeply committed to his technique of working with plant fibers and he strives to further develop it in collaboration with local artisans from Nabeul, a coastal town in northeastern Tunisia.

Photograph by Bachir Tayachi in collaboration with *MaftMag*

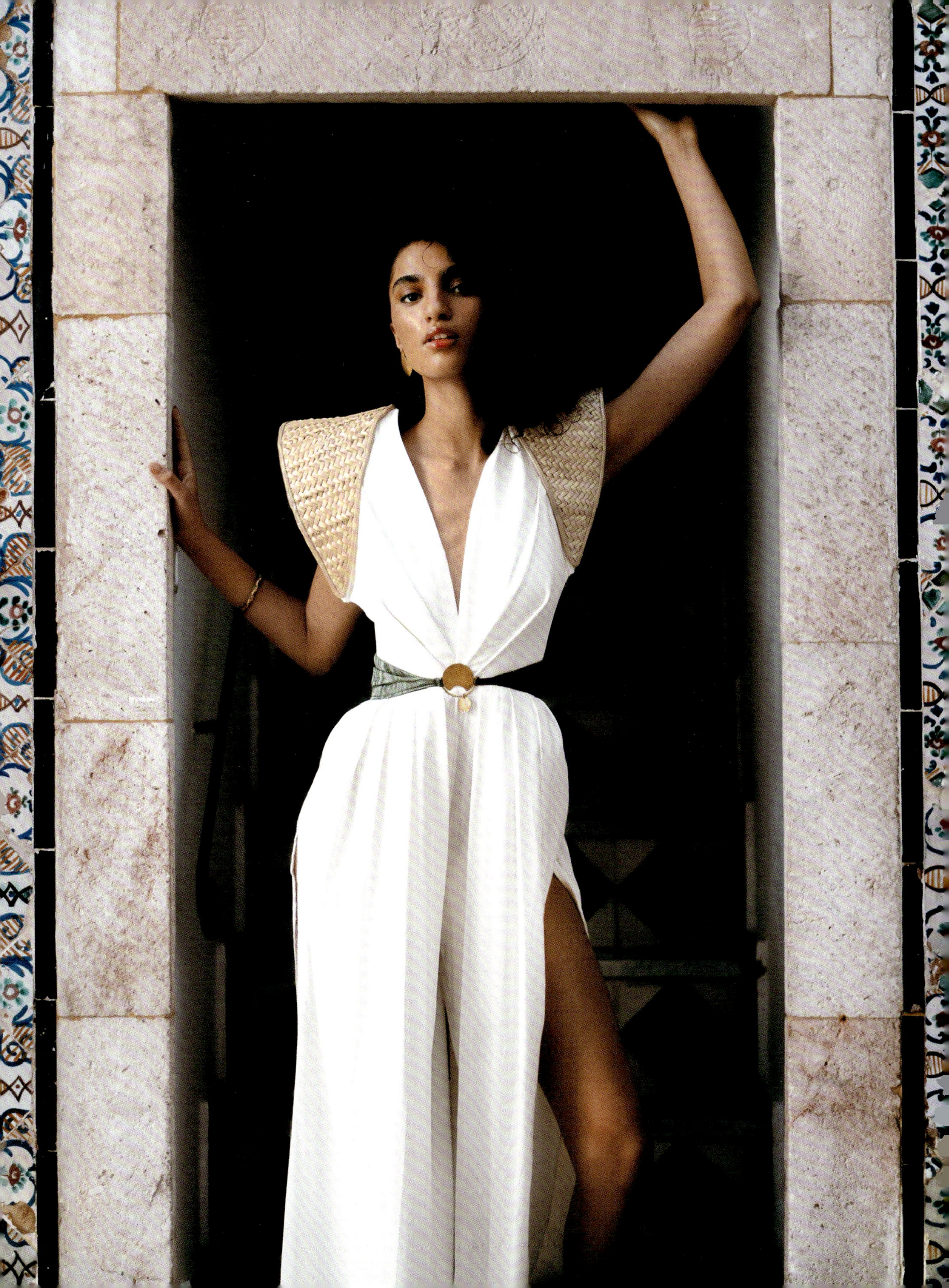

SAID MAHROUF

Images courtesy of Said Mahrouf

Born in Asilah in Morocco, Said Mahrouf grew up in Amsterdam, where he received a degree in fashion design from the Gerrit Rietveld Academy. He went on to continue his studies at Pratt Institute in New York. Initially, he focused on site-specific performances and costume design, but ultimately returned to fashion design and launched his own eponymous label. He began participating in Festimode-Casablanca Fashion Week in 2007, which ultimately led to an invitation to present his Spring/Summer collection in Paris. In addition to showing in Casablanca, where his studio is based, he has shown in Amsterdam, Cadiz, Sicily, Jakarta, Dubai, and Bangkok.

Despite his strong international presence, his clientele is primarily from Casablanca and continues to grow through word of mouth. Having lived both in the Netherlands and Morocco he has found different attitudes towards self-presentation. In Amsterdam, people want to be neutral and not stand out. In Casablanca, on the other hand, there is a great deal more desire to be original, which has aided his business of custom-made clothing. While many Moroccans would once have made trips to Paris to get their clothes, they are increasingly shopping locally and supporting the local fashion industry. Ninety percent of his business is made to measure, with the dresses made right in his studio with an average of between three and five fittings. While based in Morocco and representing the country around the world, his design aesthetic is a minimalist one of silhouettes formed by draping the fabric around the body. The pieces in the exhibition are typical of his drapery with a studied nonchalance, but made out of a handwoven Moroccan brocade edged with fringe.

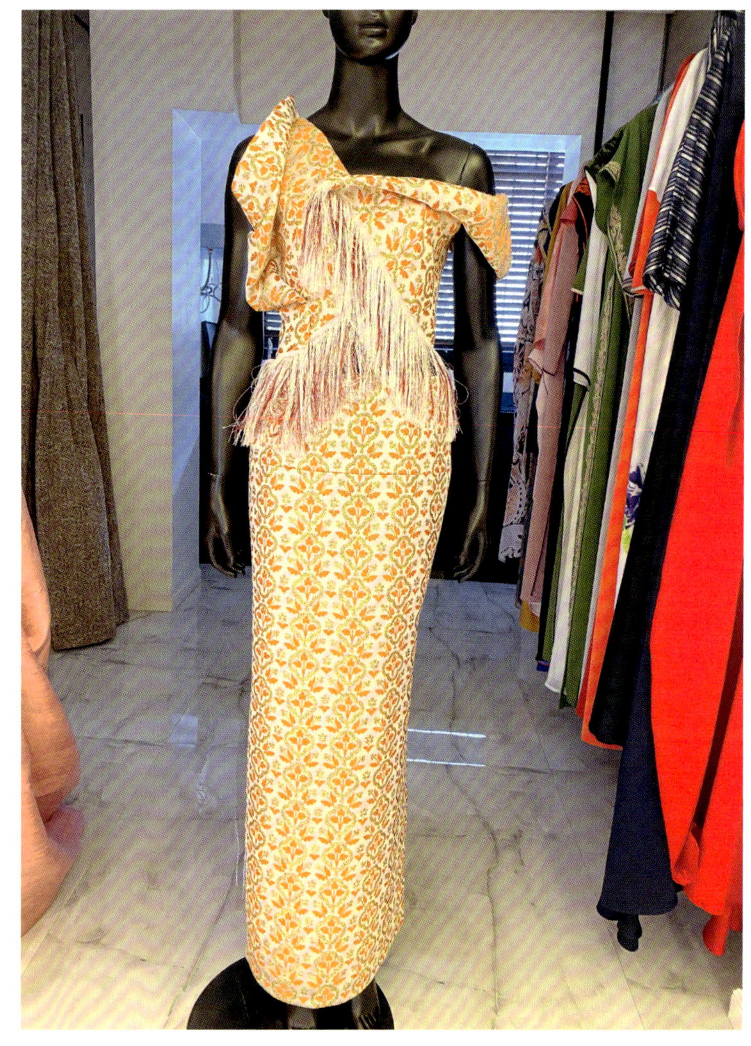

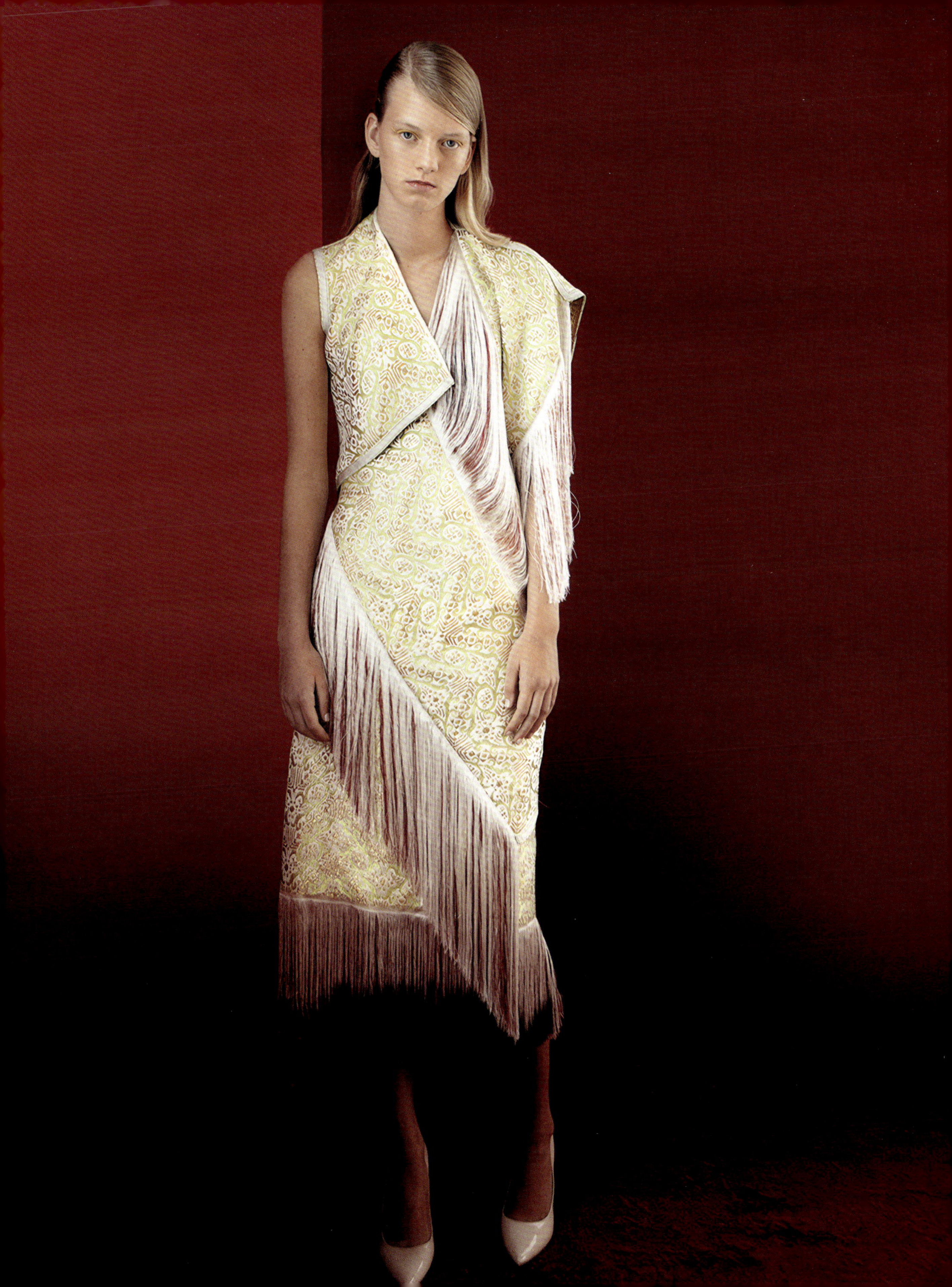

MAISON KA

KATIA GHELBOUN

The story of Maison KA is the story of a family in which the parents left everything: family, friends, and their native land, Algeria. They left to give their children a chance to live in peace, far from the injustices of the Black Decade, as the period of the Algerian Civil War from 1992 to 2002 is known. Their daughter Katia Ghelboun was born in Algeria, but was taken at the age of two and a half to France, marking the point when Maison KA was born. To be uprooted so young stimulated her thirst for culture. The opportunity to live between two cultures gave birth to a project to bring the cultures together through their know-how and tradition. Maison KA is a high-end ready-to-wear brand that brings together Amazigh and Western culture. But that is not all. Each piece is created in a limited series, encouraging reduced consumption and respect for the working conditions of their partners. The pieces are made in France in an atelier in the city of Roubaix, a former center of textile production.

Photograph by Ballers Studio, model: Nabil, clothing: Maison KA →

Photograph by Ballers Studio, model: Luiza, clothing: Maison KA ↓

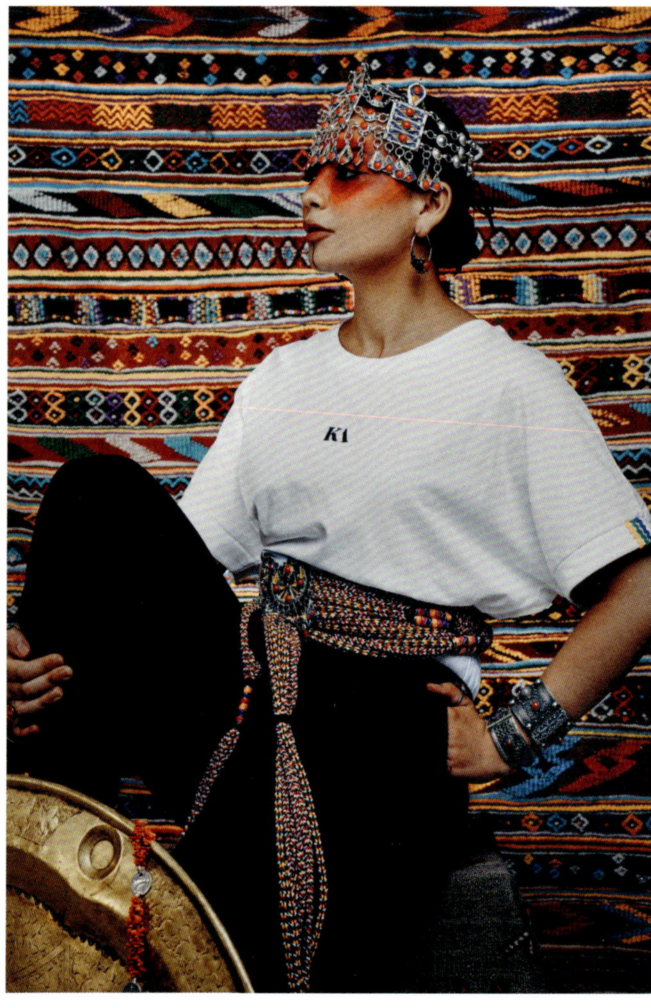

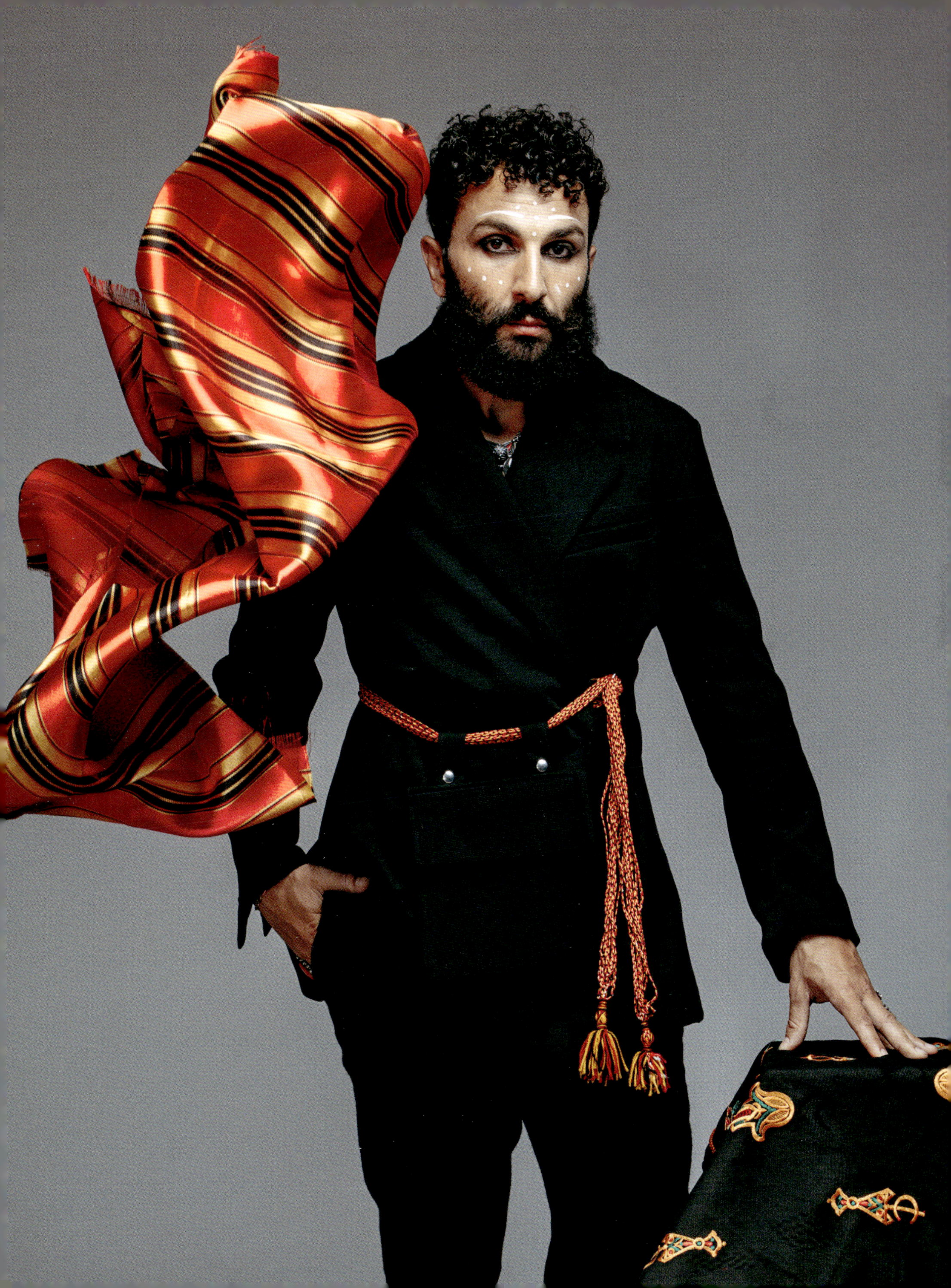

MEROË

SARAH DAWOOD AND MOUSTAFA DAWOUD

Images courtesy of MEROË

Co-founded by a sister and brother team, Sarah Dawood and Moustafa Dawoud, MEROË provides a solution to the stress of dressing. The brand creates simple, practical garments that answer to the real experiences of the everyday—designed with style and comfort in equal measure. Every piece is made to last beyond the season, with a focus on craftmanship. MEROË's commitment to sustainability is present throughout every part of the design process, from responsible sourcing and ethical production to giving a second life after ownership. All collections are made from at least 90% plant-based materials and all brand packaging is free from petroleum-based plastics. MEROË rejects the notion that sustainability is a trend and instead makes conscious fashion the heart of the brand.

Sarah Dawood studied Fine Arts and pursued numerous courses in fashion design. With years of experience in the fashion industry, she was deeply moved by the negative impact of fast fashion on both people and the planet. Consequently, Sarah decided to depart from her role as the Creative and Design Director at a fast fashion brand to establish with her brother their own sustainable fashion brand. Moustafa Dawoud originally pursued a career in industrial engineering and business management. Despite his professional success, his childhood love for fashion never waned. Embracing his passion, Moustafa studied fashion business at Style School and FAD. Alongside his sister, he founded MEROË, a sustainable fashion brand that blends his engineering acumen with a creative flair, embodying his dedication to a sustainable and stylish future in fashion.

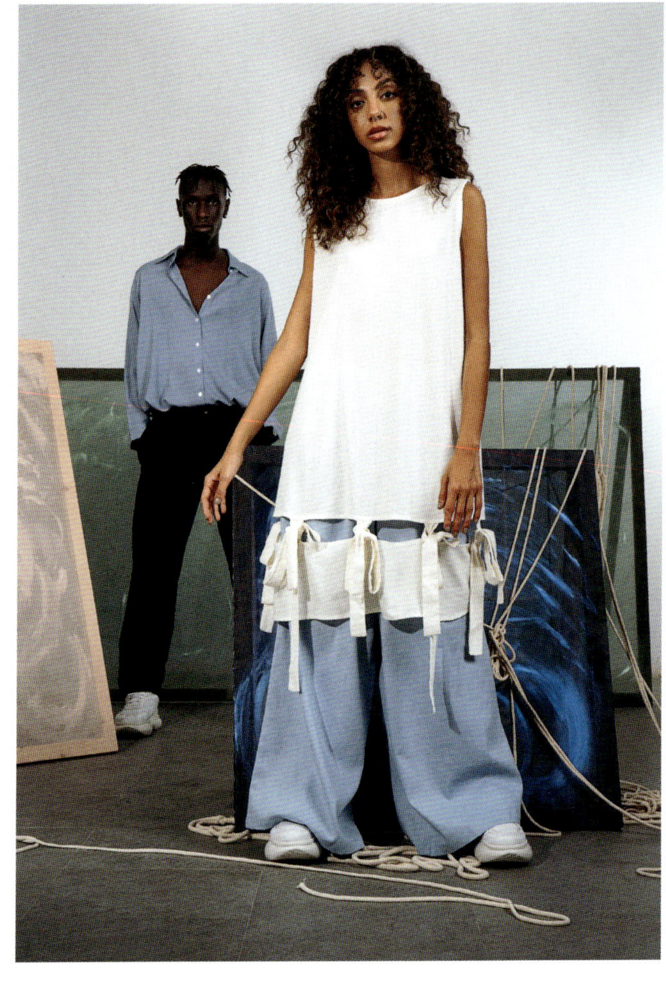

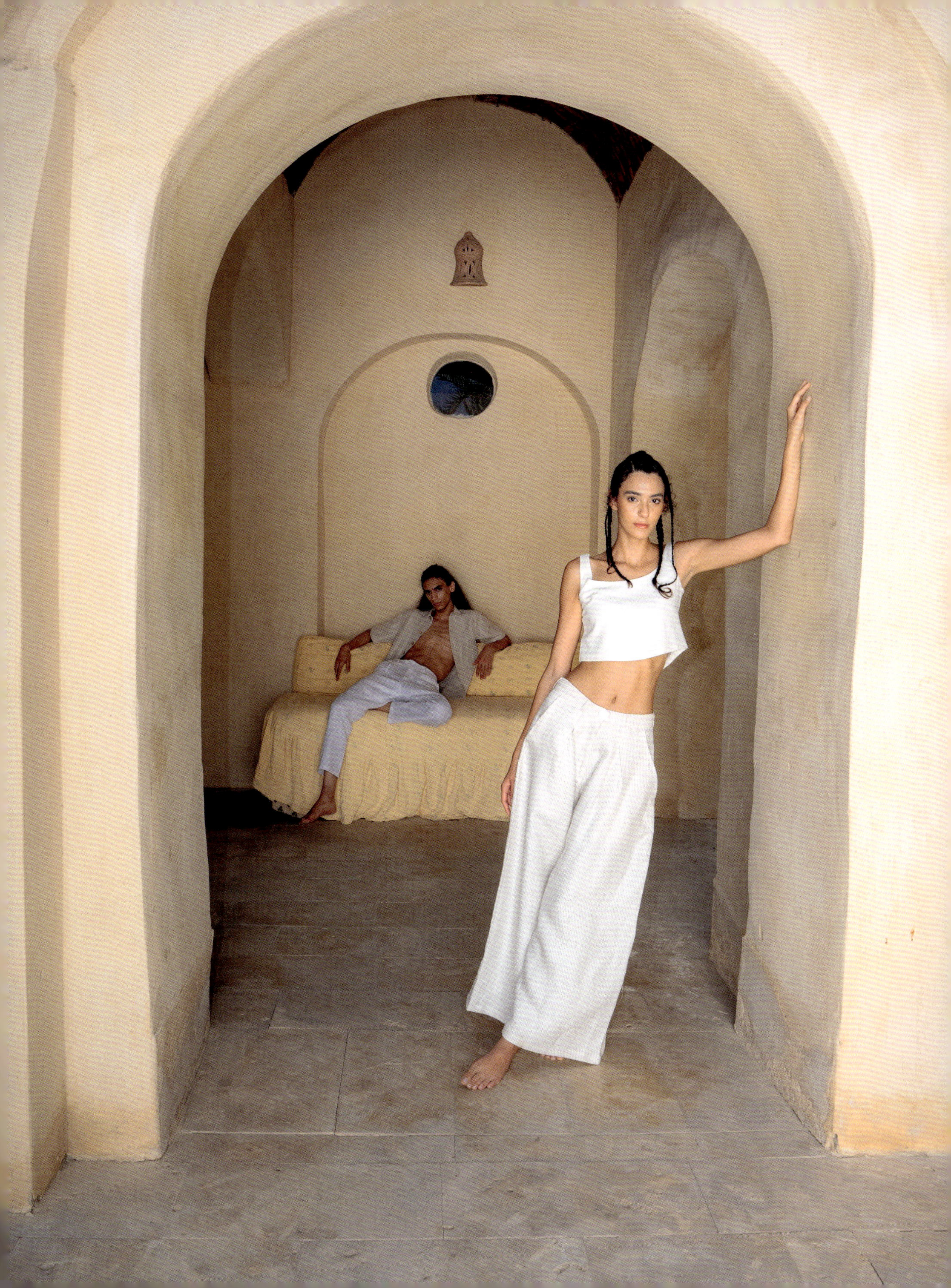

NADINE DANS TOUS SES ÉTATS

NADINE CHAMAA

Nadine Dans Tous Ses États was created by Nadine Chamaa, who was born in Lebanon but has lived and traveled around the world, ultimately basing her business in Cairo. Chamaa has learned old and traditional techniques from many different cultures, which she incorporates into her pieces. For instance, she learned Japanese shibori, indigo dyeing from Mali, and wool felting from Argentina. She focuses on using sustainable fabrics, including Egyptian cotton, linen, and upcycled materials. Chamaa often experiments with reused and overlooked materials, as well as combinations of differing techniques, creating tailored and individually unique products that offer an ethical choice to any fashion wardrobe.

For her piece Recycled Threads, which is made from leftover cottons, Chamaa arranged a photoshoot with the underwater photographer Mina Rizk and the model Saraellaithy, with help from the Bubbles Team diving instructors and Ikelite underwater accessories.

Underwater Photographer: Mina Rizk @byminarizk, model: Sara El Laithy @saraellaithy

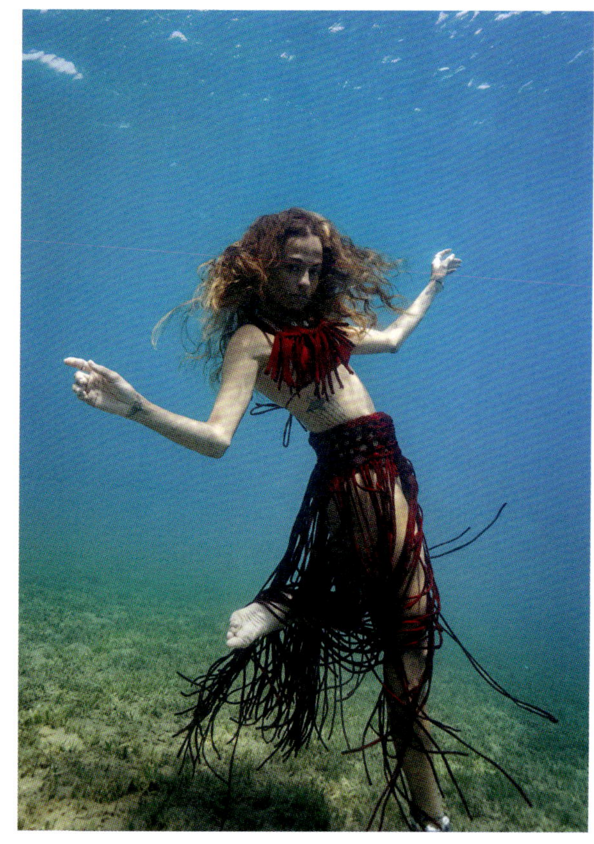

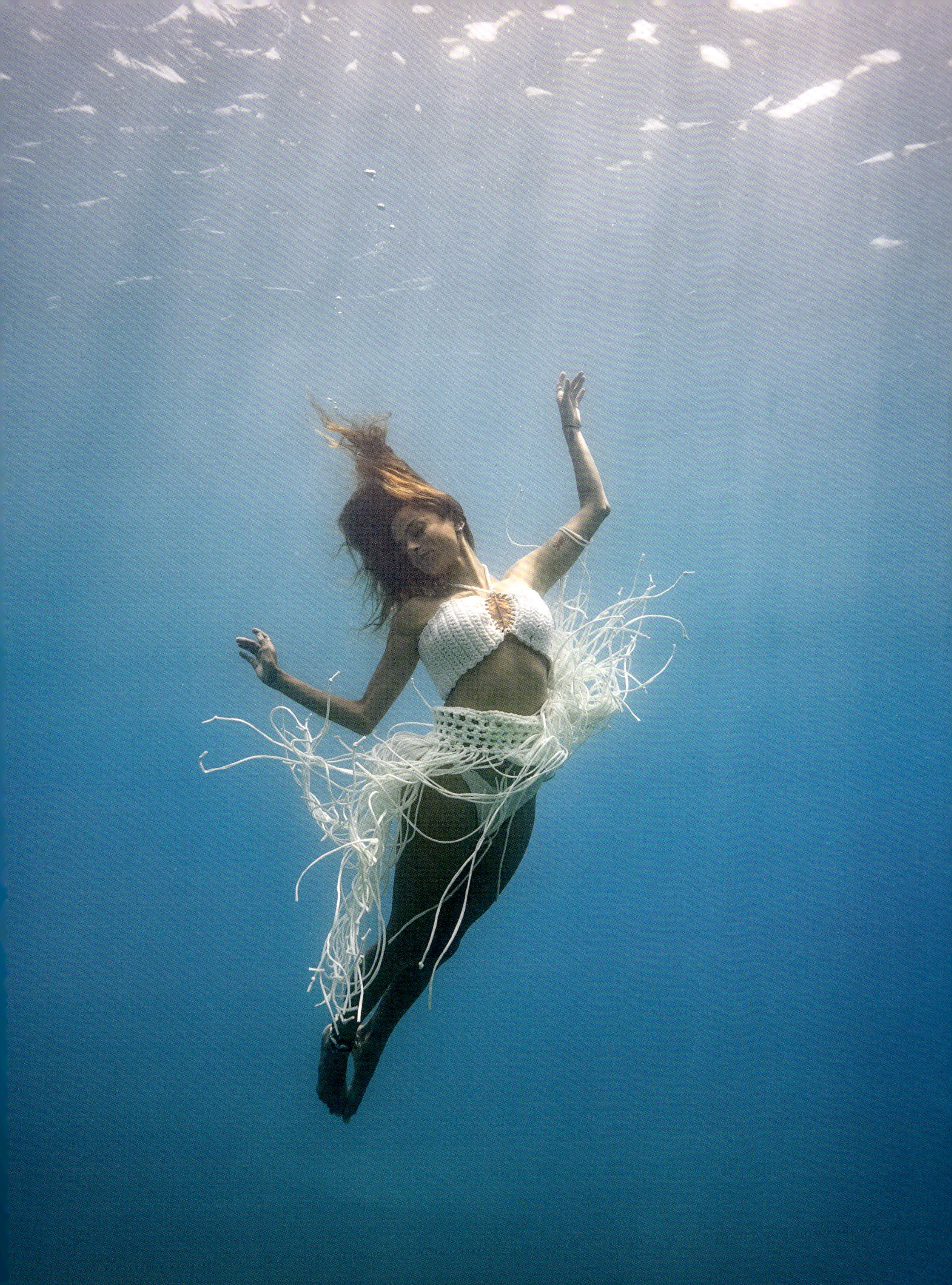

OUMLIL

HICHAM OUMLIL

Hicham Oumlil was born into a family of merchants in Casablanca, Morocco. From an early age, he was inspired by the mix of traditions, rituals and aesthetics—Moroccan and Western—flowing through the country's architecture, interiors, music, dress, and cuisine. He began his studies in Casablanca before moving to the United States. He got his start working for Hermès and Loro Piana before striking out on his own and founding his own label in 2006. Oumlil, which means white in the Moroccan Amazigh language, reflects a space open to new narratives and approaches. Focused on menswear, the brand is inspired by cultural exchange and designed for a new generation of customers with a more global outlook and a fluid approach towards life. They are not defined by career, race, or age. The world that they live in is fascinating and forever changing. While Oumlil offers ready-to-wear garments, customers also have the option of altering pieces and selecting from a curated selection of high-end seasonal fabrics and trims. The process of consultation, fittings, pattern grading, and final production takes about five weeks.

The two ensembles included in the exhibition highlight Oumlil's attention to rich, textured fabrics. In the first look, the multi-directional side and box-pleated navy double-breasted coat is shown paired with waxed cotton and linen deep single-pleat trousers, and a jewel-neck black and white ribbed cotton top. The second look combines a one-direction spaced push-up checkerboard-pleated white dinner jacket and navy blue pants with a half-button, half-banded collar blue shirt.

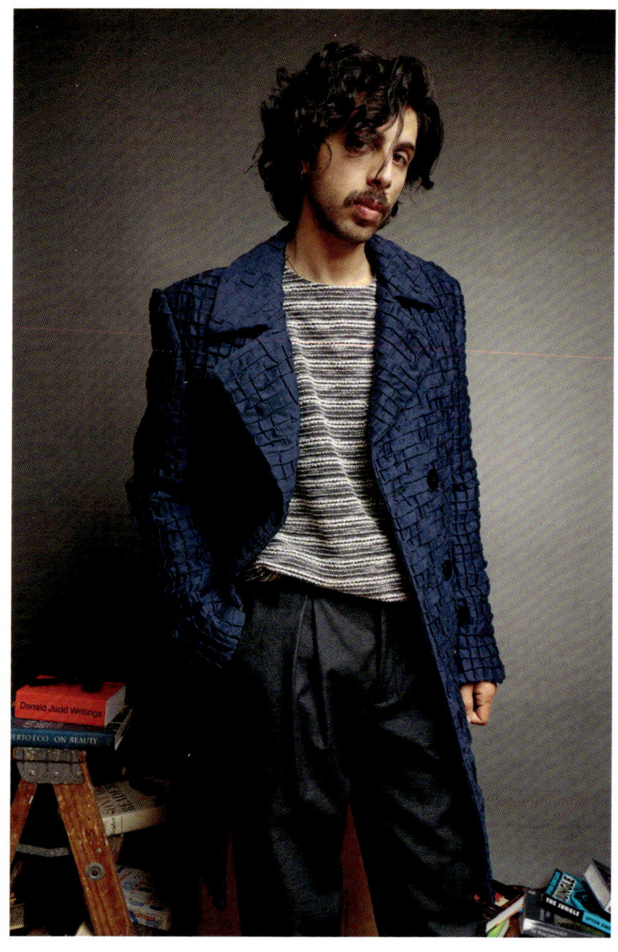

Photographer: Adrian Nina, model: Jaafar Alnabi (Iraqi-American actor/director), stylist: Hicham Oumlil, art direction: Mark Kingsley

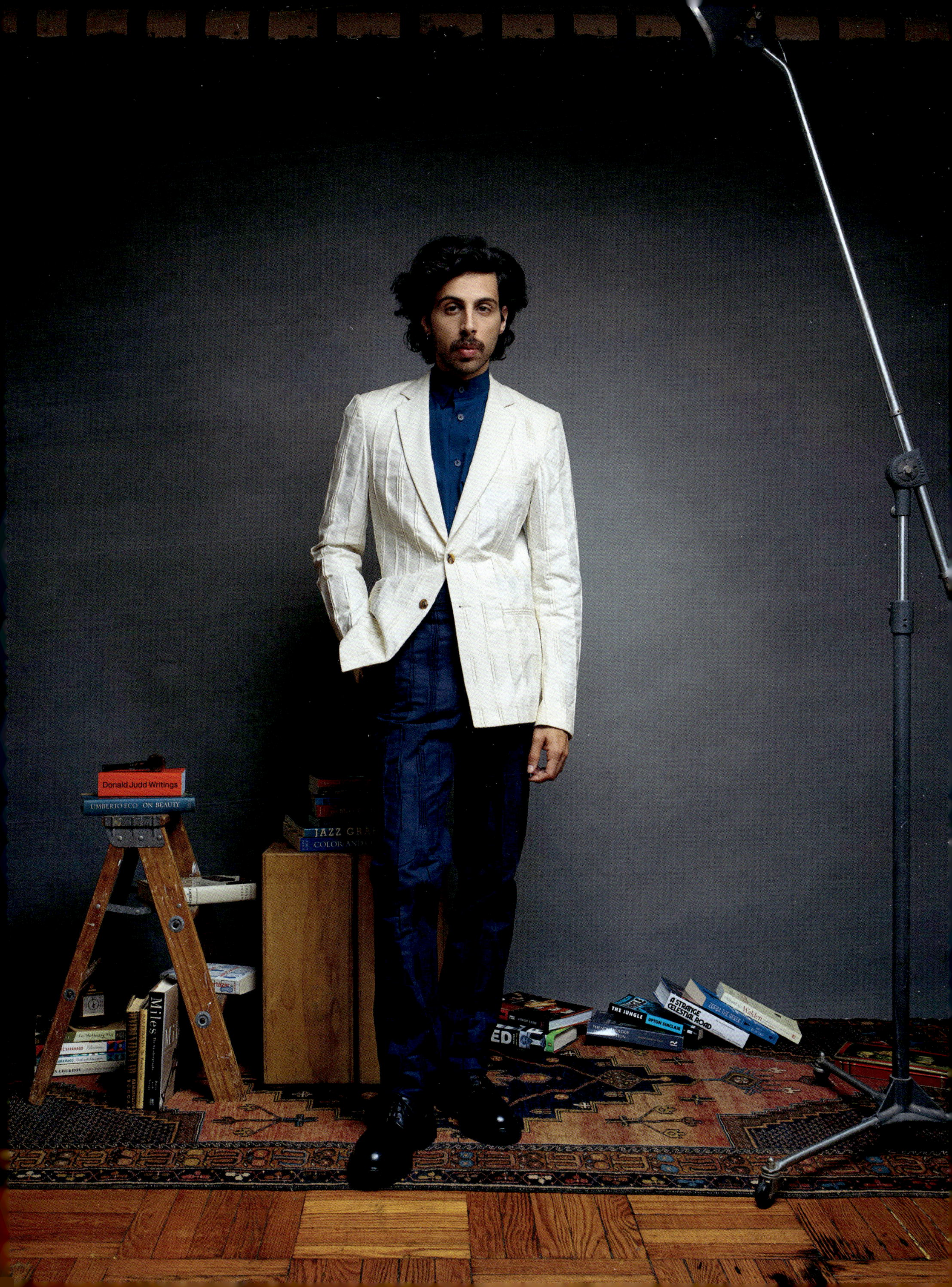
Donald Judd Writings
UMBERTO ECO ON BEAUTY
Miles
THE JUNGLE
UPTON SINCLAIR
A STRANGE CELESTIAL ROAD
Walden

SACER

MAY KASSEM AND ALI NAWAWI

Heissa collection, Emerging; image courtesy of Sacer →

Soul collection, image courtesy of Sacer ↓

Sacer is the Latin word for sacred, which this Egyptian brand chose as its name to portray the core of its mission of improving humanity and soundness of mind. The brand was co-founded by the husband-and-wife team of May Kassem and Ali Nawawi. Kassem began her career as a psychologist and Nawawi was a health economist and public health practitioner. In their desire to have a social impact they founded an eco-friendly clothing brand. Sacer creates streetwear that is eco-conscious with sustainable and ethical production practices. They use upcycled pre-consumer waste and organic Egyptian cotton to create soft, breathable, and lightweight fabrics in vibrant colors. They take pride in their supply chain being fully transparent and traceable, starting from the seed and extending all the way to the finished product. Their pieces have a wide range of inclusive styles and at the same time support marginalized groups and raise awareness about mental health. They aim to create designs that create real and honest conversations, raise awareness, give a voice to those without one, and reduce stigma.

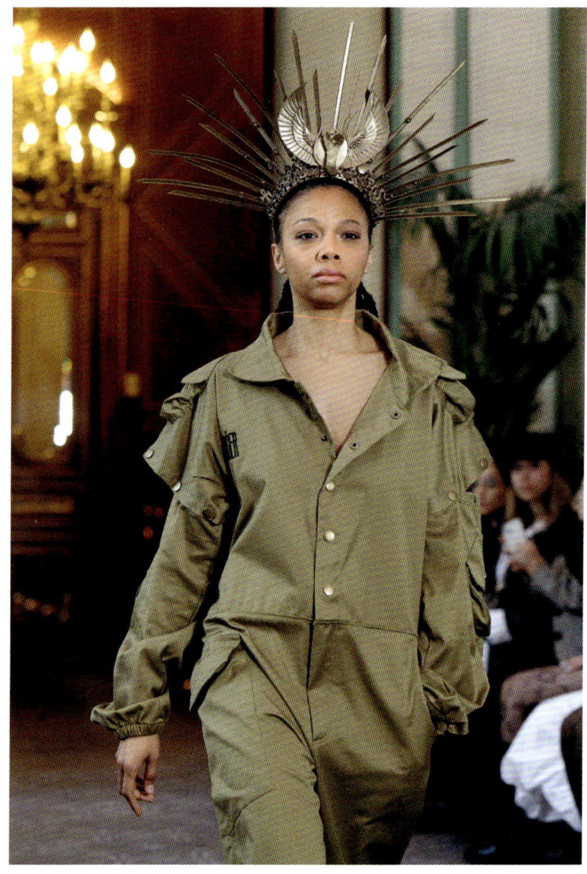

The products from the Heissa collection are inspired by the native women of Heissa Island, Aswan. In preserving the Nubian handicrafts and language passed down through generations, Sacer created products that manifest the heritage and culture of the island and its people. They implement Nubian language and handcrafts to preserve and honor their heritage and culture, including featuring the phrase "Isse Kiddibouringo Biltassi," which is used to express relief after perseverance. The Soul collection is a person's conversation with their *Ba* (soul). It is an ode to the very first recorded mental health diagnosis done by the ancient Egyptians, who divided the soul into nine parts, eight are judged and pass into the afterlife while the ninth stays behind as the physical body.

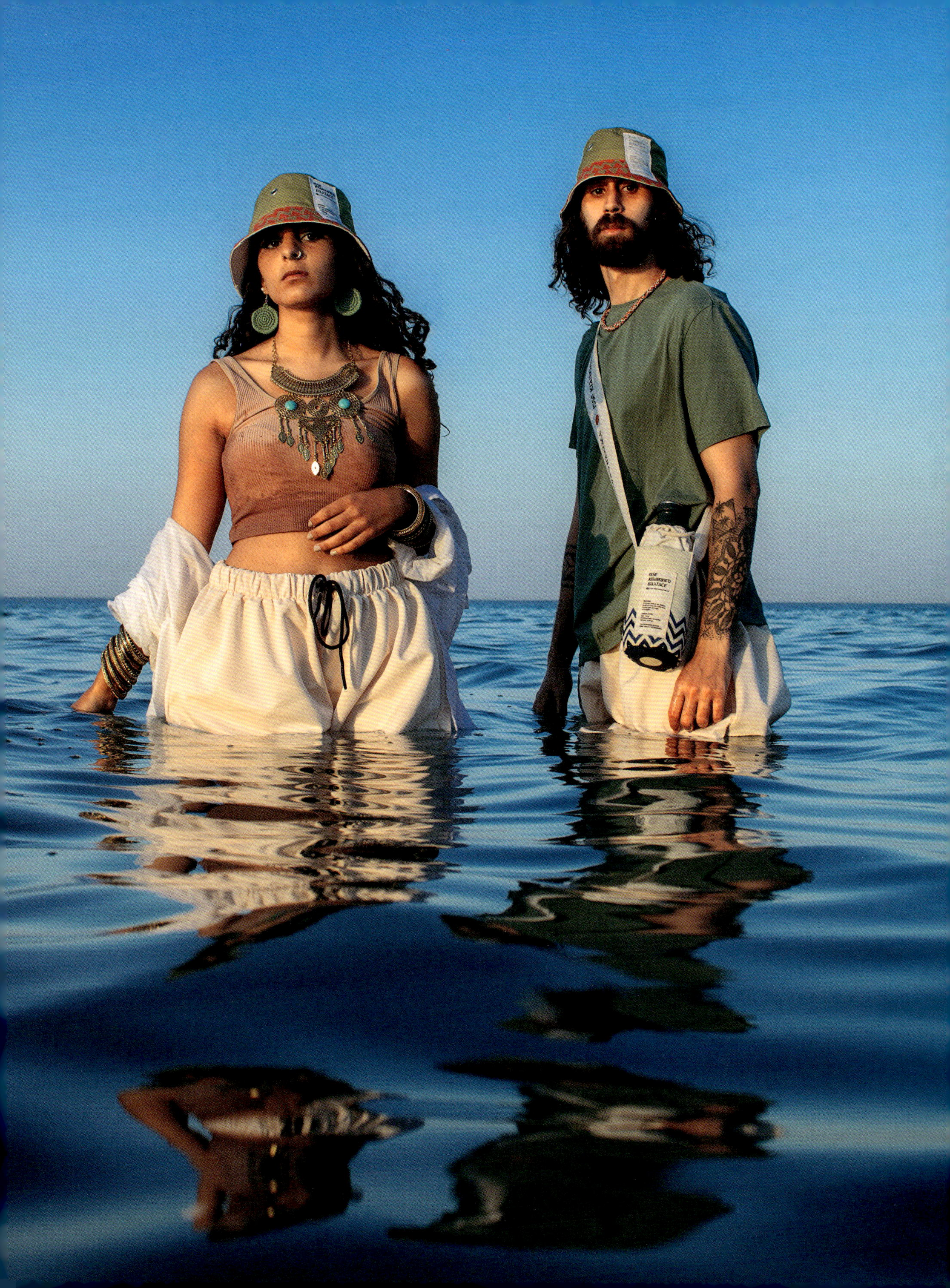

SAQHOUTE

NORHAN EL SAKKOUT

Images courtesy of Saqhoute

Saqhoute launched in 2018 as a women's ready-to-wear brand that emphasizes sustainability and Egyptian heritage. They create affordable high-end garments using Egyptian hand embroidery to commemorate Egyptian heritage and culture in pieces that are highly versatile for family, career, and personal life. Their pieces are meant to be practical staples in anyone's wardrobe, making it easier for consumers to buy fewer and more unique garments meant to be added to the basics. The founder, Norhan El Sakkout, comes from a family of architects, creatives, and academics who studied Arabic literature and Islamic arts and architecture, creating an environment that celebrated Egyptian culture and heritage. Sakkhout attended Goldsmiths, University of London, and obtained her MA in Creative and Cultural Entrepreneurship in Sustainable Fashion while focusing on Egyptian handicrafts. She also holds a finance and fine arts degree from the American University in Cairo and worked in London with designer Ashley Isham for the London Fashion week Fall/Winter 2016/17. Her strong connection to Egyptian identity led Sakkout to use garments to revive and tell the story of Egypt by reflecting on its past and present. She achieves this by using historically inspired designs and hand embroidery. She works with local artisans and maintains a slow-fashion and zero-waste approach. All textile scraps are kept, and remaining fabric goes to an embroiderer, who creates patchwork products to be sold to fund charitable causes. They produce "piece by piece" and even encourage customers to return pieces for alteration or fixing and to send back unwanted clothes to be reused, donated for charity, or used for patchwork.

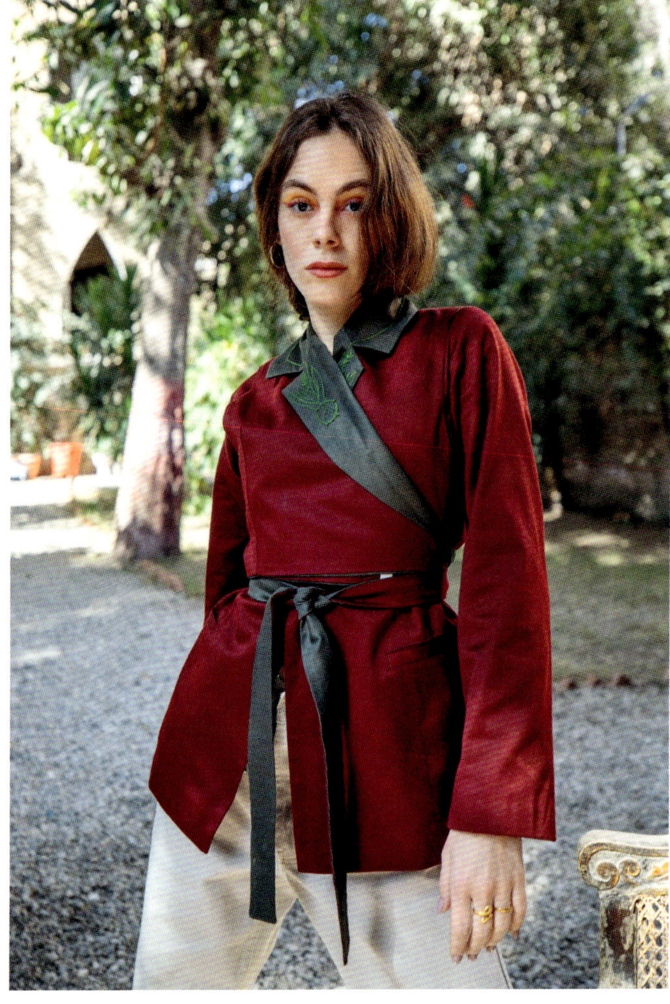

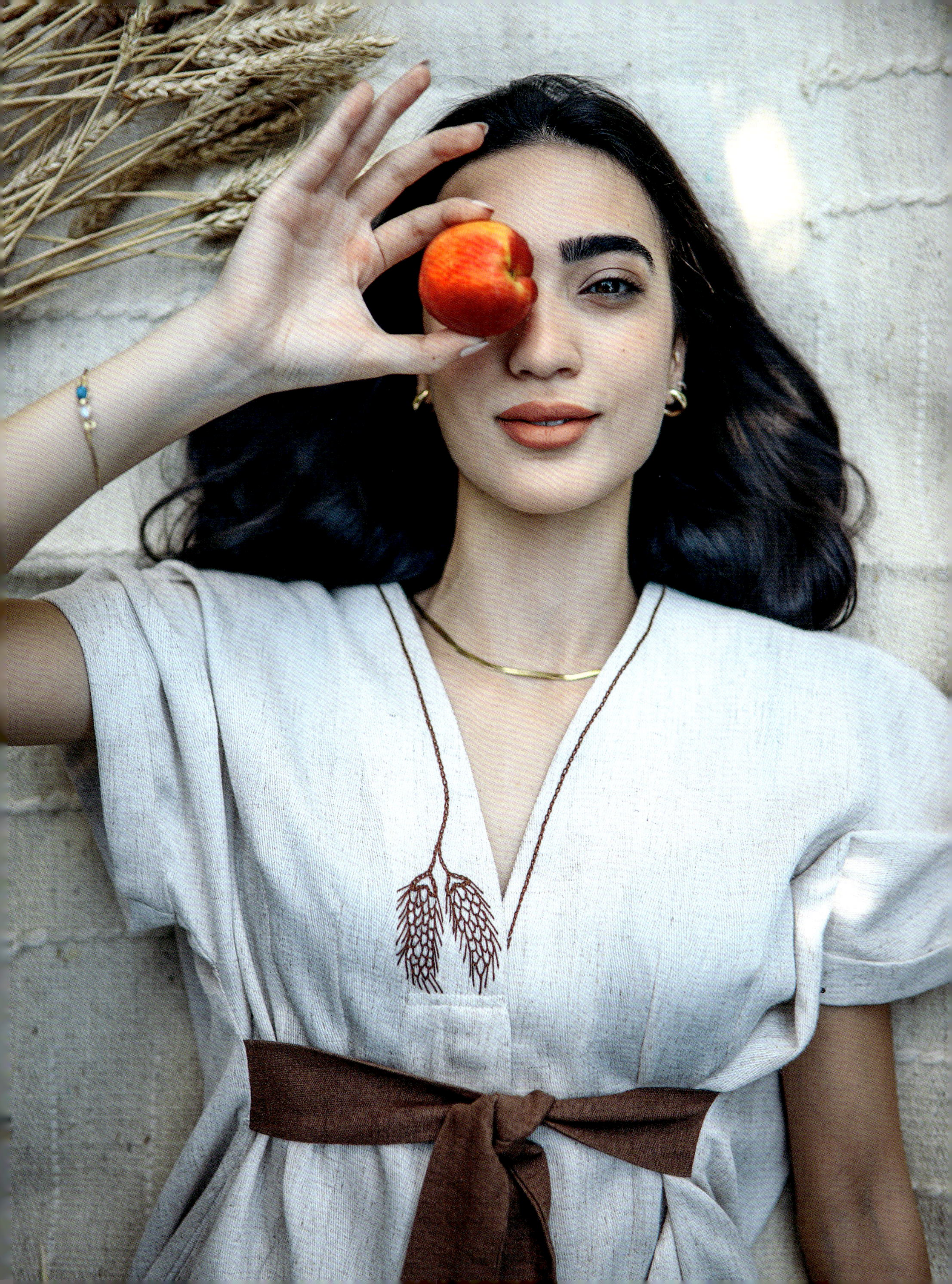

SHELL HOMAGE

RANIA ELKALLA

Shell Homage is a global award-winning sustainable brand that provides biodegradable composite materials and products made from discarded eggshells and various nutshells. It was founded by the multidisciplinary Egyptian designer Rania Elkalla, based on her bachelor's and master's research projects at the Technical University of Berlin. Elkalla was trained in product and graphic design with experience in material science and production techniques. She also works as an industrial design lecturer at the German International University. Her designs are mostly eclectic, derived from different cultures and styles. She tends to design things with humor and interaction with users.

The biodegradable material serves as a replacement for oil-based plastics and can be applied in several functional applications such as interior design, lighting design, furniture design, home accessories, consumable goods, 3D printing, fashion, and jewelry design. Shell Homage bio-composite material resembles marble, natural stone, rubber, or glass, but is made from food waste: (egg) + (nut) shells. The material properties can be controlled and modified to suit different applications. The surface of the material can vary from rough to smooth, from opaque, translucent, to transparent, and from stiff to malleable.

As Elkalla says: "We perceive 'waste' as one material being transformed into another. We see value in everything, and we want to help others see that too."

Image courtesy of SHELL HOMAGE

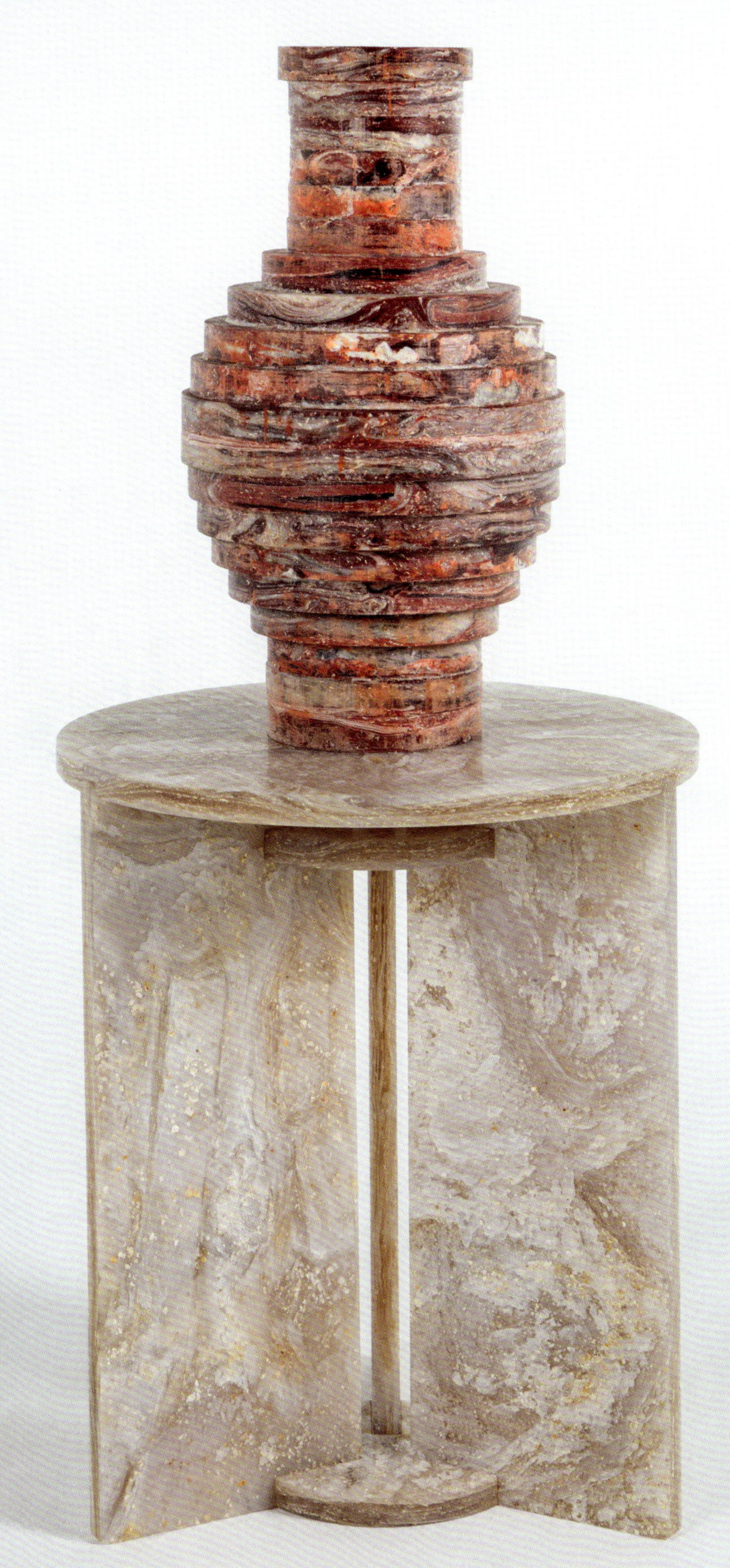

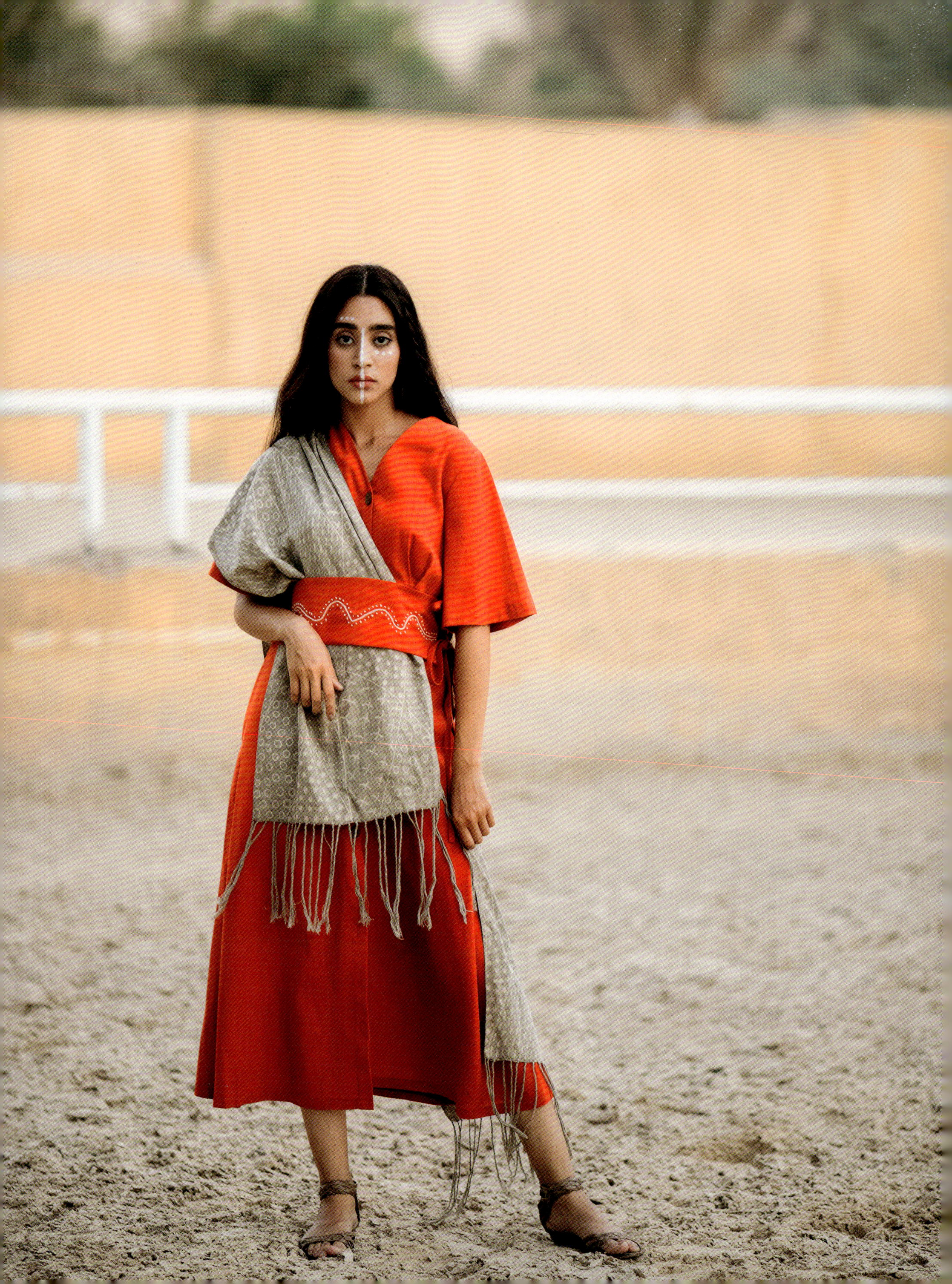

EXHIBITION CHECKLIST

DISRUPTORS

Boauna by Emna Bouaoun
Spanish-Tunisian
Gatifa jacket, Gatifa pants and white t-shirt,
Winter 2023 Petrol Collection
Brown corduroy of 95% cotton, 5% polyester;
white 100% cotton knit
Loan courtesy of the artist, L2024.5.1 a-c

Boauna by Emna Bouaoun
Spanish-Tunisian
Limestone overalls, Winter 2022 Sand,
Earth, and Mud Collection
65% polyester, 35% cotton
Loan courtesy of the artist, L2024.5.2

Bophonysse
Amazigh, Algerian
Wild-Winged Butterfly, 2021
Baby pink and fuchsia hand-painted dupioni silk, satin
Loan courtesy of Bophonysse, L2024.12.1a-e

Bophonysse
Amazigh, Algerian
Out of a Silver Shell, 2021
Hand-painted dupioni silk and satin cloak with
beaded tassel, hand-painted and beaded silk wedding dress
Loan courtesy of Bophonysse, L2024.12.2a-c

Born in Exile
Libyan
Libya Leather Biker Jacket, Fall/Winter 2021, Blood,
Sweat and Oil Collection
Embroidered leather, velvet, metal buckle
Purchase, by exchange, KSUM 2024.4.1a-e

Born in Exile
Libyan
COA shirt and pants, Fall/Winter 2021,
Blood, Sweat and Oil Collection
Printed cotton denim
Purchase, by exchange, KSUM 2024.4.2, .3

Karim Chater
Moroccan
L7atta originale, May 2022
Digital photograph
Courtesy of the artist, L2025.11.1

Karim Chater
Moroccan
Steady Clear Vision, February 2021
Digital photograph
Courtesy of the artist, L2025.11.2

Kegham Djeghalian
Palestinian/Armenian/Egyptian/Dutch
ToGather, 2022
Video, patchworked fabric and trims, wooden structure
Installation and video by Kegham Djeghalian, patchwork in collaboration with the Egyptian Clothing Bank,
film in collaboration with Abdallah Sabry, L2025.16.1

Ibrahim Gamal
Egyptian
Fashion by Amina Galal, 2023-24
Digital photograph
Courtesy of the artist, L2025.13.1

Ibrahim Gamal
Egyptian
Fashion by Shahira Lasheen, 2023-24
Digital photograph
Courtesy of the artist, L2025.13.2

Kenza Vandeput-Taleb, artistic director and founder of Kasbah Kosmic
Belgian-Algerian
"Ali La Point" shirt, upcycled trousers and reworked tarboush, 2024
Cotton shirt; cotton, linen and polyester trousers; felted wool hat
Courtesy of Kenza Vandeput-Taleb, L2024.21.1a-c

Kenza Vandeput-Taleb, artistic director and founder of Kasbah Kosmic
Belgian-Algerian
Upcycled shirt, printed sirwal and reworked cap, 2024
Polyester, cotton, plastic shirt; polyester sirwal; cotton cap
Courtesy of Kenza Vandeput-Taleb, L2024.21.2ab

OUR LAND

Anissa Aida
Tunisian
Africa burnoose, pleated tunic, sirwal, fouta/sarong skirt and balgha, 2020
Burnoose of handwoven cotton, tunic of handwoven "stacrouda" silk, sirwal of wild silk from Tunis region, fouta/sarong of wild silk, balgha of handwoven cotton and braided rope sole
Courtesy of ANISSA AIDA, L2024.23.1a-f

Anissa Aida
Tunisian
Origami coat, oversized sweater and architectural pants, 2024
Coat of wool, sweater of cotton, pants of wool
Courtesy of ANISSA AIDA, L2024.23.2a-c

Reem Atout
Egyptian
Teta Fadia Upcycled Galabia, TETA CHIC Collection, 2022
Double-knit jersey, upholstery velvet
Reem Atout, Fashion Designer, L2024.9.1a-e

Reem Atout
Egyptian
Teta Zainab Upcycled Galabia, TETA CHIC Collection, 2022
Double-knit jersey, cotton-polyester, upholstery velvet
Reem Atout, Fashion Designer, L2024.9.2a-f

Samia Ben Abdallah for AwA
Tunisian
Mirror bag, February 2023
Leather and brass
Courtesy of Architect with Artisan (AwA), L2024.4.1

Samia Ben Abdallah for AwA
Tunisian
Medina necklace, 2023
Sterling silver and enamel
Courtesy of Architect with Artisan (AwA), L2024.4.2

Joanna Ben Souissi
Tunisian
Audace, May 2018
Digital photography print
Courtesy of the artist, L2024.24.1

Joanna Ben Souissi
Tunisian
Untitled photograph from lookbook for Amjad Khalil, June 2022
Digital photography print
Courtesy of the artist, L2024.24.2

Joanna Ben Souissi
Tunisian
Untitled photograph from print editorial for Femmes de Tunisie, June 2017
Digital photography print
Courtesy of the artist, L2024.24.3

Joanna Ben Souissi
Tunisian
The Last Supper, June 2018
Digital photography print
Courtesy of the artist, L2024.24.4

Gigi Ibrahim for Bulga Footwear
Egyptian
Shalateen Khof, Summer 2021
Sheep and goat hand-braided leather top, sheep leather lining, camel leather outsole, cotton thread, glue
Courtesy of the artist, L2024.15.1ab

Gigi Ibrahim for Bulga Footwear
Egyptian
Ramsis Sandal, Summer 2021
Sheep and goat hand-braided leather, double camel leather outsole, brass buckle, cotton thread
Courtesy of the artist, L2024.15.2ab

Gigi Ibrahim for Bulga Footwear
Egyptian
Nut Slipper, Summer 2021
Sheep leather top with traditional embroidery,
foam cushion, camel leather outsole, cotton thread
Courtesy of the artist, L2024.15.3ab

Fares
Algerian
Héritage Tissé: L'Âme du Sahara en Mouvement, 2025
Repurposed Algerian Babar-style rug of sheep wool and cotton
On loan from the artist, L2025.17.1

Fares
Algerian
Tapis d'Exception: Quand la Tradition Habille le Futur, 2025
Repurposed Algerian Babar-style rug of sheep wool and cotton
On loan from the artist, L2025.17.2

Nour Chekiri (Intique)
Mediterranean-Algerian
Dzayer Oversized T-Shirt – A Tribute to Algeria, 2024
Cotton
Provided by Intique – Celebrating Algerian Heritage, L2025.9.1

Nour Chekiri (Intique)
Mediterranean-Algerian
Palestina Oversized T-Shirt – A Celebration of
Palestinian Identity, 2024
Cotton
Provided by Intique – Honoring Palestinian Culture, L2025.9.2

Ténéré Concept by Nawel Atsfaha
Algerian
Berbère je suis, 2024
Striped top, pants of black mousseline, hand-braided wool belt
Courtesy of the artist, L2024.6.1a-c

Ténéré Concept by Nawel Atsfaha
Algerian
Bedroun en wax, 2023
Wax print
Courtesy of the artist, L2024.6.2

Eya Zannad Chahed
North African, Tunisian
La Bérwiche, June 2020
Duchess satin and recycled polyester satin
Courtesy of ZANNAD, L2025.2.1

Eya Zannad Chahed
North African, Tunisian
La Carthaginoise, June 2020
Natural silk
Courtesy of ZANNAD, L2025.2.2

THREADS

Somaia Abolezz
Egyptian
Birds Coat, 2023
Synthetic wool
Somaia Abolezz – A wearable art brand, L2024.22.1

Somaia Abolezz
Egyptian
Nut and the cat, 2023
Silk
Somaia Abolezz – A wearable art brand, L2024.22.2

Somaia Abolezz
Egyptian
We Won't Go, 2023
Synthetic voile
Somaia Abolezz – A wearable art brand, L2024.22.3

Youssre Abdelkader for Almah
Egyptian
Coral Blues, Spring/Summer 2022
Blended material (Cotton, organza, polyester)
Almah by The Egyptian Clothing Bank, L2025.15.1

Youssre Abdelkader for Almah
Egyptian
Timber Threads, 2022 (top), 2024 (trousers)
Blended material (cottons, wool twill polyester-viscose tartans and pinstripes, poplin jersey)
Almah by The Egyptian Clothing Bank, L2025.15.2ab

Youssre Abdelkader for Almah
Egyptian
Fabric manipulation sample books, 2020-25
Mixture of blended material
Almah by The Egyptian Clothing Bank, L2025.15.3

Said Mahrouf
Moroccan
Yellow-green dress of handwoven silk brocade, 2019
Handwoven silk brocade, silk fringe
Courtesy of the artist, L2024.8.1ab

Said Mahrouf
Moroccan
Orange dress of handwoven silk brocade, model from 2019 collection made in 2024
Handwoven silk brocade, silk fringe
Courtesy of the artist, L2024.8.2ab

Maison KA
Algerian, made in France
Blazer KA, T-shirt KA, Pantalon KA, Turban KA, 2022-23
Blazer of polyester-elastane corduroy, shirt of organic cotton, pants of viscose, turban of polyester
Courtesy of the artist, L2024.7.1, .2, .3ab

Maison KA
Algerian, made in France
Kimono KA, Bandeau Bohemien, Sac KA, 2023-24
Kimono of linen-cotton-rayon, bandeau of cotton-Jacquard-viscose, jacket of embroidered silk
Courtesy of the artist, L2024.7.4, .5, .6

Meroë
Egyptian
Oversized linen t-shirt and loose-fit linen shorts, 2024
Linen, coconut shell buttons
MEROË by Sarah Dawood & Moustafa Dawoud, L2024.18.1ab

Meroë
Egyptian
Oversized hand-knit bag, 2024
Hand-knit
MEROË by Sarah Dawood & Moustafa Dawoud, L2024.18.2

Meroë
Egyptian
Short-sleeve linen shirt and regular fit pants, 2024
Linen, coconut shell buttons
MEROË by Sarah Dawood & Moustafa Dawoud, L2024.18.3ab

Nadine Dans Tous Ses États
Egyptian
Recycled Threads, 2024
Leftover cottons
Courtesy of the artist, L2025.6.1

Nadine Dans Tous Ses États
Egyptian
Dress inspired by Egyptian Revolution, 2020
Leftover linens and cottons
Courtesy of the artist, L2025.6.2

Nadine Dans Tous Ses États
Egyptian
Recycled necklace (plastic to fantastic), 2024
Leftover plastic hose and plastic thread
Courtesy of the artist, L2025.6.3

Nadine Dans Tous Ses États
Egyptian
Recycled necklace (plastic to fantastic), 2024
Leftover plastic hose and plastic thread
Courtesy of the artist, L2025.6.4

Hicham Oumlil for OUMLIL
Moroccan-American
Navy double-breasted coat, deep single-pleat trousers and jewel-neck black and white ribbed cotton top and signature white shirt;
coat: Autumn/Winter 2011, trousers: A/W 2024, top: A/W 2021
Cotton twill coat, waxed cotton and linen trousers, ribbed cotton top, cotton shirt;
Loans courtesy of OUMLIL, L2025.7.1a-d

Hicham Oumlil for OUMLIL
Moroccan-American
One-direction spaced push-up checkerboard-pleated white dinner jacket and navy blue pants styled with a half-button, half-banded collar blue shirt; jacket and pants: Spring/Summer 2010, shirt: S/S 2023
Cotton twill jacket, cotton twill pants, cotton shirt
Loans courtesy of OUMLIL, L2025.7.2a-c

Sacer
Egyptian
Zipper Headpiece, Dwelling Dress, The Shut (Shadow) Vest, Boots, Up-cycled Soccer Ball Bag, 2023-24
Polyester and metal headpiece; polyester-cotton blend dress; vest of upcycled gaberdine made from military uniforms; boots of cow leather, rubber soles, cotton laces and nylon side panels; bag with polyester straps, metal accessories and rubber
Courtesy of Sacer, L2024.16.1a-f

Sacer
Egyptian
Bucket Hat, Dwelling Vest, Basic Oversized Basic Tee, KA the Vital Essence Pants, Boots, 2023-24
Hat of GRS-certified recycled PET bottles; vest of 100% organic Egyptian cotton, polyester-cotton blend; t-shirt of 100% organic Egyptian cotton; pants of up-cycled gaberdine made from military uniforms; boots of cow leather, rubber soles, cotton laces, and nylon side panels
Courtesy of Sacer, L2024.16.2a-f

Saqhoute by Norhan El Sakkout
Egyptian
The Lotus Dress, September 2016 (updated September 2018)
TR suiting fabric and satin lining
El Saqhoute for Garment Design & Eco Fashion, L2025.8.1

Saqhoute by Norhan El Sakkout
Egyptian
L'Eau du Nil Set, July 2024
100% Egyptian cotton body, 100% Egyptian cotton lining, cotton perlé embroidery thread
El Saqhoute for Garment Design & Eco Fashion, L2025.8.2ab

Norhan El Sakkout (of Saqhoute) & Youssre Abdelkader
(of Almah – Egyptian Clothing Bank)
Egyptian
On Slowness: An immersive experience on handicrafts and sustainability in fashion, May 2023
Video projection; camera; dress made from upcycled fabric waste, embroidery thread, and various synthetic materials donated to the Egyptian Clothing Bank including cotton, linen, different embroidery threads, and appliqué accessories
El Saqhoute for Garment Design & Eco Fashion, L2025.8.3

Manar Hilal (Talalya), Moustafa Dawood (Meroë),
Norhan El Sakkout (/aqhoute), Sarah Dawood (Meroë),
Youssre Abdelkader (Almah)
Entangling Paths – Between Design & Craft, December 2022
100% linen fabric from waste materials, cotton and linen embroidery thread, cotton perlé thread, macrame cotton, and jute thread
Courtesy of the artists, L2025.8.4

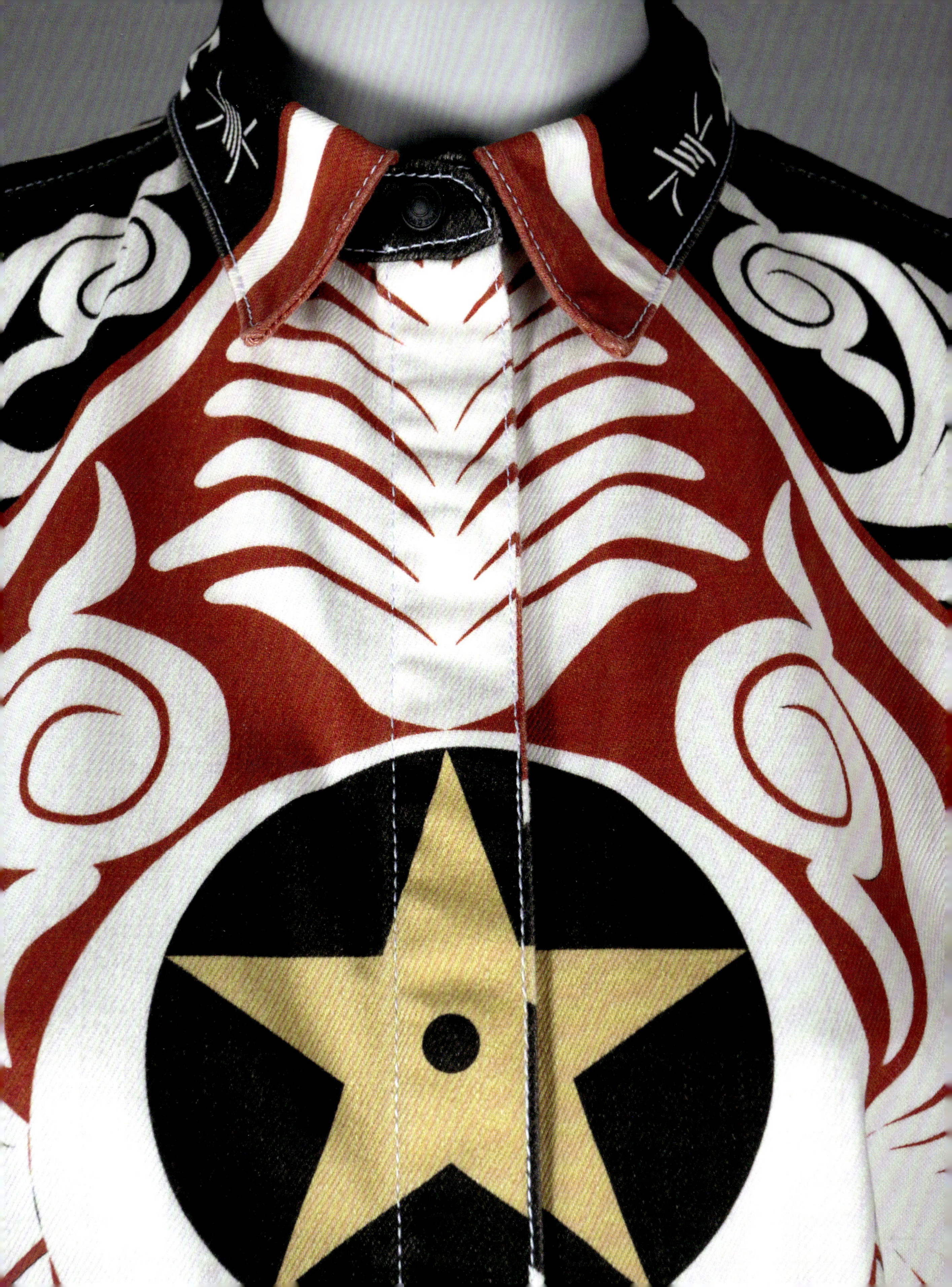

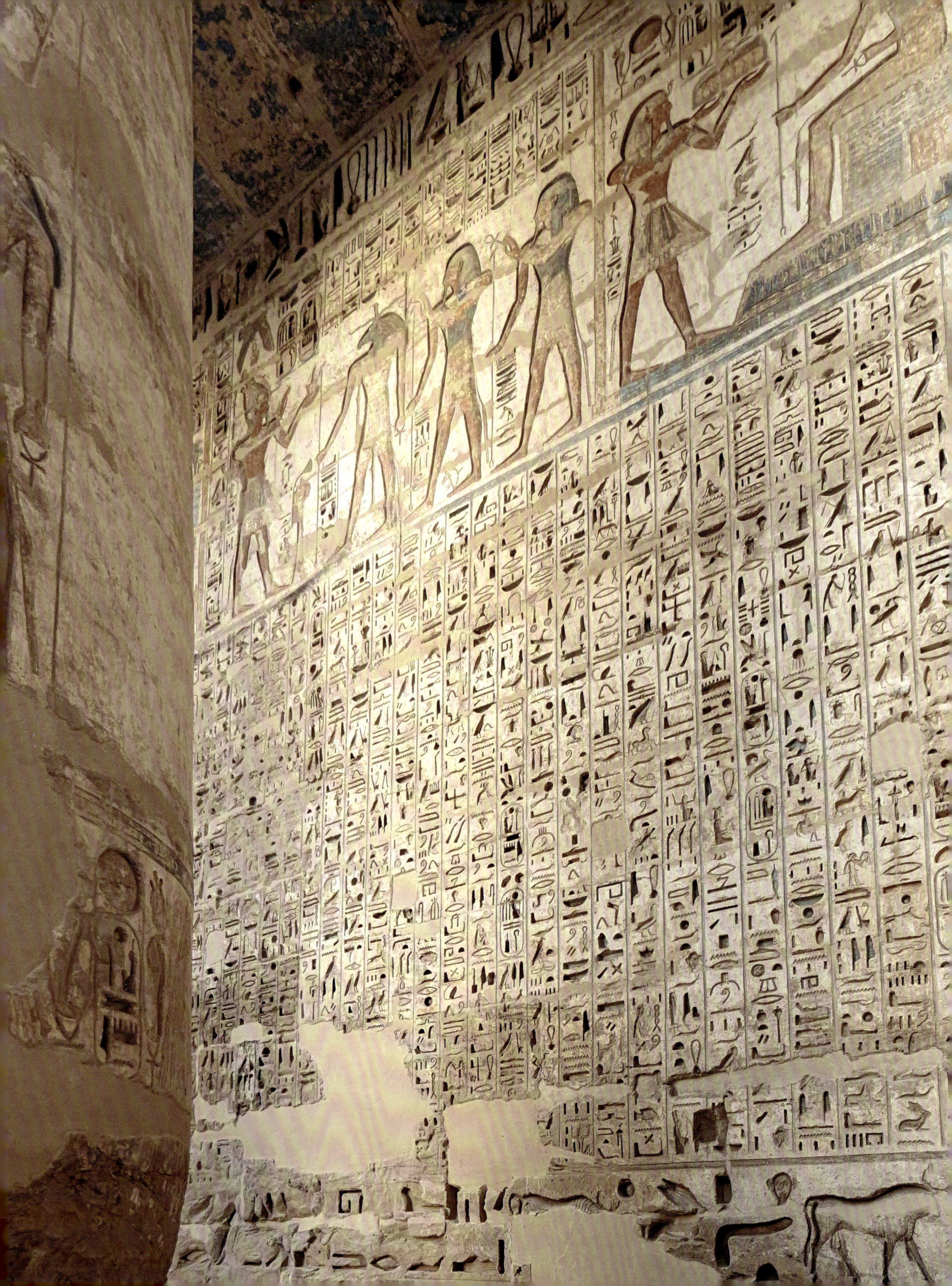

BIBLIOGRAPHY

Abaza, Mona. "Shifting Landscapes of Fashion in Contemporary Egypt." *Fashion Theory: The Journal of Dress, Body and Culture* 11, no. 2-3 (2007): 281-287.

Akou, Heather. "Stories behind the Collections and Why They Matter: Examples from Indiana University." In McGregor, *Creating African Fashion Histories*. 229–51.

Avruch, Kevin. *Culture and Conflict Resolution*. Washington DC: United States Institute of Peace Press, 1998.

Barber, Aja. *Consumed: The Need for Collective Change: Colonialism, Climate Change and Consumerism*. London: Penguin, 2021.

Blanchard, Tamsin, ed., *Fashion Craft Revolution*. London: Fashion Revolution, 2019.

Carter, Rodney G. S. "Of Things Said and Unsaid: Power, Archival Silences, and Power in Silence." *Archivaria* 61 (Spring 2006): 215–33.

Casakin, Hernan, and Fatima Bernardo. *The Role of Place Identity in the Perception, Understanding, and Design of Built Environments*. Sharjah: Bentham Science Publishers, 2012.

Chen, Xuandong, Hifza A. Memon, Yuanhao Wang, Ifra Marriam, and Mike Tebyetekerwa. "Circular Economy and Sustainability of the Clothing and Textile Industry." *Materials Circular Economy* 3, no. 12 (2021), https://doi.org/10.1007/s42824-021-00026-2.

Corbett, Sarah. *How To Be a Craftivist: The Art of Gentle Protest*. London: Unbound, 2017.

Entwistle, Joanne. *The Fashioned Body: Fashion, Dress and Modern Social Theory*. Cambridge: Polity Press, 2023.

European Environment Agency. *Private Consumption: Textiles EU's Fourth Largest Cause of Environmental Pressures after Food, Housing, Transport.* 2020. https://www.eea.europa.eu/highlights/private-consumption-textiles-eus-fourth-1.

Evans, Martin, and John Phillips. *Algeria: Anger of the Dispossessed.* New Haven: Yale University Press, 2007.

Fanon, Frantz. *The Wretched of the Earth.* Trans. Constance Farrington. New York: Grove Press, 1963.

Fletcher, Kate, and Matilde Tham. *Earth Logic: Fashion Action Research Plan.* London: JJ Charitable Trust, 2019. https://katefletcher.com/wp-content/uploads/2019/10/Earth-Logic-plan-FINAL.pdf.

Greef, Erica de. "Refashioning Clothing Collections in South African Museums." In McGregor, *Creating African Fashion Histories.* 252–79. Bloomington: Indiana University Press, 2022.

Jansen, M. Angela. "'There Was No Fashion in Morocco Before' (Re) Creating Contemporary Moroccan Fashion History." In McGregor, *Creating African Fashion Histories*, 187–210.

Korn, Peter. *Why We Make Things and Why It Matters: The Education of a Craftsman*. New York: Vintage, 2017.

Martin, Richard, and Harold Koda. *Orientalism: Visions of the East in Western Dress*. New York: The Metropolitan Museum of Art, 1994.

Masri, Safwan M., and Lisa Anderson. *Tunisia: An Arab Anomaly.* New York: Columbia University Press, 2017.

McGregor, JoAnn, Heather Akou, and Nicola Stylianou, eds. *Creating African Fashion Histories: Politics, Museums, and Sartorial Practices.* Bloomington: Indiana University Press, 2022.

Mignolo, Walter, and Catherine Walsh. *On Decoloniality: Concepts, Analytics, Praxis.* Durham: Duke University Press, 2018.

Miller, Susan Gilson. *A History of Modern Morocco*. New York: Cambridge University Press, 2013.

Peeren, Esther. "Language Cannot Be 'Cleaned Up.'" In *Words Matter: An Unfinished Guide to Word Choices in the Cultural Sector*, Wayne Modest and Robin Lelijveld, eds. 42–45. Amsterdam / Berg en Dal/ Leiden/ Rotterdam: Tropenmuseum, Afrika Museum, Museum Volkenkunde, Wereldmuseum, 2018.

Morgan, Andrew, dir. *The True Cost*. Untold Creative, Life Is My Movie Entertainment, 2015. Film.

Niinimäki, Kirsi. *Sustainable Fashion: New Approaches*. Helsinki: Aalto University, 2013.

Ouano, Jessica. "Cultural Sustainability: Colonialism, Appropriation, and What Justice Looks Like." *Good on You*. October 6, 2024. https://goodonyou.eco/cultural-sustainability/.

Perkins, Kenneth J. *A History of Modern Tunisia*. Cambridge, UK / New York: Cambridge University Press, 2004.

Rocamora, Agnès. *Fashioning the City: Paris, Fashion and the Media*. London: IB Tauris, 2009.

Said, Edward. *Orientalism*. New York: Pantheon Books, 1978.

St. John, Ronald Bruce. *Libya: From Colony to Revolution*. Oxford: Oneworld Publications, 2012.

Tarlo, Emma. *Clothing Matters: Dress and Identity in India*. Chicago: University of Chicago Press, 1996.

Vatikiotis, P. J. *The History of Modern Egypt: From Muhammad Ali to Mubarak*. 4th ed. Baltimore: Johns Hopkins University Press, 1991.

PHOTO CREDITS

Page 1
Photograph by Ibrahim Gamal; fashion by Amina Galal; art direction: Ibrahim Gamal and Amina Galal. Image courtesy of Ibrahim Gamal.

Page 2
Drip de Bled by Karim Chater (Style Beldi); Creative Director: Karim Chater; December 15, 2022. Image courtesy of Karim Chater.

Page 3
Architectural knit top, architectural pants, origami coat by Anissa Aida, photograph by Photokolach. Image courtesy of Anissa Meddeb.

Page 4
Joanna Ben Souissi
Image from print editorial for *Femmes de Tunisie*, June 2017; photograph by Joanna Ben Souissi. Image courtesy of Joanna Ben Souissi.

Page 5
Image from lookbook for Amjad Khalil, June 2022; photograph by Joanna Ben Souissi. Image courtesy of Joanna Ben Souissi.

Page 6
Ensemble for Boauna by Emna Bouaoun; photography: Hamza Ben Nour; stylist: Emna Bouaoun Carrasco. Image courtesy of Emna Bouaoun.

Page 7
The Last Supper, June 2018; photograph by Joanna Ben Souissi. Image courtesy of Joanna Ben Souissi.

Page 8
Ensemble by Zannad; model: Hiba Hkimi; location: Dar Traki home in the medina of Tunis. Image courtesy of Eya Zannad.

Page 10
Siwa Nut shoes by Bulga; photograph by Gigi Ibrahim. Image courtesy of Gigi Ibrahim.

Page 12
Mirror bag by Samia Ben Abdallah for AWA. Image courtesy of Creative Tunisia.

Page 134
Kadada Sienna Dress from MARKINGS Collection by Saqhoute. Courtesy of Norhan El Sakkout at Saqhoute.

Page 145
Detail of COA shirt by Born in Exile; collection of the Kent State University Museum, KSUM 2024.4.2; photograph by Sara Hume.

Page 146
Photograph by Gigi Ibrahim. Image courtesy of Gigi Ibrahim.

Page 152
Ensemble by Oumlil; photograph by Adrian Nina; model: Jaafar Alnabi (Iraqi-American actor/director); stylist: Hicham Oumlil; art direction: Mark Kingsley. Image courtesy of Hicham Oumlil.

IMPRINT

This book has been published on the occasion of the exhibition **A Meeting of Cultures: Fashioning North Africa** ملتقى الثقافات: أزياء شمال أفريقيا

Kent State University Museum
Kent, Ohio, USA
September 5, 2025 – May 10, 2026

EXHIBITION

Curators:
Dr. Sara Hume
Nada Koreish

Exhibition Design:
James Williams

Collections Manager:
Joanne Fenn

Student Assistants:
Kathryn Anderson, Sophie Bessell, Sefra Protch, Sabrina Adjiri, Olivia Carpenter, Likitha Kalla, Babz Glines, Art Mooneyham, Vic Williams

KENT STATE UNIVERSITY MUSEUM

Director:
Dr. Sarah Spinner Liska

Curator:
Dr. Sara Hume

Senior Exhibition Designer and Preparator:
James Williams

Collections Manager and Registrar:
Joanne Fenn

Security Supervisor:
John Puntel

Special Assistant:
Bianka Hausknecht

Kent State University Museum
515 Hilltop Dr.
Kent, Ohio 44242

www.kent.edu/museum
@ksumuseum

PUBLICATION CATALOGUE

Edited by:
Sara Hume

Senior Editor Hirmer Publishers:
Elisabeth Rochau-Shalem

Project management:
Hirmer Publishers
Rainer Arnold

Copy-editing:
David Sánchez Cano

Graphic design, typesetting and production:
Sophie Friederich

Prepress:
Reproline mediateam GmbH&Co. KG, Unterföhring

Paper:
Gardamatt Art 170 g/m²

Typefaces:
Arbotec, Semplicita

Printing and binding:
optimal media GmbH, Röbel/Müritz

Printed in Germany

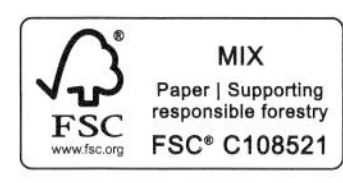

Bibliographic information published by the Deutsche Nationalbibliothek
The Deutsche Nationalbibliothek lists this publication in the Deutsche Nationalbibliografie; detailed bibliographic data is available on the Internet at https://www.dnb.de.

ISBN 978-3-7774- 4428-4

Hirmer Publishers
Managing Director:
Kerstin Ludolph
Bayerstraße 57–59
80335 Munich
Germany

hirmerpublishers.com
hirmerpublishers.co.uk

Cover image:
Two ensembles from the Teta Chic collection by Reem Atout, image by Baiba Photography

Back cover image:
Mirror bag by Samia Ben Abdallah for AWA. Image courtesy of Creative Tunisia

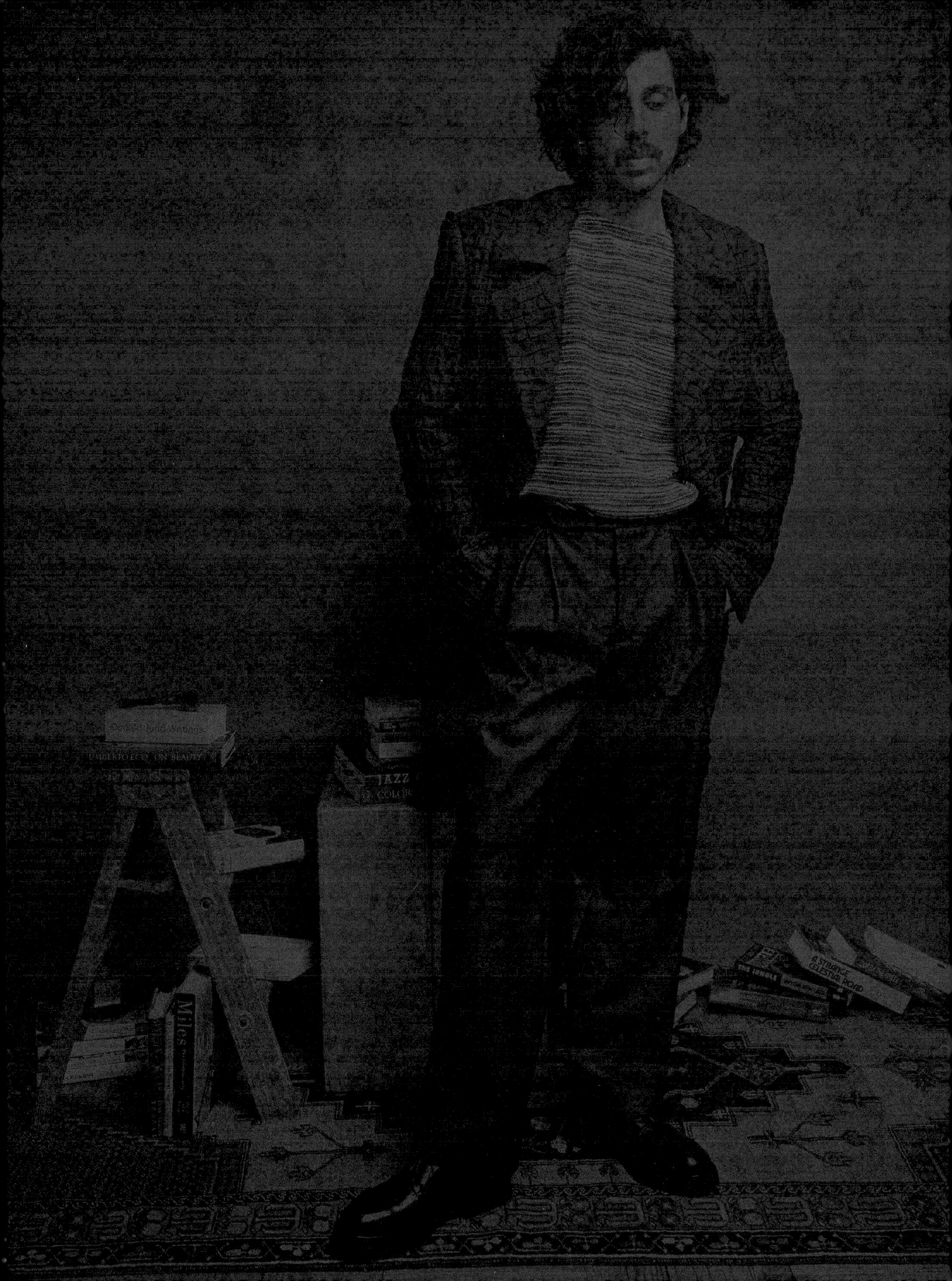
UMBERTO ECO ON BEAUTY
JAZZ
Miles
A STRANGE CELESTIAL ROAD